Restoring
The Christian
Family

by
John and
Paula Sandford

Logos International
Plainfield, New Jersey

Scripture quotations are taken from the King James Version of the Bible unless otherwise noted as: RSV (Revised Standard Version); TAB (The Amplified Bible); and NAS (New American Standard Bible).

RESTORING THE CHRISTIAN FAMILY
Copyright © 1979 by Logos International
All rights reserved
Printed in the United States of America
Library of Congress Catalog Card Number: 79-64977
International Standard Book Number: 0-88270-347-1
Logos International, Plainfield, New Jersey 07060

This Book Is Lovingly Dedicated to Our Children:

Loren and his wife, Beth
Amilee and her husband, Ron
Mark
John and his wife, Marty
Timothy
Andrea

And Our Grandchildren

Angela
Charity
Jason
Nathan
Reah
Mike
Joshua Paul

CONTENTS

Foreword

People who pioneer are threatening to those of us who resist change. Like prophets, they often have to make their way across the wilderness alone, dodging stones from friend and foe alike. Yet what the majority of us, sitting back home in our theological rocking chairs, may describe as the "fringe," may indeed be the cutting edge instead.

That's where I classify John and Paula Sandford. On the cutting edge. Perhaps it's the Indian blood. More probably, it's the prodding of the Holy Spirit which keeps thrusting them out, beyond the routine, into the exciting sphere of fresh revelation.

Pioneers look for new worlds to conquer, new heights to ascend, new depths to plunge. Spiritual pioneers do all this, plus believing that in these places one can find a fresh revelation from God. Realizing the sacrifice of venturing beyond the ordinary, they raise the banner and march forward—determined to prepare the land for those who will one day follow.

The Sandfords did that in their first book, *The Elijah Task*. Some of my theological friends (the rocking chair variety) had problems with that book. They could not accept the fact that God was reestablishing the office of prophet in the contemporary church. Their response went all the way from a shaking of the head with a solemn "tsk, tsk" to a fist-slamming anger which categorized the book as heresy.

But the Sandfords were right. Prophets are emerging, wandering in from the wilderness and speaking forth the word of God as clearly as Elijah, Amos and John the Baptist. *The Elijah Task,* prophetic itself, has helped prepare the way for these modern prophets.

Now John and Paula have reappeared, this time with a book on the Christian family. In it they fulfill, again, the prophetic role. This book, like *The Elijah Task,* will make some angry, cause others to think. And for some, it will be the salvation of their homes. It is far beyond the ordinary leftovers served up by most who write in the area of the family. Here the Sandfords are once again pioneering, exploring new territory, daring to suggest that our concepts of God are much too small.

True prophets, they are far ahead of most of us. But sheep, as you know, are valley-loving creatures. In fact, left alone, sheep will remain in muddy pens the rest of their lives. It's only when some daring shepherd scales the peak and begins to play his flute, that the sheep follow.

So it is with the Sandfords. They have gone ahead. Now, in these pages, they are calling back, and with the mellow refrain of the music of the Spirit, are beckoning the rest of us to "come on up."

Jamie Buckingham
Melbourne, Florida

Preface

Behold, I will send you Elijah the prophet before the coming of the great and dreadful day of the Lord: And he shall turn the heart of the fathers to the children, and the heart of the children to their fathers, lest I come and smite the earth with a curse. (Mal. 4:5, 6)

God intends to restore the family, the central unit through which He will raise His sons. The Lord will not fail (Isa. 42:4). Someday all of heaven and earth and every creature everywhere will know itself to be one family under God, for the knowledge of the Lord will cover the earth as the waters cover the sea (Isa. 11:9).

When we use the word "restore," we do not mean to patch up what once was good and failed to function. By "restoration" a Christian means nothing short of full death to self with Christ on the cross, and reformation into a new heart and mind and style of life (Gal. 2:20). Death and resurrection—not teaching of principles nor correcting behavior—are the essence of restoration. Christian restoration is therefore always totally evangelical, always a more complete conversion. It is a continuing process of dying daily to our striving by receiving His gift.

Though we may lay out standards of behavior, describe roles for family members, and exhort others to obedience, we know it all leads to that confession of hopelessness in our flesh by which, and only by which, the hope of the Spirit in us can live. We are not soul-builders. Neither is the family, though the soul is formed in it. Only Christ is the chief cornerstone, and we are *being built* into a lively house by Him as we submit to His government (1 Pet. 2:5). We are not laying down guidelines by which the family may restore itself. Rather, we are laying down those understandings by which our instances of repentance may be more full, continuous, and joyous, that our redemption may be more complete. In no other way can we be restored.

Even though He taught, our Lord did not come to be a teacher. He did not come to be an example, though He was. He did not come to be a healer, though He healed. He came to die and be raised. Therefore, the purpose of this book is to demonstrate the need for individual death and resurrection and the consequent release of the Holy Spirit in us which will restore the Christian family.

PART I

1

THE DEMON THAT
RISES WITH US

To us, the most important thing happening in Christianity today is the restoration of the family. Wherever a Christian goes today he hears speakers say, "If we do not make it in the home, we aren't going to make it anywhere. If we don't live in Christian love in the family, our Christianity will be meaningless." We believe that. To that end we write.

A destructive way of thinking has encroached upon Western minds. It is commonly called materialism. Usually people think materialism refers to "things." We hear sermons about having too many cars and houses, TVs and boats. But possessions mean little, one way or the other. Materialism is far more vitiating than that.

Materialism is a way of looking at life, a *Weltanschauung*. A Weltanschauung is more than a philosophy; it is a way of seeing which virulently controls and determines our thinking. It's a process which prescribes what we shall see, experience, and value in the reality which surrounds us. Materialism as a Weltanschauung is an apprehension of life which accords reality solely to that which the five senses or test tubes can detect. That only is real or practical which one can see, touch, hear, smell, or taste. Accordingly, we say, "No matter," or "It doesn't matter," or "It didn't materialize"; to us that means it

3

wasn't real, it did not become that which we recognize and value—"matter." Such thinking omits nearly everything which Christians value. Things such as love are thereby relegated to a degree of lesser reality—love can't be seen; we can't hear it; no one can feel it materially; we can't taste it or smell it. Yet without love nothing "matters." Because of the materialistic mind-set, men in the world may give lip service to hope, desire, loyalty, honesty, truth, philosophy, principles, ideals, and faith, while in actuality they trust only those things which can be seen and managed—things which lead to success in the world's terms. Consequently, real belief seems to the worldly to be a departure from the sensibility of reality, rather than being the true apprehension of reality it actually is. The end result of materialism has been the destruction of our society's understanding of what it is to have a spirit and a soul. Spiritual development is God's sole intent for creating the family. The family's greatest and first enemy, Satan's first tool in the destruction of the family, is materialism, a carefully-created, mesmeric mind-set which subtly instructs families in how to view life. The born-anew must sift all their thinking according to the Word. Throughout this book we will be shaking out the rotten fruit of materialism from the tree of family living.

One might ask, "Why did God create families in the first place? Why did He create the earth? Why did He create people?" He had already created angels, but apparently they could not express to Him fulness of individual love and response. Something more was needed. In the God-man, Jesus, God planned to bring to birth the first of a new order of sons, fully spiritual, fully human. He could have created some other sort of beings programed to give back to Him love and worship—everything He desired—but that's just the point, they would have been programed. To have sons, God had to create an environment in which they could exercise free will. There is no other way for them to mature. Since He is the Father God who would have sons become like Him, He must create fathers to have sons. God is interested in the spirit and soul of each individual in the family. It is within family relationships that He is building character and personality. The kind of character development which happens in the soul is His primary interest and purpose.

People ask, "Why does evil exist?" We cannot answer that question fully, but we do see that by putting man inside sinful families, inside a broken people, God is able to raise sons who will have problems. Through their struggles, the sons of God will become alert and strong. If nothing else, our sinful nature smashes our pride, and this is a lesson worth everything in human experience. Therefore, the title for the chapter: "The Demon That Rises with Us."

The first and basic Scripture for child-raising is this: "Train up a child in the way he should go: and when he is old, he will not depart from it" (Prov. 22:6). And from the New Testament we read: "Children, obey your parents in the Lord, for this is right. Honor your father and mother (which is the first commandment with a promise), That it may be well with you, and that you may live long on the earth. And, fathers, do not provoke your children to anger; but bring them up in the discipline and instruction of the Lord" (Eph. 6:1-4 NAS).

The inner self or carnal nature has an independent evil life of its own. Sometimes when we look at the way our children behave, we are certain of this. At other times, when we look at a child asleep, we think, "My, such an angel. How could I have thought the inner self has an evil life?" Yet the Scripture is unequivocal: "You have not heard, you have not known. Even from long ago your ear has not been open. Because I knew that you would deal very treacherously; And you have been called a rebel from birth" (Isa. 48:8 NAS). All have sinned. Our nature *is* sin. From the moment of our children's conception, our corruption becomes theirs—genetically, environmentally, behaviorally, scripturally, in every way, from the beginning—our sin affects our children's lives!

To understand how we develop in the family, we will begin with a Havighurst-and-Ellis concept called the developmental task. This theory explains that we grow from deep inside according to a blueprint and timetable which our inner being is set to follow. Each person evolves from his own unique plan, his own peculiar timetable.

In the first mental year of his life, a child learns, among all his specific achievements, one fundamental, pervading lesson called "basic trust." In this instance, Havighurst and Ellis do not use the word trust in its usual meaning. It does not refer at all to the ability to believe in another person—that he tells the truth, that his behavior will be consistent, or that he can be relied upon. Rather, it is the capacity to hold the self open to others, to receive and give affection. As unconditional love gives without regard to any other's behavior, so basic trust is the specific ability to hold the heart open to the very people one cannot believe. It is the capacity to risk sustained heart-to-heart involvement with imperfect people. If mankind were trustworthy, holding the heart open would be easy. Basic trust is an inner strength and resilience necessary to human relations. Since we must remain vulnerable and interact with others who can and will fail us or hurt us, basic trust is the essential building block of character, without which nothing consequential can be securely founded.

In the first six years of his life a child learns more than he will learn in all his remaining years, even if he earns several degrees. That learning is more intense in his first year than in all the rest. "Train up a child in the way he should go" does not mean that one begins to train the child's mind when he is six. Training begins when the child enters the womb, continues when he is born, and accelerates and intensifies as he first experiences life in this world. It is in those very first years that his character and personality are formed. Life itself, not the classroom, is the teaching ground. If we would understand the Christian family and its uniqueness, we need to see clearly that those two primal parts of the soul—character and personality—are formed in the first six years. All subsequent learning is simply framing and embellishment upon that foundation. Understanding this fact may effect changes in our entire approach to child-raising.

We tend to think that what happened in the past belongs only to the past. "So let's forget about it. It isn't important now. It can't affect us." But that is not true. What happened in our first year affects us all our lives. As Christians we are not so much interested in what happened in our first moments of existence as we are in how we reacted in our spirits, and what kind of automatic patterns of response we have built into our natures.

If a child of two were to fall and break a leg, which didn't mend well because the bone was not set properly, the child might well limp the rest of his life. We can understand that easily because we can see the malformation on the x-ray. Somehow we have failed to think as concretely about the inner psyche. A familiar proverb says simply, "As the twig is bent, so the tree grows." Assuredly, not to receive affection, to lose a father or mother, not to be nursed, or to be toilet trained too soon are injuries as real as breaking a leg. These are injuries to the inner psyche. Reactions to emotional wounds are as real and vivid as reactions to broken legs, and they are often far less temporary. People sometimes limp emotionally throughout their lives from sinful reactions to events in the very first moments of life! Moreover, when a particularly damaging event occurs, and is repeated a number of times, the character may become structured to habitually respond in automatic, defensive or hurtfully aggressive ways.

A baby lives by primal senses in his spirit. He feels the presence of people and their absence. We don't know if we began when we entered the womb or always existed with the

Father in the heavens. We do know a baby has been affected by all that happened in the emotional and psychological experiences of the parents during his life in the womb, by coming through the shock of being drawn out of a warm womb into the noise and light and cutting and unfamiliar grasping of strange hands. A sleeping baby breathes many little sighs because he has been wounded and needs to be held and loved and comforted. This is the first thing a Christian family needs to understand, that much physical affection brings needful healing to the child. He cannot survive emotionally without physical embraces. He lives by those gentle touches that call forth and train his spirit to reach out to receive and to give back love and affection. In the first few weeks and months of his life the capacity to relate is formed. The soul, a living structure of character through which the spirit expresses life, from that time forward either enables or prevents the spirit to embrace another through the body.

Medical science has learned that if a baby is born through Caesarean section, the doctors and nurses need to rub the muscles in his arms and legs. They know the baby needs the pushing of the mother's muscles against his body, and if he does not experience this, he will have the muscles, but they will not be fully activated. In the same way we are born with the capacity in our spirits to reach out through our bodies to embrace another, to be enfolded, to give and take. But that power is not fully awakened unless the baby receives the warmth of touching and holding in the first year. Call that faculty basic trust, because basic trust is the ability to open the heart and mind to give and receive. And that is the fundamental capacity to be human. The ignorance of our parents, our divorces and broken homes have raised an increasingly inhuman, incapable generation.

"And the Lord God formed man of the dust of the ground, and breathed into his nostrils the breath of life; and man became

8

a living soul" (Gen. 2:7). We acquired a human spirit simply by existing. God breathes His own spirit into us, but we become a living soul. That implies a process. We believe that as our spirit enters into relationship with the spirits of others, our character and personality are formed. If a person receives continual warmth of affection, ways for the spirit to continue such joyous embraces are formed in the soul. But neglect and abuse either fail to form the structure by which such interchanges can happen or cause crippled structures of response. We do not without nurture acquire capacities to relate humanly; they have to be built into us over a long period of time. The human baby remains helpless longer than any other species.

Unfortunately, parents have too often seemed to think of babies like seeds in the wild, as though infants, untended and untouched, would grow like trees in a forest. A heifer does not require a cow to learn to moo, nor does a kitten to mew or a puppy to bark. But a human infant cannot learn to talk unless talked to. In similar fashion, a human animal cannot acquire many of the sensitivities and skills of human interaction without human nurture. The quality of nurture greatly determines what kind of character and personality will be formed. A human being has to be walked to walk, talked to talk, loved to love.

In the first six years we are called upon to learn how to walk, how to talk, how to eat, how to handle our emotions, how to control our bladders, how to control what we say, all the basic motor and human skills, and we learn those things only as they are imparted to us by other human beings. How important that is! "Herein is love, not that we loved God, but that He loved us" (1 John 4:10). That is true psychologically as well, for if we do not first receive love, we cannot give it.

We Christians have too long let it be thought that a mother could give birth to her baby, and rush out to get a job. Almost totally unaware that her own physical presence is absolutely vital, she hires a baby-sitter or puts the child in a nursery. She thinks the baby doesn't yet have a mind, so it could not "matter." Trained in this materialistic culture, she is too often unaware that her baby has a spirit which can sense her presence or absence. Consequently the baby is not given her presence in those first six months when her nearness is so critically important. That breeds future parents who are incapable of human warmth, who raise others yet more incapable, who raise others, and so humanity spirals downward. Only the mercy of the Lord stops the destruction of humanity.

Because of the influence of our materialistic culture, most fathers are unaware of the role they were created to fulfill in the lives of their children. Ignorant of the life of the spirit and formation of the soul, they fail to appreciate that all of their actions and attitudes affect the character formation of their children. A boy learns what it is to be a man by watching his father. Girls learn how to embrace a man or close off from him. Countless habitual unconscious practices (see Col. 3:9 RSV) for relating are built into children as they live with their fathers. If fathers knew their importance, would they not be more inclined to discipline themselves to express the life of Christ for their children's sakes?

For example, we took great pleasure in the fact that all of our children slept most of the night on my (John's) chest when they were tiny. This experience taught them the comfort and security of the embrace of the father's strength, that their daddy was there for them when they needed, that it was not a fearful thing to trust themselves so close to someone who could by size and strength overpower them. Fathers need to know that their temper or compassion when forced to walk the floor with a six-month-old colicky baby affects the security of the child. Some of our counselees have discovered that their fear to come to us is derived from their early fear of their fathers.

Now let us speak of the second mental year. A chronological

year is simply twelve months; a mental year may consist of two or three chronological years. Some children mature much more quickly than others. The rate of development is nothing about which we ought to be either proud or ashamed. Geniuses often mature emotionally and socially more slowly than others (Albert Einstein, for instance). It is important to know that a child should not be required to accomplish a skill, for instance toilet training, before he is ready. Surprising as it is to our materialistically trained minds, when we are teaching about such down-to-earth human things as toilet training, we're talking about the formation of spirit and soul. Faith and religion are not divorced from life. Spirituality is expressed not merely in worship, but in the little, common daily acts of life. The way and time a thing is done affects and trains the nature of the soul. Some mothers have been taught that a child *must* learn potty training at age one. Filled with all their tension about being good mothers, they force their children, ready or not, onto the pot, to perform. That is blind insensitivity. While the child is learning to control his bladder, he is receiving something far more important. He learns to fear the heavy hand of instruction, and anxiety sets in. Fears of inadequacy, an inordinate desire to please, compulsory performance orientation, feelings of unworthiness, and a rigid definition of what he is as a person develop. Such a person may later learn with his mind that grace is a free gift, but for years thereafter his spirit will struggle to overcome a message from the early training in his soul, "If I don't do right, God won't love me." Most likely he will be unable to relate to God in a different manner from the early responses he learned to give to maternal authority. Many truly believing, born-anew Christians are still locked into a performance orientation with God, not realizing that that "trip" was built into them before age two! The best kind of training comes from a sensitivity to the child, to his timetable. When the child is ready, mother can assist in helping him to remember, and that without forcing. Psychologists tell us that if a child is forced into toilet training too soon, he becomes in most cases censorious, judgmental, fastidious, stingy, uptight, nervous, a high-strung person. Such a person is called an "anal personality." Unfortunately many mothers are not trained about such things.

All this about potty training is just one example among many hundreds of possibilities to show the way children develop within their own timetables. Myriad lessons we have to learn as infants demand loving parental sensitivity. That sensitivity is nothing else but constant momentary death of self in the power of what Jesus accomplished on the cross, so that the love of Christ may cause us to respond to what the other actually needs in any given moment. Without that self-death we impose our own inappropriate demands, misshaping the other's soul.

Havighurst and Ellis entitle the basic lesson of a two year old, "Independence." By this they do not mean the fulness of mature independence, but the beginning of the process of individuation. (See diagram A.) A two year old reveals who he is by saying "no." Our Tim loved ice cream, and so we would ask him, "Timmy, you want an ice cream cone?"

"No!"

He wanted one; he was only practicing. It is important for a child to say no. When he says no he is defining his own person, saying, "You stop there; I stop here." It is imperative to individuality to learn how to say no, to the other person and to the self. Many fathers and mothers have not understood this. What happens then is that when the child begins to say no, such parents feel threatened, and squelch the negativity, thinking they are doing what they should to correct such behavior. Already seeds of rebellion are sown, and the "demon" begins to rise.

There is a fine distinction concerning freedom which parents need to know. The child must be free to say his no, but not thereby free to escape consequences. Discipline is necessary but should come as a simple and natural consequence concerning something important, not as an attempt to coerce the child into a mold which prevents him from saying a no. Our son Loren used to stand and look at a particular no-no he wanted to do. We could see him measuring the fun of the crime versus the punishment he knew he would get. But he knew he was free to make his choice—and free to take the consequences.

The saying of no, this independence, is dependent upon basic trust. Picture a two year old. He stands about how high? Two feet? Not much taller. He looks up and what does he see? Noses, hands, kneecaps, and rear ends. To those giants from whom comes everything he needs—love, affection, food, clothing, shelter—he must say, "no." That takes trust! A lot of it! So you see, unless the child learns the first lesson, he cannot learn the second; and it is crucial to learn the second.

There is a generation of children who were raised during World War II when both parents were gone from the home. Mothers were working in the factories and daddy was at war. The children were not given adequate parental expressions of love and affection. Many did not learn basic trust. As a result, they did not learn independence. And so for the first time we know of in America we reaped a generation of teen-agers who *had* to be with the gang. If the gang wanted to go to a "beer bust" and get drunk, they *had* to. If the gang said, "Let's wear this kind of clothing," they wouldn't be caught dead without it. The reason for the compulsiveness was that so many of that generation had not learned independence in the second mental year. They could not "differentiate" or "individuate." They had never learned to make a distinction between themselves and others. They could not stand alone because they had not learned basic trust.

Applying this to the Christian family, we see it is important for a mother and father to understand their two year old, to give him plenty of warm human affection, and to let him say his no when it is necessary. Again, that calls for momentary self-denial and life in Christ. If the parent has not given the Holy Spirit sufficient control, he will wind up in a never-ending, self-defeating frustration trying to make the child become what he wants him to be.

We want to clarify that what we have said about teen-agers is not true of all. Some teen-agers can adhere to the fashions of the day without compulsion. Some can freely seek the belonging of the gang without loss of freedom. The difference seems to lie in the nature of the family. In the First World War grandparents still were a part of the home. To a lesser extent the same was true of World War II, and since then it occurs less and less. Incapacity to individuate has increased in ratio to the loss of the close interconnectedness of the nuclear family with all other blood relatives. Mobility has isolated parents from the support and supply of relatives and close friends, so that when some parents were made incapable, their children were left in a vacuum.

Humans raised without affection cling to their peers, afraid to differentiate. We detest the horrendous concept rising among some sociologists who say we should have common nurseries in which all mothers and fathers should place their children. They say in essence that since some are better equipped to care for children, others should be released to work by committing their children to their care. Here is another evidence that the materialistic mind-set totally misses the uniqueness of each parent to his own child. Such blind counselors would eventually lead to doing away with the family altogether.

When the Bible was written, family structure was much more cohesive, and the sense of the spiritual in daily living had not been lost. Therefore little was said directly in the Bible concerning the life of the spirit within the family; it was taken for granted. But much is implied. Do you remember when Mary left her place and came to visit with Elizabeth?

In those days Mary arose and went with haste into the hill country to a city of Judah, and she entered the house of Zechariah and greeted Elizabeth. And when *Elizabeth* heard the greeting of Mary, the *babe* leaped in her womb; and Elizabeth was filled with the Holy Spirit, and she exclaimed with a loud cry, "Blessed are you among women, and blessed is the fruit of your womb! And why is this granted me that the mother of my Lord should come to me? For behold, when the voice of your greeting came to my ears, the *babe in my womb leaped for joy.* And blessed is she who believed that there would be a fulfilment of what was spoken to her from the Lord. (Luke 1:39-45 RSV)

How did John the Baptist, encased in Elizabeth's womb, know that anything at all had happened outside? That Mary had entered the room? And was pregnant? Even to adults, Mary would barely have been showing—if at all. How did John the Baptist know? And that it was Jesus in her womb? The Holy Spirit revealed these things to John. We can testify that in countless counseling cases we have dealt with people who have been influenced some months before their birth.

Scientifically, what a fetus experiences in the womb cannot be demonstrated, apart from physiological development. But our teaching here is based upon eighteen years of experience in counseling. In those years, by revelation of the Holy Spirit, we have been led to pray for thousands of traumas *en utero*, treating these as factual. Dramatic results in mental, emotional, and physical healings, and transformed behavior testify to the reality of such en utero traumas. In the beginning of our ministry, we were only willing to postulate the possibility that our spirit has a mind with which to comprehend. Now not to believe such subjective revelation would require denial of observable results. We do not see how those results were obtained by any other means than the simple inviting of the Lord Jesus to touch and heal the wounds and fractures so described.

Common examples are:
1. Unreasoning fears of death traced to:
   a. threat of abortion.
   b. identification with the mother's fears that she might miscarry because of previous miscarriages.
2. Deep-seated feelings of rejection and unworthiness traced to:
   a. illegitimate conception.
   b. unwanted pregnancy.
   c. strong desire for a girl when a boy was being formed, or vice versa.

Some hatreds and violences remain unconquerable when all known psychological factors have been dealt with. When the Holy Spirit revealed violences which had occurred between the parents while the counselee was still in the womb, and appropriate healing prayers were said, these were immediately overcome. Likewise some lusts and fears of sex remained entrenched until influences of parental sexual confusions and traumas while the counselee was en utero were revealed and relieved by prayer. To teach how to heal such things is not our purpose in this book, but we share these understandings that Christian parents may become aware that their lives greatly affect their children in the womb.

Because questions so often have been asked of us, we ought not to leave this subject without mentioning it is for this reason that adopted children need healing prayer. Adopted children know in their spirits the loss of their own mother and father whether their minds know it or not. Infants and small children are not prepared to talk directly about such things; it is not necessary to pray aloud for them in their presence. How we talk with and pray for older children depends upon their maturity and openness and the wisdom of the moment.

Many fathers have come to us saying, "I'm sure that if we separated, my wife would find someone she would be happier with, and the children would have a much better home life. I think it would be best for the children if we were divorced." There is a living Lord who can change that quarreling to blessing. Better a struggling home than one without you! You cannot be replaced. God sent your child to *you*. If you die, that cannot be helped, but no separation ought to be allowed that can be prevented.

In the third mental year, a child learns initiative. Remember that a mental year is not a chronological year. The third mental year may normally be from about two to six. Initiative is the ability to live among the peer group. A child at first plays *alongside* others. For a child to commence playing *with* other children, he must have independence and basic trust. He must be able to say yes and no to the group. Sometimes a child gives away his toys. We praise that child, thinking he is being unselfish. That may be, but in many cases it may mean that the child has failed to learn independence. Parents were busy earning things. They knew nothing of the Christian function of physical affection, talking, sharing. They seldom bounced the baby on their laps, played with him, or even presented themselves to him. What they did give were things. The child became a market-oriented personality. Subliminally the child thinks, "My parents bought me; I must buy people." He gives things to win friends. He may never understand that he is himself already a friend, merely by existing, because that was not built into him.

On the other hand, sometimes we see a child of that age who won't share anything. We tend to think the child is selfish. We may even spank him and demand, "You share. . . ." Our own picture as parents is threatened, so that the child must be made to be unselfish. But it may only be that our child was learning independence. He is practicing being his own person, not at all ready to move into initiative. If we stand by him and help him to share without a tremendous "ought" behind it, he may soon learn initiative and start sharing. The familiar refrain for parents is again self-denial and life in Christ. Only Jesus gives the strength to let ourselves be embarrassed by a "selfish child," and not to overpraise the seemingly unselfish. "He shall not judge by what his eyes see, or decide by what his ears hear" (Isa. 11:3b RSV), must be true of us as parents as well.

In all of the foregoing we were demonstrating how important the first six years are, but that may leave some of us with heavy burdens of guilt. We often see the results of what we did with our children in those first six years and pray in repentance. If we remember what our parents did with us, and theirs with them, and so on, we can see how sin is passed on from generation to generation. We can understand how the incapacity to function rises with us, how indeed the "demon" rises with us. What we are talking about is original sin in real terms. We are incapable of giving our child a perfect nature because we are not perfect parents, and we are not because ours were not, and theirs weren't, and theirs weren't, all the way back to Adam and Eve. Only the cross stops this pattern, and that only by conscious *daily* invitation. "If any man will come after me, let him deny himself, and take up his cross, and follow me" (Matt. 16:24b).

Suppose we had all been perfect parents. The demon would yet have risen with us. Junior is in bed, hungry. In the beginning a baby is more honest. He cries because he is hungry. We hear and go running to him. We give him the breast or the bottle, comfort and hold him. Oh, that feels good to the baby! Another time he is hungry, so he cries again and we go and feed him. Now he has the idea, "If I cry, mama comes and I am comforted." He isn't hungry. He isn't wet. He doesn't need anything, but he has learned, "If I scream,

18

Waaaaaaaaaaaa—mama comes!'' Already we have a liar. We may laugh at that, but it's actually a serious matter. Children before six months already have learned to be manipulators and exploiters. We were born with a corrupt nature; we are sinful merely by entering into human nature. Jesus was the only perfect human.

Much of what we have said seems to imply that we are putting the blame on parents for our sinful nature. If we did that, we would do away with the cross. We would destroy individual responsibility. There are those who have insisted that no one can be accounted as a sinner until the "age of accountability." The doctrine of the age of accountability did not declare no sinfulness before a certain age. It held merely that until the conscious mind is mature, we are not held accountable. We have found no scriptural ground for this tenet except for some inferences. Certainly we have found none for setting the age of accountability at age eleven or twelve. Perhaps Jesus' visit in the temple at Jerusalem can be used as an indication but not as a proof. We do think it wisdom not to hold men fully accountable for their own lives until eleven or twelve. We have nothing therefore to say for or against that as a practice. But we believe the entire church should awaken to the fact of the sins of our own personal spirits in the earliest moments of existence. The Scriptures contain continual references to sinful nature and deeds of sin within our own personal spirits. "Blessed is the man to whom the Lord does not impute iniquity, And *in whose spirit* there is no deceit!" (Ps. 32:2 NAS). "Create in me a clean heart, O God; and renew a *right spirit* within me" (Ps. 51:10). No need to put a right spirit in us if there is nothing wrong with the first one. Ezekiel 36:26 says, "A new heart also will I give you, and *a new spirit* will I put within you. . . ." Again no need for a new spirit if there is nothing wrong with the first. St. Paul writes to born-again Christians, ". . . let us cleanse ourselves from all filthiness of the flesh *and spirit* . . ." (2

Cor. 7:1). Scripture is clear that we can and do sin in our spirits.

Too long we have too much arrogated the process of decision-making to the conscious mind. We need to realize that our decision-making is influenced, indeed may even be controlled, by deeper hidden areas of our beings. Else Jesus would not say, "For from within, out of the heart of men, proceed evil thoughts, adulteries, fornications, murders, Thefts, covetousness, wickedness, deceit, lasciviousness, an evil eye, blasphemy, pride, foolishness: All these evil things come from within, and defile the man" (Mark 7:21-23). Note that the first influence from within is "thoughts." We are called responsible by the Lord himself for what proceeds from within. Therefore, let it be axiomatic, and never forgotten, that though we describe dramatically and forcefully the sins of parents in child-raising, we must never allow that to obliterate individual responsibility. We are not *tabulae rasae*, on which life is written (Descartes). We are individual free spirits in God's kingdom, responsible for the way we react to whatever we find here, however horrendous the circumstances. With the Lord, we can never get away with saying, "He made me do it." Or, "My circumstances forced me."

The fallacy that we are only responsible for what our conscious mind knows has become part of our court procedures. If a man can be proven insane, he is no longer held accountable by our society. Perhaps that is as it ought to be, for the expression of mercy among men. But in our relationship with the Lord, Jesus simply says, ". . . that servant, which knew his lord's will, and prepared not himself, neither did according to his will, shall be beaten with many stripes. But he that knew not, and did commit things worthy of stripes, shall be beaten with few stripes" (Luke 12:47, 48a). Note that in the Lord's fairness the unaware are not treated so harshly as the aware, but the unaware do receive a beating. Jesus sternly rebuked the Pharisees, "Woe to you, scribes and Pharisees, hypocrites! For you clean the outside of the cup and of the dish, but inside they are full of robbery and self-indulgence. You blind Pharisee, first clean the inside of the cup and of the dish, so that the outside of it may become clean also'' (Matt. 23:25, 26 NAS). This then is our plea to parents. Christian parents must first cleanse the inner cup of their own hearts, daily. The great arena of battle is inner space, not outer. Christian parents are called to see beyond the surface of what their children do to bless and discipline for the nurture and admonition of the heart. For this reason Elijah is sent to "turn the *heart* of the fathers to the children" (Mal. 4:6).

My father used to say, "No, Jack, that is not what you really thought. Here is what you really thought. Here is what you actually were saying by what you did. . . ." Almost invariably he was right. I was furious at the moment, and later would have to agree and be grateful. My father held me accountable for where my heart was, and disciplined me accordingly. And so did my mother. Paula was equally fortunate. I can still recall my mother's words, "Just remember, Jack, if we didn't get it right this time, and we are disciplining you for something you didn't do, you just apply it to all those times you weren't caught!" Neither of our folks were about to excuse a guilty heart from correction. "Folly is bound up in the *heart* of a child, but the rod of discipline drives it far from him" (Prov. 22:15 RSV).

On the other hand, we Christian parents must learn to look upon our children and ourselves with the dispassionate judgment of the Lord. There should be an absence of condemnation in Christian parents who understand our formation in sin. We need not fear our imperfection. God loves us as we are. His lordship means that He will perfect us, in His own good time. Blame attaches appropriately only to those who, already having been set free, again choose enslavement and crucify the Son anew on their own account (Heb. 6:6). We have all too often transferred into our discipline and upon ourselves condemnation which is inappropriate. The habit of connecting criticism and blame, praise and approval, to our sense of belonging is a destructive habit carried forth from our infancy and foisted upon the present. It is not discipline which needs to cease: "He who spares his rod hates his son, but he who loves him disciplines him diligently" (Prov. 13:24 NAS). It is the false motives attached to the way we discipline which need to be purged out of us. We ought never to discipline by saying, "Where did my child go? This isn't my little _____." Nor by "I can't love you when you act that way." Children need to know they belong and are loved no matter what they do. Discipline should have its base in love. "Furthermore, we had earthly fathers to discipline us, and we respected them; shall we not much rather be subject to the Father of spirits, and live? For they disciplined us for a short time as seemed best to them, but *He disciplines us for our good*, that we may share His holiness" (Heb. 12:9, 10 NAS).

Identical twins raised in the same environment evolve differently in character and personality. Because every child decides uniquely how he will react, discipline must be tailored to each individual. If we rest in the Lord Jesus Christ, His love will naturally cause us to discipline each child "for his good."

From the beginning God knew exactly how, when and where you and I would fall. He knew in His wisdom that should He step in to prevent, none would become sons of God. He knew then just how we would bless our children—and louse them up—and He sent them anyway! Though some parents fail by not trying hard enough to nurture their children rightly, we see that devoutly Christian parents more often fail by trying too hard. Seeing those Scriptures which call us to "bring them up in the nurture and admonition of the Lord" (Eph. 6:4b), taking that as our mandate to control their behavior, we often fuss and overprotect, squelching the child's own life. As God paid the price for free will, so must we.

Lately many Christians have become aware of that Scripture which says of a bishop, "One that ruleth well his own house, having his children in subjection with all gravity; (For if a man know not how to rule his own house, how shall he take care of the church of God?)" (1 Tim. 3:4, 5). Too many of us, especially fathers, have fallen into fear, misunderstanding that text and plunging into desperate attempts to corral normally rebellious teen-agers, lest we be deemed unworthy of office. But that Scripture is not a call to dominance and control. The call is to know *"how* to rule." The Father God lost every son to profligacy save one only. Does that disqualify Him for rule? Did He not know how? Every disciple of Jesus deserted Him and one betrayed. Is Jesus thereby unfit to rule the household of God? The Father rules by humble service. He pays the cost of hurt for us; love "beareth all things, believeth all things, hopeth all things, endureth all things" (1 Cor. 13:7). Jesus is the Master by being as the least, laying down His life for our freedom. Whatever parent learns to lay down his life in loving service for his family, repenting before God for his children, will rule as Jesus did. Jesus still rules today by love, not demand. Children who are secure in love will return from profligacy, stronger and wiser.

If a parent could raise a perfect child, what need would our children have of a Savior? Our children will mature imperfectly no matter how perfectly we try. It's the nature of mankind. We have misread that Scripture, "Train up a child in the way he should go." We take it as a command to shape our children the way we think they should go. That is not what it says. "Train up a child in the way *he* should go" is a call to us to die to our own pictures of what we want our children to be, so that through us the Father may call forth what He created them to become. Our task is to stop our attempt to make them fulfill something we failed in or always wanted to be. As Michelangelo saw in the stone the sculpture which begged to be set free under his chisel, so we are ordained to find and set free what God would create in the child. "For we are His workmanship, created in Christ Jesus for good works, which God prepared beforehand, that we should walk in them" (Eph. 2:10 NAS).

Muslim families love their children. So do Buddhists. Even atheists love their children. We are not different in that. Other families discipline their children. Hebrew families were noted for good discipline. So were the Chinese. Many families discipline their children better than we. But the Christian family knows one thing which no other organization, family, group, race or creed knows. We know, through Jesus Christ, death of self on the cross and rebirth. Our task, then, is to die to self so that we become sensitive to what God is unfolding within each child's plan of development. We are to so love that the child may grow in *his own way*.

What is a Christian family? It is simply a unit of warm human love where God raises His imperfect sons. Truly we *are* called to give affection, pray with our children, attend church with them, discipline, and live before them an exemplary life, but it is God who will do the rest. In whatever ways we fail to do these simple things, it is God who will redeem. The Christian family is distinctive then in its ability to rest in the middle of all its difficulties. By faith in Christ it is also distinguished by joy and celebration. It is unafraid to make mistakes, and live life. We rest in the knowledge that God has all the "mess" in hand.

To Christian parents we say then: Be present to your children; give *you* to them. Touch often. Hold them. Read stories. Play. Pray with them. But relax. Don't try so hard. Rest in your mess. God has it. He always has. Praise God for the mess. He will turn it to glory.

Your children are not your children.
They are the sons and daughters of Life's longing for itself.
They come through you but not from you,

24

And though they are with you yet they belong not to you.
You may give them your love but not your thoughts,
For they have their own thoughts.
You may house their bodies but not their souls,
For their souls dwell in the house of tomorrow, which you
cannot visit, not even in your dreams.
You may strive to be like them, but seek not to make them
like you.
For life goes not backward nor tarries with yesterday.

(*The Prophet* Kahlil Gibran)

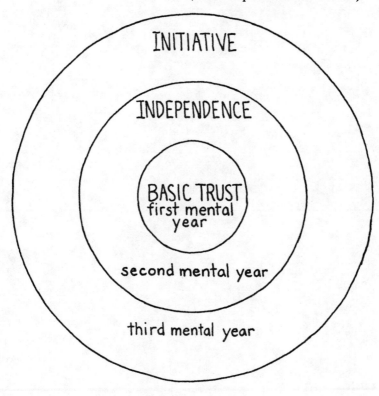

DIAGRAM: A

2

A HEART OF FLESH
FOR A HEART OF STONE

A new heart I will give you, and a new spirit I will put within you; and I will take out of your flesh the heart of stone and give you a heart of flesh. (Ezek. 36:26 RSV)

What we have said about becoming emotionally crippled as we are formed sounds deterministic. Insofar as we all respond sinfully, such results are inescapable. Perhaps the most cogent law in all the Bible is the fifth commandment: "Honor your father and your mother . . . that it may be well with you and that you may live long on the earth" (Eph. 6:2, 3 RSV). The Ten Commandments and all the other laws in the Bible are not merely a collection of rules we ought to live up to but often don't. They are God's description of the way reality works. If we drop a pencil, it falls because of gravity. If the pencil had a mind and chose to hang in the air, that would have no effect on its falling whatsoever. By the same operation of law, we are rewarded in spiritual matters. If we lie, we must reap painful results. It makes no difference what our minds think or our emotions feel.

So long as we have not repented, in the same way a pencil must fall according to the law of gravity, so by spiritual law we must and will reap. Likewise, no matter how understanding

God and we may be that a child did not want to be angry or judge his parents, if forgiveness and the cross do not intervene, that act of judgment must be reaped. Countless counselees have complained to us, "I swore I would never treat my children the way my parents did—and I am doing the very same things!" Why? Because law is law: "Judge not, that ye be not judged. For with what judgment ye judge, ye shall be judged: and with what measure ye mete, it shall be measured to you again (Matt. 7:1, 2; see also Rom. 2:1).

On the other hand, this operation of law also works to blessing. We have seen cases where a husband and wife loved and took care of their parents, and found themselves blessed by the Lord with everything they needed—happiness, good health, and a wonderful place for their own retirement. That is the simple, irrevocable, impersonal law of sowing and reaping. Chapters eight and nine of *The Elijah Task,* our first book, speak of this more fully.

Jesus quoted the law, "He who speaks evil of father or mother, let him surely die" (Mark 7:10b RSV, quoting from Exod. 21:17). Loving and merciful as He is, Jesus knew that dishonoring the parents brings death. That death may not be physical, but it can destroy the abundant life. Even if a child is unaware of this law, and represses his anger, the law still pertains. It will not be well with him to the degree of his rebellion. This is a problem to which counselors must minister again and again.

It is easier to bring healing to those who have had recognizably evil parents. Forgiveness is then a conscious work. But the hurts of the children of good parents who failed to give affection are extremely difficult to see. How can a child know what is wrong? As a sunflower turns its head to follow the sun for life, so a child, by the inner promptings of his spirit, turns to his parents for life-giving affection. That easy trust, looking for loving nurture, is most likely what Jesus meant when He said, "Except ye be converted and become as little children, ye shall not enter into the kingdom of heaven" (Matt. 18:3). God's kingdom people, like little children, have died to pride and can look humbly to others for love and sharing.

Going back to our analogy, if we cover the sunflower, so that it cannot find the sun, it searches for light. When it finds none, it wilts. Children whose parents fail to give affection become like the sunflower; they wilt and die inside. Normally the child's mind does not comprehend this loss. It loyally protects the parents. The inner spirit does know, and usually rebels in anger. Resentment and bitterness then set into the soul and eventually infect the very life of the person.

Lest some cry "unfair!" let us explain it is not as though the victim had no chance. Even as little children we make choices. When we repress our hurts, we are choosing to lie to ourselves. "Oh, what tangled webs we weave when first we practice to deceive." When we fail to admit to our consciousness what our spirit faithfully sends up, we build a web of dishonesty. Eventually the inner spirit tires of letting us know where we really are and quits sending messages. Trouble does not set in until and unless we have too long said "peace" to ourselves where there is no peace (Jer. 6:14; 8:11). It is then that the inner heart can no longer find access to our mind for healing. Bitternesses resulting from judgments made by us run like an underground river, unchecked, and spring up in full floods somewhere later in life. That is why children bereft of affection are apt then or later to start doing mean things. Somehow, somewhere sins of judgment sown will draw retribution upon such children unless the cross of Christ intervenes. The law is inexorable. "Judge not, that you be not judged. For with the judgment you pronounce you will be judged, and the measure you give will be the measure you get" (Matt. 7:1, 2 RSV). The worst facet of the problem is its invisibility. Whenever someone comes to us confessing marital trouble, we immediately ask,

"What was it like with your parents?" If the trouble is not identical, we can easily recognize similar roots. Every time we choose wrongly, even as tiny children, the law is inescapable; it is deterministic. That is God's Word. But consider how many hundreds of blessings are reaped by the operation of that same law.

Seeing that the laws of God are that real and effective, people have often said to us, "Well, good grief, I'm filled with guilt. What can I do? What have I done to my poor children already?" Praise God and hallelujah, that is why we have Jesus. That is what He came to do—to forgive our sins, to heal our broken places, to carry our sorrows and bear our griefs (Isa. 53:4). We can invite Him to go back into our lives and those of our children to transform all our errors into glory. Whoever is downcast, let him take heart; Jesus is real. His forgiveness is available to all.

Now let us turn to the subject of the heart of stone. Ezekiel 36:26 says the Lord will take out of us the heart of stone and give us a heart of flesh. What is the heart of stone? Let us remember that the growing child who comes with an imperfect, rebellious spirit to imperfect parents usually does not receive enough affection or understanding. Therefore, he begins to build defensive walls. While earlier we spoke of the sinful reaction of the child and how he became a liar, now we speak of his hurt. How purely defenseless a baby is. How often we pick up a baby and say, "Oh, I could just crush him," because he melts our heart. We feel how open and vulnerable he is. But then baby gives and papa doesn't respond, or wants to be held and mama puts him down and goes off somewhere else, and there is hurt. That happens in the best of homes again and again. Each time the baby has to handle that hurt somehow. The baby has no knowledge of confession, the cross and forgiveness. What can he do with constantly repeated frustrations? The baby wants the breast, but mama changes the diaper, or baby has diaper rash, but mama sticks the breast in his mouth. How can a baby say what he really wants? He doesn't know how to forgive and be cleansed. His spirit becomes more and more loaded as hurt is stored in him. Each instance adds to the building of checks into his nervous system until eventually he has built a way of turning off his feelings. Emotions begin to be no longer out in the open. He has built a hiding place within himself. In the beginning his walls are flexible, but they become increasingly strong and rigid as the pressures of repressed emotions increase.

In families in which there is much love and affection, the heart of stone is warmed and eased. In unaffectionate families, the heart of stone ossifies in time. Such people may find themselves able to *give* love, but they do not dare to receive. The person with a heart of stone subconsciously is incapable of divulging his inner being to another. The act of receiving is a far greater risk than giving. Defensive walls prevent others from getting to us. Defensive practices are soon forgotten but remain effective throughout life because the inner heart has become a petrified forest of automatic hidden patterns.

We need to understand here what an autonomous complex is. In the beginning as we learned how to walk, for instance, we had to concentrate on making our feet go. We learned to control wayward muscles while keeping precarious balances. Now that we have learned to walk, we do not have to think ''walk'' again. We just simply go without thinking about the process. We might walk with a loping step if we were raised in Texas. In Japan we might learn to walk with short steps. By the same token, we speak with inflections, drawls, slang phrases and colloquialisms. We do not try to have an Ozark twang; it happens because of autonomous complexes within us. An autonomous complex is an independent automatic reflex system. Without the economy of autonomous complexes we would wear ourselves out trying to do the simplest things like walking, talking, eating. Once built, such patterns are forgotten. They operate without our thinking. In exactly the

31

same way we learn how to open the heart and *give* and how to *receive* affection, how to sense underlying meanings in conversations, how to read what is in the heart of another, and how to hold the heart open to the other.

The fact of the automatic, hidden operation of our ways gives us the context of the Christian struggle for sanctification. "But now put them all away: anger, wrath, malice, slander, and foul talk from your mouth. Do not lie to one another, seeing that you have put off the old nature *with its practices* and have put on the new nature, which is being renewed in knowledge after the image of its creator" (Col. 3:8-10 RSV). A born-anew Christian has not ended the problem with self; he has only begun the work of sanctification, the daily bringing to death of the practices of the old nature. "Autonomous complex" is the psychological term for what the Bible calls "practice," or "habit." Jesus died to set us free from these.

Praying families tend to keep the heart more melted. Bible reading, and attending churches where the Word of God is preached, continually expose the heart to the sword of truth. In such families, if the milieu of love enables, the heart is less hardened than in families in the world. But we are all locked up to some degree.

Often we are unaware that we have a heart of stone because the outer nature remains so obviously loving. For example a wife who embraces her husband, prepares nice meals, dresses well for him, and gives her body to him whenever he asks, may yet be encased in a heart of stone. The telling mark is that she can't let down and cry on his shoulder. She is unable to claim his lap when she needs comfort for herself. She wants to minister to him but can't let him minister to her. Often such a woman fails to climax sexually and thinks that's all right because she is giving to her husband, and to her that is all that matters. She cannot see she actually defeats him by denying him the fulness of giving to her. More commonly it is the man rather than the wife who cannot admit his mate behind his defensive walls to melt and fill his heart.

We must learn both to help and to be helped. We have observed that elderly people who have been independent and strong, who have insisted on helping others all their lives, frequently have debilitating illnesses for numbers of years before they pass on. Though it is not His first will, God, in His mercy, places the elderly in a vulnerable position where they have to learn to receive. Faithful ministers of the gospel commonly suffer from a heart of stone, for the minister's concept of his office seduces him to value giving but not receiving.

The heart of stone is not always something hidden. When it becomes so hardened that we don't want to do things for others, everyone recognizes it. We say, "He's such a selfish man, so self-centered." In such a case, sin has proceeded to its fulness. The heart of stone has imprisoned the man.

The scriptural promise is to take out the heart of stone and give us a heart of flesh, but that word "flesh" gives us trouble. "Flesh" has a tremendously bad press in the Bible. "To set the mind on the flesh is death" (Rom. 8:6 RSV). Or "The mind that is set on the flesh is hostile to God" (v. 7 RSV). Or Galatians 5:16, 5:16, "Do not gratify the desires of the flesh" (RSV). Or "He who sows to his own flesh will from the flesh reap corruption" (Gal. 6:8 RSV). However, the flesh is not always something negative. As in Ephesians 5:29, "No man ever hates his own flesh, but nourishes and cherishes it" (RSV). The word "flesh" is used in many varying contexts in the Bible, and there are many theological confusions about it. We often think wrongly about the flesh; wrong ways of thinking about life are built into us just as Southern drawls of Northern accents are.

St. Paul says, "I know that nothing good dwells within me; that is, in my flesh" (Rom. 7:18 RSV). Knowing the flesh is bad, we set out to crucify it, but we sometimes think erroneously that that means we should block off all desires of

33

the body. So when we read that Jesus will give us a heart of flesh, we think, "What kind of promise is that? That sounds like He's going to take away our nice peaceable dead thing and give us a living serpent. Who needs flesh? I thought we were to get rid of it!"

There is, however, another use of the word flesh:

> Husbands, love your wives, as Christ loved the church and gave himself up for her, that he might sanctify her, having cleansed her by the washing of water with the word, that he might present the church to himself in splendor, without spot or wrinkle or any such thing, that she might be holy and without blemish. Even so husbands should love their wives as their own bodies. He who loves his wife loves himself. For no man ever hates his own flesh, but nourishes and cherishes it, as Christ does the church, because we are members of his body. "For this reason a man shall leave his father and mother and be joined to his wife, and the two shall become one." (Eph. 5:25-31 RSV)

So the flesh in this case is not something bad.

The Scriptures do give revelation as to what the flesh actually is:

> For we are the true circumcision, who worship God in spirit, and glory in Christ Jesus, and put no confidence in the flesh. Though I myself have reason for confidence in the flesh also. If any other man thinks he has reason for confidence in the flesh, I have more; circumcised on the eighth day, of the people of Israel, of the tribe of Benjamin, a Hebrew born of Hebrews; as to the law a Pharisee, as to zeal a persecutor of the church, as to righteousness under the law blameless. (Phil. 3:3-6 RSV)

Because Paul has said not to put any confidence in our flesh, we have acquired confused feelings and thoughts about our bodies. That is not what he was talking about; he was speaking of heritage and belonging.

For John Sandford, confidence in the flesh could be expressed as follows: American; part Osage Indian; half English; born a Congregationalist of Congregationalists; raised a liberal; in his pride taunting believers as naive and radical; a Pharisee trained to conform himself to the image of goodness he supposed was set forth for him to be. As Paul was trained under Gamaliel, John was taught in Congregational schools, both college and seminary.

For Paula, confidence in the flesh would be pride and confidence in her Baptist background; her upbringing in a solid church-going, Bible-believing family; proper training from the age of two weeks in a church which preached the gospel, a church which upheld the moral laws of God and taught tithing. A Pharisee, she rested in doing things the right way.

The flesh is never apart from the body, except when we die. Flesh, another way of saying "the self," "the carnal nature," "the old man," is trained into our bodily responses.

For example, if I feel an urge to embrace my wife, the Holy Spirit may be prompting that. But I also embrace her *through* my flesh, for the flesh is what I think and feel, including all the unconscious hidden nature, about what it is to be a husband and to have a wife. The Holy Spirit flowing through my body and spirit comes through clean and free, but through my unredeemed flesh, love becomes corrupted by all my carnal nature. Body desires need to be corraled by moral discipline, but insofar as they flow morally, they are good and clean and holy passions. That is the good flesh spoken of in Ephesians 5. Such passions do not need to be mortified and stopped. Too many families have dried up by trying to stop them. It is the built-in, wrongly motivated ways that have to be mortified. Purification changes bad flesh to good flesh as we in fact incarnate the Lord Jesus anew in us. "Every spirit that confesseth that Jesus Christ is come *in the flesh* is of God" (1 John 4:2b). We see this as more than a doctrinal test; Jesus has come in the flesh when a man hugs his wife or a mother and father truly love their children.

In the world our flesh has become corrupted as inheritance and the culture have structured wrong ways into us. St. Paul said, "The gospel . . . is the power of God unto salvation" (Rom. 1:16). Salvation refers to more than redemption. It includes the entire sanctification process. The gospel is the primary tool of God to weed the garden of our nature. It is His instrument to purify our flesh. "Wherewithal shall a young man cleanse his way? by taking heed thereto according to thy word" (Ps. 119:9). "The law of the Lord is perfect, reviving the soul" (Ps. 19:7 RSV). Our task as a family is to devour the Word so that, sharper than any two-edged sword, it may pierce to the dividing asunder of spirit and soul, joint and marrow, discerning the thoughts and intents of the heart (Heb. 4:12). As the flesh cannot be fully transformed apart from the cross of our Lord Jesus Christ, neither can it be unless we become workmen that need not to be ashamed, rightly dividing the word of truth (2 Tim. 2:15).

There are times when we use the word "flesh" to refer specifically and solely to the body, as in Shakespeare's "a pound of flesh" (Shylock). In such usages, there should be no overtones of evil. For Jesus has died to cleanse the earth (Acts 10:15).

The Ezekiel 36 prophecy that Jesus would give us a heart of flesh means of course a redeemed heart. He became that malformed flesh and died for it, so deeply ingrained in us. He puts on us His own character. Consequently what our flesh expresses is the glory of Christ. Jesus was resurrected in the flesh. That means both in body and flesh. He alone has perfected flesh. All His nature, belongings, motivations, instincts, understandings are perfect and perfectly express through every mechanism of His resurrected body. His promise to raise us means that both in body and flesh we are to be made like Him, to mature into the likeness of Christ. That is what the term "salvation" means, to be given fully redeemed flesh, a new heart of flesh.

Many Christians, confused about the flesh, find it difficult to imagine being raised in the body. Such confusion affects also our present living. For that reason St. Paul wrote 1 Corinthians 15. And we write the following, for nothing is more destructive to the family today than our unscriptural conditioned responses to the reality of living as a spirit in a body.

There are two ways of viewing what we are as spirit and body. These ways form patterns of behavior built by our culture into our nature, and affect all our life, whether we know it or not. The first way is the Hebraic-Christian. Present confusions cause most Christians to reject the Hebraic-Christian way as being unchristian. The second way is that of the anti-Christ. Unfortunately, that way pervades our Western culture and is accepted by most as being Christian.

The Hebraic-Christian way of thinking says that both spirit and body exist and flow together in oneness. Oneness is not a monism. Monism coalesces spirit and body so that one or the other ceases to exist. True faith supports a dualism, but sees no basic antagonism between spirit and body. All parts of being, however separate in nature or function, flow together in unity. Through Jesus Christ all of nature and the physical body of mankind is clean and the Spirit of God flows in and through all. Both matter and spirit are to be respected. Both are to have full life together. Fulfillment comes as spirit is expressed most fully in body and matter.

In the anti-Christ way, spirit is seen as good, matter as bad; therefore the human body is defiled. There is a dichotomy so that anything of spirit is thought of as separate and antagonistic to matter. The gnostic Marcion taught that a lesser god or "demi-urge" had created the earth; therefore, it was defiled. Against such gnostics John stated resoundingly that the Word was with God, and the Word was God, and everything was created through Him (John 1:1-3). In anti-Christ thought, since matter and body are unclean, the struggle is to mortify the body, to kill its passions, and to return to being a pure spirit. The passions of the body defile the spirit. Such thought is totally opposite to the Christian desire to be fulfilled within the body.

During the centuries in which the Bible was written, geographically all around Palestine almost everyone held that split way of thinking. Still today Hindus believe mankind has become trapped in the body, in the wheels of dharma and karma. Each person regretfully must continue to be reincarnated until the spirit can be purified of its fleshly attachments and returned to being a pure spirit, away from the body. The Hindu hope is to escape the body, not to be fulfilled within it. For this reason, Christians should have nothing to do with Eastern mystics who teach meditation. Their way is to block out all feelings and thoughts. That splits life apart. The Christian is never more alive in every faculty of his entire being than when in prayer. The Christian way is unity and fulfillment. That means life abundant, not resignation.

Let us expose the historical base by which the anti-Christ way of thinking has become so dominant in our culture. It began in the mythological stories of creation apart from the Word of God.

The Babylonian story of creation says that Marduk, a god, fights with Tiamat, his mother. He stuffs the four winds into Tiamat's mouth, whereupon her belly distends and she dies. Taking out his knife, he slits her belly and lifts the top half, which becomes the heavens. The remaining blood and intestines become the earth. That's creation. Would a man be inclined to respect material life with that story? Could he honor his own body?

In Egyptian mythology, there is a slimy mud flood. In the midst of the muck there arises a mud hillock. On that miry mound arises a man who spits. That spit is creation. With that belief, who could respect the earth? Or love his body?

Contrast those with the Hebraic concept. In the beginning, God, a holy and loving Father, created the heavens and the earth. The earth was without form and void and darkness was on the face of the deep, and God said, "Let there be light." And behold there was light. *And God saw that it was good.* What a blessed contrast! Six days He created and each day He saw that it was good. On the sixth He took that good, clean dust of the earth and molded it into the form of a man, and breathed His own holy and loving breath into that form. And man became a living soul. "And God saw every thing that he had made, and *behold it was very good*" (Gen. 1:31). How beautiful that story of creation is! In the Hebraic-Christian belief all of earth with all of its creatures is redolent with the beauty and breath of a good and loving, holy God. It is no accident that wherever true Hebraic-Christian faith has appeared, reverence for life has followed.

It was into the Hebraic way of life that Jesus came as God incarnate in the flesh. The Eastern mind could not receive that fact. Easterners were scandalized by the concept of the Incarnation. From that conflict sprang many heresies. To them it was scurrilous to think that God himself would come in a human body, that the Prince of Peace would be born through a woman's womb. That the promised Counselor would have to be suckled at the breast? Horrors! Therefore, such men as Cerinthus, Elipandus and Felix came up with Adoptianism. This held that Jesus was not in fact born of a woman; God found a grown man and adopted him. To them Jesus was a man possessed by God, not truly the Word *become* flesh. Then came Docetism, from the Greek word *dokein*, "to appear." It was too repugnant to think God came naturally and fully into a human body. Docetists said that He only appeared to have a body, as a theophany (an appearance of God in human form), and returned to heaven. Resistance to the body created resistance to belief in the Resurrection. St. Paul wrote 1 Corinthians 15 to disabuse Greek believers' minds from the false notions of the Mithraic cults, to whom the blessing of death was to rid oneself of the body. The body is not a mortal coil to be shuffled off. It is not temporary. It is not a disposable can from which God removes the spirit for use in heaven. The body is itself a part of the new creation. We are to be resurrected within our natural bodies. If we die, and lose the body, we will be given new bodies in heaven.

Confusion came into Christian thought through the Greek mentality, mainly through Aristotle. Aristotle attempted to elude the mystic, but nevertheless perpetuated and elaborated the split way of thinking which was its base. Through Thomas Aquinas and others, that framework of thought rather than the biblical approach pervaded the life of the church. The Aristotelian wrong way of thinking consequently infected all of Western mentality—our science, philosophy, economics, politics, and sex. Since all our thinking is corrupted by it, so are all the common daily actions by which we relate to each other in the family.

If we attend the theater, all too often we see something like "Hair," or some other denigration of life. At the movies we are frequently exposed to pornography even in PG, to say nothing of R- and X-rated films. What we seldom see portrayed is a true and honorable attitude toward sex. We do not see the Hebraic-Christian concept of sex but the opposite is expressed. "Were they ashamed when they had committed abominations? nay, they were not at all ashamed, neither could they blush" (Jer. 6:15). Because of anti-Christ confusion, men think the body is only a body, so why not display it and exploit it sexually? Truly God's people are destroyed for lack of knowledge (Hos. 4:6 RSV). They do not reverence the whole person, body and spirit, as one wondrous and holy being. People have actually said to us, "Truly spiritual people would not have sexual feelings, would they?" What tommyrot! In Christ we believe the glory of God shines *through* every man and every woman. A Christian who understands this does not want to defile the goodness of the body and the wholesomeness of sex by using it wrongly. Sex for the Christian is a gift of God, a most hallowed and exciting fulfillment of spirit and body.

Anti-Christ confusion causes men to think that being spiritual is something distinct from the practical issues of living. For them, if spirit exists, it is something foreign, strange, over there somewhere, and what we do in church is something mystical, obscure, kooky—"religious." A "real man" would of course be physical and practical, sexually an animal. This sets up total confusion for the Christian layman at work. He thinks his Christianity must be something he can "do." He fails to understand that the Spirit of Christ naturally flows through everything he is and does. Casting about and finding nothing specifically Christian he can "do," he wonders what is missing, feels shame-faced and guilty, somehow less than he ought to be. Whereas if his mentality were steeped in the truly biblical, he would know that the Lord blesses everything he touches, that he is a blessing purely because he is. He would clean up his language, stop his dirty jokes, carry the burdens of his fellow-laborers in his heart, and find ways to be kind to all around him. Honesty and integrity would gird his loins. He would work beyond his pay. But these common things hardly seem dramatic and different enough. He cannot see the common as Christian because his mind, trained in anti-Christ before his conversion, calls that secular, not religious. The word "secular" cannot be found in the Bible. It is a fiction of the devil. Nothing is secular.

There is no separation of body and spirit. No man can touch a woman without touching her spirit. St. Paul wrote: "Do you not know when you lie with a woman you become one with her?" (1 Cor. 6:16, author's paraphrase). Only Paula has been consecrated or tuned by God to fulfill John's body and spirit. Because we know that, we do not *want* any other. No one else can have it for us, however beautiful in personality or body. The full glory of sex can happen only between married couples. Absolutely nowhere else. Not understanding that, men think to gain and only lose. A man thinks that sex is only something body to body, so "I might as well find a better body and enjoy it." Even if he never commits adultery, that wrong way of thinking causes him to miss the glory. He never becomes aware that he has a spirit that can meet and be thrilled in the embrace of his wife's spirit. A holy glory surrounds a man and wife making love. But because of the anti-Christ way, most of our grandparents thought sex was nasty. "Sex is only for procreation." "You shouldn't do it unless you want to have children." "If you enjoy it, confess. You are being sinful." Contrast that with the beauty of "Adam *knew* Eve his wife; and she conceived" (Gen. 4:1). And "Even so husbands should love their wives as their own bodies. He who loves his wife loves himself. For no man ever hates his own flesh, but nourishes and cherishes it" (Eph. 5:28, 29 RSV).

Our entire scientific technology is based on the Aristotelian split of life. We see matter as being dead and inert. We fail to relate to matter. We impose our will, willy-nilly, on the things around us. We push, pull, use, manipulate, and destroy. All things are mere "its" to us. We are totally insensitive to anything less than human or animate. We are about to deplete and destroy fair earth, partially because we can think in no other terms than these. Such thinking carries over into family living. Martin Buber points out that we also tend to relate to each other as objects, as "its" (Martin Buber, *I-Thou*). Mothers dutifully feed bodies food, three squares a day—but let their children starve emotionally and spiritually. Fathers relate all day to objects of their work as "its," unfortunately also to other men likewise as "its," and come home to treat their families the same way—and wonder why it doesn't work. Politicians count votes and miss people as persons. Sociologists count statistical noses, oblivious to the primacy of each man's spirit. Programs are fomented both in the world and church which further tear apart the fabric of the spirit's and soul's life in the family. Anti-Christ thinking is not merely a dead and inert philosophy, as we tend to think of all objects. It is an archetypal form, having a life of its own, a demonic thing wielded by the principalities of evil, a mesmeric construct by which Satan blinds the eyes of men to keep them from seeing the light of life in all things and in all people (2 Cor. 4:4).

It is crucially important for families to comprehend that this anti-Christ way of thinking affects the way we relate to each other every single moment of our lives. Only by such knowledge can we come to true and joyous repentance, and let Him change all our thinking. We need to be aware that when we touch one another, whomever we touch, we do so as one whole being to another whole being. Jesus wants to give us a heart of flesh so that we may refresh one another, so that each soul may be formed and reformed daily in Him.

The spirit and soul must have touch, laughter, light and joy, work and sweat, tears and games, boredom and excitement, rest and strife. Spirit and soul are not a machine, or a thing apart from the body. As we touch one another in the family, the soul is being formed. It is that formation, constant death and reformation, which is the primary product of life in Christ in the family. The child's spirit must have its own mother and father whenever possible—not substitutes. Human passion is not opposite to spirit-life; it is the very milieu in which the spirit grows to be fully human, fully God-like. It is in the melee of life that the spirit learns to choose between the wrong passions of the flesh and the pure passions of the spirit in the body. That is what life is all about.

3

MAN AND WOMAN
BECOMING ONE FLESH

Man and woman becoming one flesh means that we enter into a commonality of feelings, one way of thinking, one set of goals. We do not become each other. We do not lose our identities in each other. We enjoy a unity of love in which each person can become all that he is meant to be. We also become one body, in the sense that the physical body of one does not seem complete without the other. Being with each other in spirit unites and completes each individual.

"Be subject to one another out of reverence for Christ" (Eph. 5:21a RSV). To be subject means "to be cast under," but "out of reverence for Christ." The only way we can subject our prideful flesh to one another is through reverence for Christ. We will not accomplish it any other way. Note that the command is not merely to women, but that we all should be subject to one another.

Consider the little word "as" throughout the following: "Wives be subject to your husbands *as* to the Lord. For the husband is head of the wife, *as* Christ is head of the church." How are we subject to the Lord? Freely, through love for Him. Submission is voluntary, we want to submit out of our desire to give to Him. So is the wife submitted to the husband. Christ is head of the church purely because He is who He is. In love He invites us to let Him rule, and His rule sets us free to be our own persons. He never domineers or forces. His lordship means He makes himself servant to all mankind. A husband's headship makes him servant to all his family. It does not make him a controller nor give him a right to dominate. A father's life in the family should set the wife and children free to develop. "*As* Christ is the head of the church, his body, and is himself its Savior. *As* the church is subject to Christ, so let wives also be subject in everything to their husbands. Husbands, love your wives, *as* Christ loved the church and gave himself up for her, that he might sanctify her, having cleansed her by the washing of water with the word, that he might present the church to himself in splendor, without spot or wrinkle or any such thing, that she might be holy and without blemish. Even so husbands should love their wives *as* their own bodies. He who loves his wife loves himself. For no man ever hates his own flesh, but nourishes and cherishes it, *as* Christ does the church, because we are members of his body" (Eph. 5:23-30 RSV). The husband is called to love *as* Jesus loves us. His task is to lay down his life for the benefit of his family, day in and day out.

"For this reason a man shall leave his father and mother and be joined to his wife, and the two shall become one" (Eph. 5:31 RSV, quoting Gen. 2:24). That is a three-stage process, for if we do not leave the father and mother emotionally as well as physically, we cannot be joined to each other, and the process of becoming one cannot begin. Hundreds of times we have counseled couples who could not mature into oneness because one or the other or both had failed to leave home. Perhaps it is significant that the command to leave home is given to men. Far more often we find men unable to do so rather than women. But the Lord also speaks to women, "Hear, O daughter, consider, and incline your ear; forget your people and your father's house; and the king will desire your beauty" (Ps. 45:10 RSV).

When I (John) watch young people marching down the aisle

at a high school or college baccalaureate, my spirit is crushed with grief. I weep because I see that in this commercial, materialistic culture we have taught our young people everything external and nearly nothing internal. We give them the mechanics—reading and writing and arithmetic. We may have taught them some government, history, sociology, and a little psychology. But they know almost nothing about the skills of forgiveness. They know next to nothing about the art of hearing each other in true communication. They comprehend even less of the skills of sensitivity. About themselves as spirit and soul, they are tragically destitute, and what they do know confuses them. Worse, they are nearly completely unequipped to upbuild and nurture each other. I cannot help but hang my head in shame at our failure to fulfill the commandment of God: "And these words, which I command thee this day, shall be in thine heart: And *thou shalt teach them diligently unto thy children,* and shalt talk of them when thou sittest in thine house,

DIAGRAM ONE

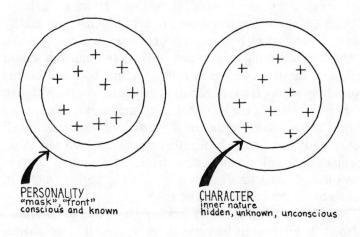

PERSONALITY
"mask", "front"
conscious and known

CHARACTER
inner nature
hidden, unknown, unconscious

47

and when thou walkest by the way, and when thou liest down, and when thou risest up'' (Deut. 6:6, 7). I know that when those young people marry, most of them will make a shambles of their lives. Their innate selfishness will destroy their marriages and their parenthood. We desperately need to know how to become one in Christ.

In diagram one, the two sets of concentric circles represent two people. We live on the outside and on the inside. The word "personality" comes from the Latin *persona* which means "mask" or in our modern slang "front." It is not necessarily phony that we have a front. We can't go around "letting it all hang out" all the time. We have to put forth a best face. We are working at being a person to other people. That is our exterior, known, overt personality, represented by the exterior circles.

On the inside is the character. Character comes from the Greek word *charakter,* meaning "engraving tool." Character means our "inner" nature, which surely is engraved or written into us by the hand of God (Jer. 31:33; Rom. 5:1-5 RSV). Our inner nature is largely hidden. It is mostly unknown and unconscious (Col. 3:3; 1 John 3:2). "Unconscious" does not mean "knocked out," nor does it mean asleep. "Unconscious" refers to anything in us of which we are usually unaware, which may be a construct, complex, instinct, habit, or any automatic thing which acts in and through our motor reflexes. The unconscious is active and motivational behind everything we do. It has hundreds of devices and traits within it. The closest term in the Bible for it is "the heart." We use the word "unconscious" rather than "heart" or "subconscious" because so many people habitually connect heart too much with feelings, and think of any word with the prefix "sub" as having less value. What is inside of us is as valuable, perhaps more so, than what is conscious and known.

We did not put into our diagram little circles for pearls of wisdom and diamonds for gems of truth, as well as the crosses which represent trouble spots, because that would overcrowd the picture. A great deal of what is inside of us is hidden diamonds and pearls. Most of what we bring to marriage is the positive within us. And the most glorious mystery of God's mercy is that every one of our sore spots is to be transformed by the Lord Jesus Christ into pearls of wisdom and diamonds of truth.

We all have hidden within us vast unknown incapabilities. As we have said in chapter two, we may be unaware that we may be unable to give or receive affection. Until parenthood reveals this to us, we may not know how critical of our children we will be. It may be a shock to find ourselves disciplining entirely differently than we thought we would. Sudden fears and angers may crop up. And so on it goes, ad infinitum.

It is amazing how the little things get to us. Where does he drop his socks? Does he leave a ring in the bathtub? Is he forgetful? Does she set the table like mama did? Or burn the bacon? Are the sheets always wrinkled? Is the house too messy or too clean? These are also represented by the x's in the circles.

When a man and woman enter marriage one question faces them. It makes no difference whether they are sixteen, twenty-one, or fifty, nor whether this is their first, second, third, or fourth marriage. All face the same question. Will they learn to drink from each other's strengths and overcome each other's weaknesses, or drink from each other's weaknesses and overcome each other's strengths? Will they learn to upbuild and nurture each other, or tear each other apart? Will they find those hidden gems and pearls and polish them? Will they uncover their broken places and let the Lord heal them and turn them into gems? Or will they reveal, nurture and build up their incapabilities until they have made themselves into inhuman demons dwelling in self-made hells? We all take the same test: will we overcome for each other or succumb to mutual destruction?

In our culture we have grown up too much entertaining a foolish romantic idea: "If I love somebody, I have only good, romantic love feelings. I always want to be kind to my mate. If I begin to have bad feelings, or no feelings, I must be 'falling out of love.' If I hate somebody, surely I can't be in love." All of that is a delusion. Since human love is corrupted by the inhumanity of sin, we also entertain feelings of hate for whomever we love. David, Saul, and Jonathan were involved in real love. Saul wound up hating David, and David struggled not to return it. Jacob and Esau were brothers who loved and therefore also hated. Rachel and Leah, two sisters who loved the same man, were also filled with jealous competition, hating each other. Wherever unredeemed love is, there is hate. Love and hate are not opposites; they go hand in hand. Because the flesh is corrupted, we cannot love without hating and we cannot hate without loving.

Love is a risk relationship. Major differences exist between secondary and primary relationships. At work or with friends, we have secondary relationships. We brush shoulders. If they insult us, we get over it. We may hate for a moment, but we soon forget. A primary relationship involves a much more vital risk. A primary relationship is with a father or mother, brother or sister, husband or wife, and children. If people in a primary relationship say the same words in the same way as secondary people do, we are either blessed out of our socks or torn to shreds. Primary people have access to us. What they are and do defines us to ourselves. These are the people on whom we are emotionally dependent. If they don't express love, we are undone. If a person in a secondary relationship fails us, so what? We can get over it. The same is true if one insults us. But a primary person can cut us to the quick. If a stranger says to me (John), "I don't like you,"—okay, I'll get over it. But let Paula say that to me, and without copious help from Jesus, I am not going to get over it. So, to the degree of our involvement, we experience risk and are often hurt. The response to hurt is anger. Anger becomes resentment, then bitterness. The name of that game is hate.

The first thing we need to understand is that without Jesus Christ and His skills of forgiveness, we are not going to stay together. Life is too painful without Him because we enter into too many risks without the opportunity for redress. The second is that old saw, "Marriage is no bed of roses"—unless we remember that roses have thorns. We need to drop our romantic notions and realize that the beginning of trouble does not signify the end of love.

As married couples are time-exposed to one another, the individual masks cannot be kept in place. We begin, whether we want to or not, to penetrate behind each other's fronts. In diagram two below, the expanding, interpenetrating spiral indicates ever-deeper involvement in one another. Eventually we commence to tap into hidden sore spots. We are land mines

DIAGRAM TWO

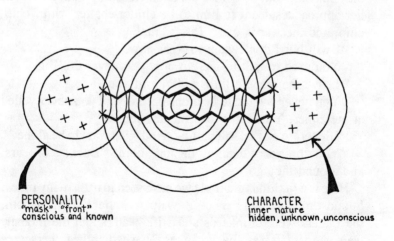

PERSONALITY
"mask", "front"
conscious and known

CHARACTER
inner nature
hidden, unknown, unconscious

51

waiting to be stepped on. When a hidden habit or wound flares up, we most often strike into a counterbalancing grievance in the other—and the battle is on! The jagged lines between circles represent our arguments.

Married people are bound to disagree. If they are not arguing occasionally, something is wrong. Either they are not facing things, fooling themselves, putting on false faces of peace, being super-spook martyr Christians, or they are wrestling things out. Healthy marriages necessitate hassles.

The husband has been at work, putting forth his best to be responsible, kind, and attentive to all. He is poured out and weary. Now he wants to come home to "recollect," which means to gather his energies, rest in himself a while, and regain his composure. In the vernacular, he needs "to get it all together." So he sits down in isolation before the TV or buries himself in the newspaper. That is not really what he needs, but it is what he has chosen. The wife has been at home all day, or among women friends, talking to women and children. A part of her feels unfulfilled, waiting for her husband to come home so they can talk. But he comes home all closed up in himself. All her approaches seem to him to be chitter-chatter, chip, chip, chip, and the war is on. "Talk to me!"

"I will but I don't want to right now."

"You used to talk to me but now you never do."

"Leave me alone a little while, will you?"

"You never wanted to be alone before, and you never yelled at me either. You don't love me any more!"

"I do too. And I wasn't yelling. And I just want to be alone."

"You don't ever listen to me any more!" Buckets of tears, and around they go.

Here is a fictitious example we have seen in truth many times. Suppose a fiance and fiancee grew up in similar homes. In both, the fathers were drunkards and wife-beaters and the mothers were naggers. It was always a question whether the fathers were drunkards because the wives were naggers or whether the wives were naggers because the men were drunkards. Whichever, that was the style of life. Now the children of those couples marry. One night the new husband comes home a little tipsy. Suddenly there is an exaggerated anger in her, larger than the occasion warrants, and she blows up at him. Equally, there is a surprising fury in him, also more than the occasion warrants. What's going on?

Most people see the first level. She is afraid he will become a drunkard like her father. He fears she will become a nagger like his mother.

But something far more involved is happening. Each has judged his parents and determined not to live like that. But "Judge not, that you be not judged. For with the judgment you pronounce you will be judged, *and the measure you give will be the measure you get*" (Matt. 7:1, 2 RSV). It is an inescapable law that what we have judged *will* come upon us. Without Jesus the law is unstoppable.

Yet there is another trouble. When these two were children, say only seven, and each father was drunk and each mother nagging, and the mothers were being hit and screaming in anger and terror, both children became angry, terrified, and disillusioned. How does a seven year old tell off papa or mama? Or how does he, not yet mature in faith, release a thing to the cross by prayer? What can the children do but push it down? Because the unconscious like a good computer never forgets anything, that anger becomes like festering pus. If we multiply this one example by the countless thousands of hurts and frustrations, large and small, that happen to us all even in the best of homes, we can understand why the Scripture describes our hearts as storehouses of violence (Amos 3:10). We can see why Jesus said that out of the heart proceed evil thoughts (Matt. 15:18) and Jeremiah spoke of the heart as "deceitful above all things, and desperately wicked" (Jer. 17:9). The heart has become the storage place and festering area of all of our emotional sores. What happens between couples is that the anger, resentment, bitterness, and unforgiveness of all our youth, actually directed at our parents, siblings, and others, come out on our mates and family, regularly.

Do we see that no marriage has a chance for complete fulfillment and true happiness without the Lord Jesus Christ? Most of us can recollect having seen some seemingly successful marriages outside of Him, but what lies unresolved in the hearts of such couples? And what might they have been *with* Him? Someone has said that marriage is a twenty-four-hour-a-day, 365-days-a-year, exercise in the art of forgiveness. How true!

Because of what is in us, we are continually a fight looking for someplace to happen. Seldom are fights "clean," (i.e. actually concerning what they seem to be about). Most marital battles involve what psychologists call "projection"— problems with parents or others foisted onto the mate. We fight unseen shadows, and work out long forgotten things at each other's expense.

A young man was raised with a hypochondriac mother. It took a strong woman to get that sick. The boy detested it, and resented having to take up the slack and do whatever chores the mother's supposed illnesses prevented. When he married, if his wife became ill, even to running a 103-degree fever, his mind said, "She is ill. Help her." But no way could he in fact perform what his mind said. His heart said, "She's faking it." Powerful confusing feelings welled up. He found "valid" excuses to be elsewhere, helping someone else.

"He will make my feet like hinds' feet, and he will make me to walk upon mine high places" (Hab. 3:19). The mountain deer or hind is able to go safely in high places because its rear feet track exactly where the front feet lead. Mountain guides know not to use some horses because they have been around humans too long. Their rear feet, like a puppy running sideways down the street, do not track as they should. Some mountain trails are so precarious that if the hind feet do not step exactly in the track of the forefeet, horse and rider could plummet to death. Our front feet are our will to be married and the conscious mind's determination to live in Christ with one another. But if the Lord has not brought us to sufficient purification in Him, if He has not ferreted out those sore places in sanctification by His Spirit, our rear feet, the heart and feelings, will not track. Our marriage and family relationships plummet down.

It will not do to find another, with whom we might supposedly be more compatible. What is in us will soon come out. Therefore, we cannot ascend the high places of successful marriage. Whoever marries takes a "pig in a poke." We have no idea what we are stepping into, either in the other or in ourselves. Until marriage brings it out, we shall not know what is locked up inside. That is the risk we take! Marriage is fraught with surprises.

Our culture has taught us to think we ought to marry someone with whom we are compatible. While some compatibility may help, usually we discover ourselves to be so different we could almost agree with the quipster who said, "About the only truth behind compatibility is that if the husband keeps on bringing the income, the wife will keep on being 'pattable.' " We attract to us people who are opposite to us, because we need that opposition precisely in order to wrestle with it. Our romantic dream is of a couple walking off into the sunset living happily ever after. But God designs us so that by our encounter we will be unable to congratulate ourselves that we are all right, and have to face what is in us. We are lazy and unwilling to see truth. We "hide from our own flesh" (Isa. 58:7). Therefore God gives us a "beloved enemy." Peace is not always God's design. "Suppose ye that I am come to give peace on earth? I tell you, Nay; but rather division" (Luke 12:51).

In all this we are teaching concerning normal people in

normal marriages. Not the aberrational or psychotic. We write exclusively concerning Christian marriages, not the worldly. Many who are not Christian *seem* to have peaceful, happy marriages. Both the Christian and non-Christian wonder at that. But the wise will understand (Dan. 12:10). God is not afraid to embarrass His own. "He hastens and chastens His will to make known." Because they are His, and have given their wills to Him, He can bring His sword to pierce and stir until they have to confess the sin-nature which none of us otherwise wants to admit is there. "If others about you are losing their heads, and you're keeping yours, perhaps you just don't understand the problem."

The existence of problems and fusses is not itself evil. What is worse is to go through life half-dead, never having dealt with the iniquity of the heart. "And every one who thus hopes in him purifies himself as he is pure" (1 John 3:3 RSV). Both outsiders and insiders often fail to comprehend that Christians' wrestles lead to a peace which passes understanding. "For the moment all discipline seems painful rather than pleasant; later it yields the peaceful fruit of righteousness to those who have been trained by it" (Heb. 12:11 RSV).

This says something unequivocal about the modern delusion that we can live with someone awhile before marriage in order to find out if it will work. If a couple are truly married, they begin to work out their hassles in Christ. The modern confusion is hedonism: "If it's still pleasurable, it's still working. If pain starts, it isn't working, so we must not be in love any more." To a Christian that's sheer rot. True marriage is not all battles, but at the onset, there is a healthy kind of foment which is unavoidable. Therefore, to think that the beginning of struggle signifies the end is exactly backwards. It actually signifies entrance into the effort truly to become one.

What marriage does give is the security needed in order to face what we are. Suppose that everyone in the church and in society could see our flaws, standing out like splotches of blood on a white wall? What if all our fractures made themselves evident on the job, in front of the boss? How long would we keep our job? How many friends would stick it out with us? How many would turn out to be fair-weather friends? But in Christ our mate is the one person who will see what we are and still choose to love us! Marriage is a covenant relationship, "for better, for worse, for richer, for poorer, in sickness and in health." "The *heart* of her husband trusts in her, and he will have no lack of gain. She does him good and not harm, all the days of her life" (Prov. 31:11, 12 RSV). All the rest of the church may see my faults—gossip, get disgruntled, flee, persecute, whatever—but Paula will be there, scolding maybe, but choosing me, staying right there, giving herself to me by the grace of God in Christ. That is security. Security comes first from the Lord who will never abandon, but secondarily and humanly in the mate whom He causes to continue to choose us.

Psychologically that security produces what is called "ego-strength." Ego-strength is not bad. We have maligned the ego. Here, we take the liberty of identifying the ego with our own spirit. We may be in error, and people may want to argue with us, but let's not lose the meaning. Whatever we call it, if we obtain real strength inwardly, we are empowered. We can say, "No." Somebody says, "Let's go have a drink." And we know that would mean staying out late. The pressure of the gang is there but we can say no. Lacking ego-strength, we can't resist the temptation. A teen-age gang says, "Let's go smoke pot." A youth with ego-strength can say no. Whether he says yes or no, he makes his decision out of his own center. Without ego-strength, behavior is complusive. There is no freedom; the person is controlled exteriorly, and every temptation pulls him down. A husband who has ego-strength can say, "Forgive me," (another way to say it is he has "the grace of God flowing in his life"). A mate who does not have the grace of ego-strength cannot sincerely apologize. All too often, women say to us in counseling, "My husband can never say he is sorry."

We give to each other strength to be, through the nurture of love. The Bible calls it "power." "But as many as received him, to them gave he power to become the sons of God, even to them that believe on his name" (John 1:12). Grace, self-control, the ability to deny self, to be unselfish, that power to live our faith, that "something" is what we are to nurture in each other. That power comes from God himself but also through each other. We give to one another not only the strength to overcome, but also the strength to receive change. God provides that strength as we forgive and cherish, touch and love, share and talk. God's itinerary for marriage is that as we hurtle into x after x of trouble as pictured on our diagram below, His grace will overcome and transform.

DIAGRAM THREE

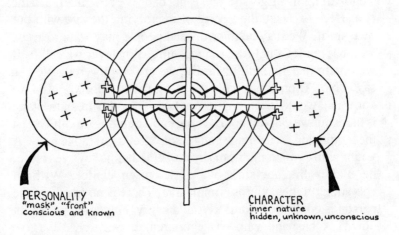

PERSONALITY
"mask", "front"
conscious and known

CHARACTER
inner nature
hidden, unknown, unconscious

Changing is painful. Staying open to each other is both

blessing and trauma. If we would remain alive and enjoy life, we need to keep growing and changing. The final product of life in Christ in marriage should be that each of our sore spots is transformed to a cross of glory. (One can see that what we say of marriage ought also to be seen in lesser degree in all relationships—pastor and church, teacher and class, foreman and workers, friendships, etc.) But because of immature reactions to hurt, many couples stop the process. They erect barriers. Consciously and/or unconsciously they agree to know each other only so far. Now they will have a secret life apart from each other. In so doing, they have unknowingly opted for silent divorce. Many seemingly successful couples are actually entrenched in silent divorce. Sometimes couples who are too perceptive to hide and too fiery in their natures, conclude their relationship in legal divorce.

Couples normally fall in and out of silent divorce. Silent divorce can be recognized easily. Before barriers come up (represented by the heavy line in the diagram below), a husband may have poker buddies or golf or business friends, but he does not look for excuses to spend too much time with them. He wants to be with his wife. He tells her, but not his buddies, all his hurts and sorrows as well as his successes. The same for the wife and her bridge clubs and sororities. Their hearts find nourishment in each other. They have no secrets. Sharing bridges are in place, and they find joy in meeting. Life is a mutually shared banquet, whether of grief or happiness. Unity has enabled an interflow of spirit to spirit in heart to heart and mind to mind.

After silent divorce barriers come up, the husband and wife find excuses to spend more time with their own individual friends. Communication bridges are down. The mate now becomes the last person we would tell what really counts in our life. That is like handing the devil a sword and saying, "Here is where you shove it in and twist to the hilt." If anyone can cut us to the quick, our mates can. Therefore, we sit in pockets of loneliness making up speeches.

DIAGRAM FOUR

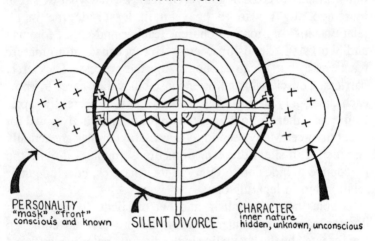

PERSONALITY
"mask", "front"
conscious and known

SILENT DIVORCE

CHARACTER
inner nature
hidden, unknown, unconscious

Silent divorce is deadly. Not only does it stop God's process of making us whole, but it makes our children feel the chill. They ache for us. Tranquility is not always a sign of happiness or God's favor. It may only mean that the marriage is making an outward show while inwardly dying. We know a couple who never had a fight for thirty-two years, and without a fight, they divorced. They had settled nothing. Their marriage was dead. Their peace had been only an armed truce.

Each time we discern silent divorce, we need to break out. Normally we cannot do this unless we talk things out. Most likely we will have to quarrel and we need to know how to have a good fight. There are good fights and bad fights. A bad fight leaves us sitting in a cave of hurt, gnawing old bones. After a good fight, we may find ourselves tired, worn-out, hurt, but sweetly so, and more in appreciation of our mate. Maybe for the first time we have understood the other *from within*. We understand how and what the other feels, what makes the mate tick. We respect the other more. We feel good about the other one, and we want to make love.

Therefore let us present some guidelines for good fights. The first rule is: Be honest. We do *not* mean, "Be perfectly honest about the *other* guy's faults." We mean, "Be self-honest." Be willing to admit that you may be at fault. Have the humility to listen. The striking thing is that the other will often point out some flaw in us right where we thought our strength was. Where we least expect it the knife comes—and rightly so most often. Where we thought we were doing so well and were proud of ourselves and wanted a compliment is likely to be where we are attacked. Why? Because normally behind our strong areas there lie hidden weaknesses. Pride has crept in, covering hidden false motivations. So a wife may set a beautiful table, prepare a delicious meal, dress well, and want a compliment, but the husband may be turned off by some kind of wrong, covert motivation. She may not understand that some clues in her manner prevent him. A man may be a good driver and want a compliment for it. But some kind of arrogance, an inner demand upon the other, a pride or insensitivity may cause her to attack him right at the point of his being a good driver. We could all list hundreds of examples. We need to pray for that kind of humility which can hear the true content behind the context.

Couples need to know the difference between context and content. Context is the freight train which carries the cargo of content, the true meaning. The words of a discussion may be all about the children, or business, dress, manners, anything at all. But the real meaning may be something else. It is quite revealing sometimes when counselors bring a quarreling couple together and stop them now and then to say, "Do you hear what he is really saying?" Frequently, for example, a wife responds, "Yes, he was complaining about the way I look!" Whereas in reality the husband was trying to give a compliment to encourage her to spend some money for herself because she has been too self-effacing. Her insecurity caused her to miss the real content, which was an attempt to help her find and express her own sense of beauty. It takes practice, skill, and humility in the Holy Spirit not to become distracted by contexts so as to hear real content. It is for this reason that couples many times need to talk in the presence of detached friends or wise counselors, who can help them to hear the true content behind what they are saying.

We need to take it on faith that the mate may be quite accurate in assessing us, even if we can't find one iota of truth in the charge against us. Probably we are merely blind. We have found that unless projectionism clouds the view, couples usually tell each other off fairly accurately. So listen! "He that hateth reproof shall die" (Prov. 15:10). Defensiveness reveals a striking, religious spirit rather than Christian grace. "He who corrects a scoffer gets himself abuse. . . . Reprove a wise man and he will love you" (Prov. 9:7, 8 RSV). There is nothing so valuable as the scolding of a mate. One of the greatest tragedies behind the recent overemphasis on submission was the silencing of the counterbalancing words of wisdom which could have come from women in the Lord. "She will do him good . . . all the days of her life" (Prov. 31:12). A husband who has learned to trust the truth of the Lord's Word will also learn to trust Him through his wife, and will treasure her ability to scold her husband appropriately. How greatly we need to hear and value what we say to each other, even when the words seem wide of the mark. If we will say to the Lord, "Show me where and how this really applies," and listen again, the Lord can help us to speak truth to one another. "Speaking the truth in love, we are to grow up in every way into him . . ." (Eph. 4:15a RSV).

If we will look behind our strengths we will find our weaknesses. And if we will look into our weaknesses, we may find some of our strengths. John was courageously foolhardy. He would always attack a problem head-on, jump into everything with all four feet, and take every dare. It took awhile for him to realize, at Paula's insistence, that that wasn't really courage but overcompensation for fear. To be attacked at the point of courage seemed ridiculous. It required the grace of the Lord to hear behind the context the true calling of the Lord's words through Paula. Paula was set to perform and needed to be affirmed. It took many hassles and the grace of the Lord for her to hear behind criticism the affirmations which were really there.

Often rich truth arrives in beggars' clothing. A confused thought many times masks a gem of truth. Christians should pray for a teachable spirit to recognize truth behind what is said. Real listening is the most difficult art in the world precisely because it calls for the most complete and constant death of self. However, some people take home guilt when they should not. They are too willing to hear criticism even when it is inappropriate. The same admonition applies nevertheless, for taking home too much criticism is just as much a flaw in the self as to refuse to hear. True listening is the art of discerning by the Holy Spirit what is true for us and what the other truly intends. "But strong meat belongeth to them that are of full age, even those *who by reason of use* have their senses exercised to discern both good and evil" (Heb. 5:14). Practicing to hear humbly with those closest to us develops those faculties of discernment which enable us to meet life for Christ in the world.

A second rule is: Never try to hurt. You will do enough without trying. If you try to hurt, if you enjoy that malicious art of the squelch, you force your mate to put up walls. No one can take constant insult. We are too vulnerable in marriage to stand continual purposeful wounding. Never try to get even. Respect, admiration, and trust must abide in a marriage. Insults destroy the capacity to cherish and keep respect alive. Be willing to quit while you're behind. Let the other have the last word. Find ways to admire and respect the other even while disagreeing. The Scripture never anywhere says, "Unbridle your tongue " It does say, "If your brother sins, rebuke him" (Luke 17:3a RSV), but the counterbalancing words are, "and if he repents, forgive him" (17:3b RSV), and "Brethren, if a man be overtaken in a fault, ye which are spiritual, restore such an one *in the spirit of meekness*; considering thyself, lest thou also be tempted" (Gal. 6:1). Moses, when challenged, fell on his face in prayer (Num. 16:4); he had become the meekest of men on earth (Num. 12:3). Meekness is not weakness, but such personal awareness of sin as to make one unwilling to attempt whatever could hurt another or override another's will. The best way to destroy a marriage is to be sure to win every argument. "The beginning of strife is like letting out water; so quit before the quarrel breaks out" (Prov. 17:14 RSV). Even if you are absolutely sure what you want to say is right and true, say it only if the Holy Spirit prompts it in love, for the other's welfare.

John's and Paula's parents both carefully trained their children never to try to insult. How grateful we are for such instruction (accomplished as much by their lives as by words). By the grace of God, in twenty-seven years, neither of us has ever hurled a word with malicious intent to wound. I (John) remember vividly my mother's words, "No man who ever hits a woman is a man at all." Nothing is so wounding to me in counsel as to hear of a husband beating a wife, both for her sake and for his. Violence should have no place whatsoever in a Christian home.

Hurt, and the desire to hurt, are more easily overcome if we remember at all times that we are loved in the Lord Jesus Christ, by Him and by each other.

We are tripartite creatures, body, soul, and spirit. In the level of our spirits the Lord Jesus Christ resides in each of us. In heart and mind and therefore also in body we may become confused and blocked, but not in spirit. Couples need to maintain that faith, that no matter how confused or incapable they become in heart and mind, they never cease to love one another. We need to believe always that in the other's spirit, no matter what actions seem to say otherwise, the other one loves us. It is on that basis that we trust and admire and respect the other. We put no trust in the flesh. We honor the life of Christ in the other. Hate is thus the flip side of love.

The third rule is therefore: When desire to hurt arrives, stop awhile. Go apart if necessary. Give yourself and the other a chance to recoup. You may say, "I need to take a breather." We do not mean to give anyone a license to cop out. You must be willing to come back to finish it. We mean, "Don't fire off half-cocked." Take time to put yourself together and regain your perspective. If listening to music does it, turn on the stereo. If chopping down trees releases the anger, chop down trees. You may live in a desert, but at least you're going to have marital victory. Whatever it takes, do it. The best recourse is prayer. Let Jesus restore your self-control. It is as though we have put on colored glasses. Everything the other does or says is now seen in that coloration. Little children lose sight of all the world and can only experience the hunger or pain which grips them in the present moment. The tensions from arguments can throw us into a regression back to childishness. In such cases we act as though the problem of the moment is all there is to our marriage and as though the problems or flaws or sins we think we see in our mate are like a drop of dye discoloring the whole vessel. We need to regain our perspective, and that is why we need to retreat from the melee. To let Jesus Christ cleanse the heart of the bitter, poisoned waters of the fallen star of wormwood (Rev. 8:11) so that we can see again the blessed totality of our mate and life together.

We need to walk in the other person's moccasins awhile. We should turn the argument around, seeing it from the other person's point of view to try to see what the other was thinking and feeling, given the best plausible motives, not the worst. If we can truly get inside the other, we can return and say, "Honey, it was all my fault." And when the mate says, "It's all my fault," we can argue the other way around!

Suppose the husband does something wrong. He comes to the wife and says, "Honey, I am sorry." One of the greatest tragedies is that most couples do not know how to respond. Most say, "Oh, that's okay." Or, "Oh, that's all right." It is *not* okay! It is *not* all right! The fourth rule is therefore: Always say those three important little words, "I forgive you." To say that it is okay is both a lie and an insult. Until the cross of Christ cleanses, there is no okayness, no matter what we think or feel. If John does something to hurt Paula, and comes to say, "I'm sorry," and she says, "No matter," that tells John he is unimportant, that he couldn't hurt her if he tried. John needs to be important enough to her that what he does *can* hurt her.

For the sake of being "nice," many couples wreck their marriages. Not wanting to hurt, they fear to speak truth. But truth is never destructive when the heart is right. "Better is open rebuke than hidden love. Faithful are the wounds of a friend; profuse are the kisses of an enemy" (Prov. 27:5, 6 RSV). Only if couples recognize their guilt can their grievances arrive at the cross. They must learn the art of speaking the truth in kindness. It is one art to hear, but a more important one to learn how to say hard words so compassionately that the other welcomes it and thanks you. "A word fitly spoken is like apples of gold in a setting of silver" (Prov. 25:11 RSV). Such apples were actually a fruit used to refresh welcome travelers. Truth fitly spoken refreshes. Potential arguments become embraces when kind words find their way to the heart. "A soft answer turns away wrath, but a harsh word stirs up anger. The tongue of the wise dispenses knowledge but the mouths of fools pour out folly. A gentle tongue is a tree of life, but perverseness in it breaks the spirit" (Prov. 15:1, 2, 4). Sometimes we must say the truth knowing it will hurt, but our intent should be to comfort and heal. "Blows that wound cleanse away evil; strokes make clean the innermost parts" (Prov. 20:30 RSV).

Though we should and sometimes do say those all-important words, "I forgive you," it is not easy to accomplish forgiveness. We cannot make the heart perform what the lips say. Only the Lord Jesus Christ can reach and transform the heart. We may say we forgive but a week later when the mate repeats the offense, we shout, "You've done it *again*! You *always* . . . !" One way or another we discover that what we said hasn't happened. "Without the shedding of blood there is no forgiveness of sins" (Heb. 9:22b RSV). A couple who are not practiced in prayer have little chance to apply the power of the cross to the depths of their hearts. We will teach more fully about forgiveness in chapter nineteen. Suffice it to say here that the ability to completely forgive is perhaps the most needful skill requiring restoration in family life today.

There are three legs to the stool of marriage: one, communication; two, prayer; three, sex. I (John) used to milk a cow, sitting on a three-legged stool on soft earth. I can tell you by sad experience that if one leg goes down, the others will also, no matter how good they may be. I've been under the milk, under the cow more times than I could say! It matters little whether communication, prayer, or sex fails first, the others will soon follow. As a man can use his own legs for the third leg of the stool, so we can strain to keep the marriage going. But sooner or later the other two will have become so eroded that the whole marriage sits hard in the dust. Some find it difficult to think of prayer and sex as interrelated. But Christians find that the more their spirits are refreshed in prayer and informed by sharing, the more glorious the act of sex becomes.

Communication does not mean talking *at* each other. People can talk at each other a mile a minute, while erecting Gardol walls between them, with never a moment of true communication. Real communication happens when empathy from spirit to spirit and heart to heart enables mind to mind comprehension.

Prayer is not talking at God, but meeting with Him. Much of prayer is not talk at all. Prayer happens by the same kind of empathic exchange which enables communication between humans. We need to meet God spirit to spirit, and then to speak with Him in real ways. What we need is honesty with God. Here is dishonest prayer, "Lord, you know that I love that wife you gave me. You know that she is the most beautiful and most wonderful of women. But why don't you just make her do this thing or that?" Honest prayer is, "Lord, I'm mad at her, I'd like to belt her. Please come in and take this corruption out of my soul, that I might be able to forgive her. And please forgive me."

Husband and wife may have copious quantities of sex and miss true quality. True sex is meeting, union, sharing, embracing, nurturing, complete being to complete being. Obviously such cannot happen where prayer and talk have not prepared the lovers.

These three, communication, prayer, and sex, influence each other. The better our interpersonal communication the better our prayer and sex life. The converse is true as well. The better our sex life the more easily and effectively we pray and communicate. Prayer, aloud, together, humbles and opens our hearts to each other, improving freedom of communication and uniting our spirits for sex. Lack of communication shuts down sex. The wife feels used, not met and cherished. The husband feels isolated and unfed. Both conclude in self-martyring pity parties.

Marriage is a pilgrimage from individual self-centeredness to ever fuller corporate life. The essence of marriage is the laying down of one's life for the other, not in self-martyring but in the joy of service. Fifty-fifty is a formula for divorce. One hundred percent given for the other is an equation for blessedness. A man who still thinks it's *his* job and *his* money is not yet married, no matter how long ago the wedding service. It's *our* job, whoever does it; it's *our* money, whoever brings it home. Not *my* children but *ours*. Not *my* house, but *ours*. Corporate life is the sign of maturity. A child is sweet but totally self-centered. An infant interrupts for his own need in the midst of any party or worship service. He has no awareness of the needs of others and therefore no consideration for them. Maturity demands death of self in service to others and therefore brings real life. "Whoever seeks to gain his life will lose it, but whoever loses his life will preserve it" (Luke 17:33 RSV). We can measure our distance from real life in Jesus by the degree of our regression into selfish thought and demand. Conversely, proximity to Jesus is told by its fruit in the ease of our giving and sharing.

If a couple are not to become delimited to the confusions of the moment, they will need a goal which transcends the years. Jesus warned not to take thought or be anxious for the morrow (Matt. 6:31-34) but He himself met on the mountaintop with Elijah and Moses to speak of how He was to accomplish the cross (Matt. 17:2, 3 and Mark 9:2-4). He did not inveigh against taking thought for the future but against selfish ambition and the anxieties which are born of distrust. Couples who do not have goals cannot escape self-centeredness. Paradoxically only those who have a plan for the future are free to live in the moment. Some couples confuse ambitions with goals. An ambition is a selfish desire for gain or glory. We use the word "goal" to refer to a calling of God for purposes other than selfish matters. A goal draws and empowers sharing; an ambition creates selfish striving. In seminary I (John) studied group dynamics. There we discovered that if a number of individuals sat down and said, "Let's become a group," we were soon at each other's throats. We never became a group. But if we were given an important task to do, we soon found ourselves becoming a group, losing our selfish desires in the joy of doing something together. Unity was a by-product of the struggle for the task. Many couples have shattered their marriages simply by trying to be married without a common goal. We know a couple who said, "We will raise good children." They were a success at it; they raised good children. But when the last child left the home, they discovered they didn't like each other any more and so they divorced. They had never had a goal, only an ambition. A goal outlasts life, is larger than can be accomplished by the couple alone, and calls forth all the latent energies of both partners. We knew a couple who wanted to create a successful business. They were enthused to sacrifice and work hand in hand until the moment of success. Now they are divorced. That dream was incapable of overcoming selfish glory-seeking.

If a man sees that his wife's desires never really get beyond the confines of her own struggle for fulfillment, even in the noble aspirations of raising children, after a while he can no longer pour all he is into that. It is like pouring the glory of the Jordan into the Dead Sea. If a wife sees that her husband's energies, however seemingly spent for others, are really only to enhance his own self-image, after a while she can no longer give all she is into that. We need to be Seas of Galilee, refreshed by cool waters from the mountains of prayer, sustaining the life of our family, and poured out for the life of the valley below. I (John) become engrossed in my work, insensitive to my family, and sometimes cross and tired. Before we were given to the Lord so completely as a team for the common goal of serving, I had the same tendencies to crossness and tiredness. Paula's ability to forgive and embrace was hampered by her perception that my tiredness was born of my own striving for vainglory. But now that we are in harness together, and have died to vainglory by counting even our goal as loss for Christ (Phil. 3:7), forgiveness is borne upon wings of mutual respect and admiration. Our goal enables us to see the life of Christ at work in each other and prevents us from becoming confined to this moment.

The only goal which truly outlasts life is to be given to the Lord Jesus Christ for service. A couple who still go to church to *get* something have not discovered the secret of life. "I appeal to you therefore, brethren, by the mercies of God, to present your bodies as a living sacrifice, holy and acceptable to God, which is your spiritual worship" (Rom. 12:1 RSV). The *New American Standard Bible* puts it, "which is your spiritual *service* of worship." True worship and the secret of life are one and the same, to be given upon the altar of life for others. A couple so given are founded upon the rock who is Jesus, and the floods of great waters shall not reach them (Ps. 32:6). It is not enough to have a Savior. That is still self-centered. A family needs to be given into His lordship, in which His headship is not words only but fact.

4

ANIMUS AND ANIMA

Perhaps the most important prerequisite to restoring the Christian family is communication. People talk but cannot hear, and sometimes hear in subliminal levels but fail to find words which adequately convey the heart's meaning. As a prophet cannot speak for God unless he truly hears, neither can a couple meaningfully serve each other's needs unless they can accurately hear one another. Perhaps the most difficult task we have in marriage is to learn how to decipher the three levels of meaning in what we say. We speak with the mind, with the heart, and with the spirit. The spirit speaks from embrace, desire, or loneliness, but it must express itself outwardly through the body, through our feelings and the conscious mind. The heart often warps and twists what comes from the spirit, and the mind is servant to both. The mind thinks it is objective, but any counselor can testify to countless instances in which counselees came to discover that their conscious minds had all along been serving hidden motives. A mate must learn to read the other's spirit, hear the heart, and weigh what the mind says accordingly. Continual prayer aloud together makes possible a flow of spirit to spirit which enables each mate to read the heart and comprehend the mind of the other.

It is extremely difficult to really hear what another says. For example, suppose a husband walks across a floor his wife has recently scrubbed. She exclaims, "Just look! Mud all over my clean floor!"

Usually a husband will say, "Sorry, I didn't notice."

The wife becomes even more upset because he didn't notice, and says something like, "What's the matter; are you blind?" She really means, "That's the trouble, you didn't notice."

The typical husband answers, "Well, you married me, and if you don't like it, you can lump it!"

Neither heard the other. What her entire being actually broadcasts is, "Everything I do is tedious! I do the scrubbing all the time and people don't notice me. I need attention. I need you to see that I'm worth something. I need a compliment." If she were to say, "Give me a compliment," that would defeat the virtue if he did respond. She could say, "I need to be hugged," but while that is sometimes helpful, there are also times when if it is asked for, it is spoiled because she needed to feel chosen and sought after without asking. The man in our example missed the content and answered only the context. If he says as some do, "Why the hell is it so important?" or "I'll scrub it up again" or even if he says, "I am sorry, I will clean it up," he has still missed the point. He failed to read and respond to her heart.

Our Lord has given us in the Word of God what is necessary to our faith and salvation, but He did not attempt to cover every exigency of life. The Word of God is applicable to every area of life, but some things must be seen by inference. Except for a few verses in Proverbs, the Bible exhorts us to speak to each other but contains little instruction concerning how to do so. A strong inference can be drawn, however, from Colosians 3:4-11 (NAS): "When Christ, who is our life, is revealed, then you also will be revealed with Him in glory. Therefore consider the members of your earthly body as dead to immorality, impurity, passion, evil desire, and greed, which amounts to idolatry. For it is on account of these things that the wrath of God will come, and in them you also once walked, when you were living in them. But now you also, put them all aside: anger, wrath, malice, slander, and abusive speech from your mouth. Do not lie to one another, since you laid aside the old self with its evil practices, and have put on the new self who is being renewed to a true knowledge according to the image of the One who created him,—a renewal in which there is no distinction between Greek and Jew, circumcised and uncircumcised, barbarian, Scythian, slave and freeman, but Christ is all, and in all." Necessary to communication is a putting aside of all the things of our carnal nature, the self-centered traits, images, and "practices" that keep us from hearing each other. Indeed it is necessary to put aside those things because they cause us to "lie to one another." As we grew in body we also developed a mental screen, a way of interpreting whatever approaches us. That screen is a part of the self, the carnal nature with its practices. If we do not put it off, we will see everything around us through those dark glasses.

Most people think the first function of the mind is to regulate or reason or decipher. But that is not so. The first function of the mind is to block out. Even as you read this page, multitudinous signals approach your brain simultaneously. The ears catch other sounds inside and outside the house. The seat sends messages of comfort or distress. The feet say, "I'm cold" or "Jiggle me, the leg's nerves are going dead." Light streams from a bulb or the sun. Clothes may bind or pinch or feel good somewhere on the body. From deep subliminal reaches, the inner being may be sending worry signals about some relative you heard about yesterday. Silence may nag at our minds until we suddenly think, "Oh, now what are the children into?" The ringing of the phone may be breaking into your consciousness. If the mind does not screen the hundreds of simultaneous stimuli, acting upon some without conscious awareness, blocking out some totally, and deciding from some predetermined priority which stimuli to admit to the conscious mind, we would become overstimulated into chaos! We would hop onto our horses and ride off in all directions at once! Unfortunately the programing of our minds as to which signals to admit and how to interpret them was built before our conversion. Therefore the Word says, "And be not conformed to this world: but be ye transformed *by the renewing of your mind,* that ye may prove what is that good, and acceptable, and perfect, will of God" (Rom. 12:2). As soon as we have received our redemption in the Lord Jesus Christ, we have the mind of Christ in our spirits (1 Cor. 2:16). But that mind must wrestle against the stubborn mind of our yet unmortified flesh. "For they that are after the flesh do mind the things of the flesh; but they that are after the Spirit the things of the Spirit. For to be carnally minded is death; but to be spiritually minded is life and peace. Because the carnal mind is enmity against God: for it is not subject to the law of God, neither indeed can be" (Rom. 8:5, 6, 7). The work of the Holy Spirit throughout our life in Christ is to haul down every proud imagination and take every thought captive to obey Christ (2 Cor. 10:5). Until that reformation, our mind retains its primary programing to screen and decipher within our selfish and self-centered ways. Therefore, we do not see the reality of the other nor hear what is truly being said. Again and again Jesus said to the disciples, ". . . perceive ye not yet, neither understand? have ye your heart yet hardened? Having eyes, see ye not? and having ears, hear ye not? and do ye not remember?" (Mark 8:17b, 18). The trouble is that we do remember—the old way rather than the new.

This does not mean we need be discouraged. Our ability to hear grows in direct ratio to our sanctification. As it took Paul fourteen years before he was ready to be the Lord's apostle (Gal. 12:1), so it normally will take years of daily death and rebirth before our eyes and ears see and hear what is real between us. As there are no instant saints, neither is there instant constancy in communication. But we do need to perceive that communication is a vital area demanding study and work. To take communication for granted is to invite disaster. Hearts want to remain in loving embrace but continual misunderstanding destroys this. "A gentle tongue is a tree of life, but perverseness in it breaks the spirit" (Prov. 15:4).

The answer is not only to bring to death the old programing, but to "Put on then, as God's chosen ones, holy and beloved, compassion, kindness, lowliness, meekness, and patience, forbearing one another and, if one has a complaint against another, forgiving each other; *as* the Lord has forgiven you, *so* you also *must* forgive. And above all these put on love, which binds everything together in perfect harmony. And *let* the peace of Christ *rule in* your hearts, to which indeed you were called in the one body. And be thankful. *Let* the word of Christ *dwell in* you richly, as you teach and admonish one another in all wisdom, and as you sing psalms and hymns and spiritual songs with thankfulness in your hearts to God. And whatever you do, *in word* or deed, do everything in the name of the Lord Jesus, giving thanks to God the Father through him" (Col. 3:12-17 RSV). No better advice could be given concerning communication, because there must be death in Jesus Christ to our impetuous, unconscious demands, but more importantly an imputation of His life, if we would not judge by what our eyes see, or decide by what our ears hear (Isa. 11:3b).

God can speak truth from many sources. We now borrow from Carl Jung's work. In so doing let us insert the disclaimer that we disagree with much of what Carl Jung has said. But we find in his portrayal of the animus and anima a most apt exposition of "male and female created He them" (Gen. 1:27b). The word "ani*mus*" refers to the male pole of our being, "ani*ma*" to the female. None of us is solely male or female. We are bipolar, both male and female. We are not bisexual. We manifest mainly in one or the other pole of our being.

For simplicity of remembrance, note that the animus can be remembered as the male pole through the word "must." And you can remember that the female pole is the anima because of "ma." Both poles operate in us whether we are a man or a woman. In the anima reside feeling, nurture, care, intuition, sensitivity, receiving, spontaneity, and desire. Love participates both in the animus and the anima, but because of its association with emotion, we list it as part of the anima. Art as a skill manifests in the logic and structure of the animus. But the intuitive sense of art originates in the highest imaginative and sensitive faculties of the anima. Finally, our conscience is seated in the female pole of our being. An old joke ruefully expresses how the conscience acts from within the female pole. The story is that God was at work in His creation on the first day and rested, then on the second day, and rested, on the third day and rested, and so on. For six days He created and rested each day until on the sixth He created man and then woman, and since then neither God nor man has rested!

The other side of us is the animus. In it are logic, structure, authority, principle, idea, aggression, thrust or drive, and creativity. One sees immediately that these divisions are just too neat; you can't split people like that. We are too complex. And women's rightists might object strenuously to these arbitrary delineations of what is male or female, which actually may come more from cultural definitions than from what God created us to be. But sometimes an oversimplification gives us a springboard for understanding, so let's use it and hold our reservations as a counterbalance in the back of our minds.

These two poles are basically antagonistic. They stand in tension with each other. Suppose a man at work becomes furious at his boss and wants to tell him off. Those feelings originate in the anima. But logic, structure, and principle say, "Cool it, buddy, you want to keep your job." Or suppose the wife wants to give her husband a hug and a kiss, or the opposite, a scolding, but they are in public. Christian principles say, "Don't embarrass him in public." Often the animus must restrain the anima. A husband may come home desiring to romp with the children. He wants to hug and bounce them on his lap, tease and play with them. The wife greets him with, "The kids have been mean all day. Spank them." By principle he must back her up, but his feelings don't want to. One definition of maturity is that we learn how to express both poles without trailing off into imbalance.

We have all observed the type of man who occasionally loses control, yells at people, shouts obscenities, and makes accusations he doesn't mean in his right mind at all. He has for the moment lost the virtue of the animus and fallen into the worst elements of the anima. One can become captive to the extreme of either pole.

A number of years ago, I (John) worked at Midway Airport, Chicago, in charge of loading and unloading all Delta C and S planes at night. In those days radar procedures were not as highly developed as they are now. When fog and clouds prevented landing, planes were held in pattern, and when the skies lifted, there would be eight to ten planes on the ramp at once. As foreman, seeing what was coming, I would call my boss for authority to call in more men. "You've got ten bodies, ain't that enough?", or "You've got ten units, can't you do your job?" I never had ten *men* or ten *people*. The boss couldn't think in those terms. He was off balance, inhuman, trapped in the animus side of his being.

Remember "Bonanza"? Hoss was the type of guy who had all the feelings of a woman. But he was so big—who was going to bother him? Little Joe had all the same feelings but had to fight like a bantam rooster, defending his manhood. Many of us saw the movie *Dr. Zhivago,* in which the Russian nation was crushing the masses forward. The animus had created the great principle, the idea of communism, the total corporate man. The masses were to be type-stamped into perfection, thus into the boredom of sameness. Dr. Zhivago was a doctor who lived his feelings, had a romance, and wrote poetry. The message of the movie was that he became the people's hero because he kept the anima alive for them.

In the Second World War, the Nazis became obsessed by the vision of the Third Reich. To them that was a great principle, a great idea, and on that basis they came to think that all feeling was weakness. They would build the disciplined, structured, authoritative superman. Part of the training of an SS officer was that he was given a puppy and told to train the dog while he was himself being instructed. The graduation test was the command, "Strangle your dog instantly." If the trainee could not choke his dog to death without showing feeling, he had flunked the course. He had failed to kill his feelings. When the Nazis suppressed the anima, they slew the conscience. Having silenced conscience, they became as prophesied, ". . . Without natural affection, trucebreakers, false accusers, incontinent, fierce, despisers of those that are good" (2 Tim. 3:3). Without compunction they could cut women open and experiment with their organs, practice eugenics without regard to marital vows, and murder six million Jews while seemingly feeling nothing. Fortunately that condition was not true of all the German people, but only of those Nazis who had succeeded in the process of entrapping themselves in the animus. St. Paul says of such people, "By rejecting conscience, certain persons have made shipwreck of their faith" (1 Tim. 1:19 RSV). The Nazis not only made shipwreck of their faith, but of an entire generation.

As animus without anima becomes brutal and brittle, so anima without animus becomes flowery and frilly. We have all observed women who wear elaborately feminine clothing and excessive cosmetics, who exhibit extreme sensitivity, and sweetly overconcerned manners. To a request they may answer,

"Oh, I couldn't do that," accompanied by fluttering eyelids and a hand over the chest. Such a woman has fled into the anima. She needs more structure, logic, principle, and authority. On the other hand is the woman who bosses the women's aid society, the church, the minister, her husband, and anybody else within range. Or the woman in the business world who has become the ultimate business executive. Her voice is brisk, her walk is mannish, her manner is clipped, and she wears a smartly-tailored suit. She needs to come into balance.

Understanding imbalances may help us to be more compassionate toward the effeminate male. The man who walks with a woman's swing to his hips, extends his fingers daintily, and speaks with all the moods and inflections of a woman may simply be a captive to the anima. He may have possessed good sensitivities as a child. Perhaps he was raised by women, or the father and the world of men appeared too brutal for his gentle nature. Or perhaps he was gifted with the fine intuitiveness of the artistic. For one reason or another, he finds the male expressions of our culture inappropriate and grinding to his nature. Finding no way to express the animus, he becomes confined to the anima side of his nature. Effeminacy is an imbalance which can be overcome by counseling, prayer, and an introduction into a more acceptable definition of masculinity. Effeminacy is *not* coterminous with homosexuality. The effeminate may be passionate lovers, in no way homosexual.

Imbalance prevents adundant life. Those who are bound in the animus have little freedom to enjoy life. Paula and I attended a hilarious play with an imprisoned friend. Our friend's wife and the two of us laughed so uproariously we were holding our sides in pain while trying to keep from falling off our chairs. Our friend occasionally emitted a half chuckle, much like a man who fails to suppress a burp. He would have suppressed even that if he could. A man may become a total cool head and miss everything! There is ". . . a time to weep, and a time to laugh; a time to mourn, and a time to dance" (Eccles. 3:4). Our western society has become aggressive, thrusting, dominating, and materialistic. It will not tolerate the development of both sides of our being as we mature.* We are pushed off balance.

As a boy, a man possesses good feelings; he has a strong and active anima. But if he lets his feelings show in the midst of the gang, his peers scoff and taunt as though he had done something wrong, "Sissy! Boys don't cry!" Or if a lad happens to be a good student, likes his teacher, and enjoys doing well in school, frequently he is subjected to, "Teacher's pet! Goody-goody!" He is not allowed to manifest normal feelings in his behavior because "Guys aren't like that." What does a boy do? He must learn to run counter to his nature to get in with the gang. Feelings, which should be a blessing to him, become his enemy. He learns to choke them down and prevent them, until he can and does often become so out of touch with himself he can no longer decipher what he truly does feel. Teen-agers often still entertain genuine childlike emotions of delight, but if they discover for example a gloriously beautiful flower, a girl can exclaim effusively, "Oh, isn't that lovely?" But can you imagine a football jock on his knees above a flower saying, "Oh, isn't that lovely?" Society will not let him do that. Perhaps it was totally unconscious, but we believe male hippies chose to wear long flowing hair, headbands, beads, and bright colors, because they felt our culture had denied them half of their being. They were saying in effect, "I *am* going to express the anima side of my nature."

On the other hand, society doesn't permit a woman to become a whole person either. Two fellows can stand shoulder to shoulder, tell each other off, slap each other on the back, and go have a beer. Did you ever see two women who could do that? They are not as protected by the dispassionateness of logic and

*We recommend that the reader study Paul Tournier's chapter on temperament in *The Healing of Persons.*

authority. Being too much in the anima, what happens most often is that they begin to chip at each other emotionally, and soon they are in a cat fight. Men can take out their aggressions in a football or basketball game, or some other sport. The harder they hit, the better they like it, and come home all roughed up, laughing, bruised and happy. Usually, women are not allowed to do that. Physically, they might injure delicate organs. Our definitions of what is "ladylike" not only prevent open expressions, often they also prevent needful and appropriate, frank and loving verbal confrontations. So where do women take out their aggressions? On their husbands! Society permits too few ways for a growing girl to develop the male side of her being. Therefore when she as a mother tries to exercise authority, occasionally her voice goes up and out come the tears. The anima overcomes her. Sometimes the wife's tears are the more profuse because of her frustration that her husband's anima is so dormant he has failed to sense what was going on with the children. She feels a desperate necessity to overcome his abdication, and is carried beyond her capabilities in a task too big for her.

When we marry, we grant to our mate consciously and unconsciously the right to express the other half of our beings. I (Paula) express John's anima. He expresses my animus. Not altogether or each would fail to be a whole person, but unconsciously an identification goes on. Consequently there is a most powerful pull upon each other. I used to say to John, "You have a box you want to get me into! You're trying to program me."

"I am not. Be your own person."

"But you want me to be my own person the way *you* want me to be my own person!" It was an unconscious box; the flesh in John was determined that I fulfill half of his being as he wanted it to be. I had better be sensitive, gracious and kind, express beauty, and walk with a woman's walk. Husbands like to watch

82

their wives move about the house, hear them singing or playing the piano. They enjoy watching them undress. Most wives don't understand that. They think men are simply being dirty old men. But that isn't always so. The husband may be watching and listening to that kind of grace and supple femininity which expresses half of him. More than being stimulated sexually, he is fulfilled. Women like to have the man around the house. A wife says, "I just like for you to be here." She feels at rest watching him and listening to him, because it fulfills her being. Do you see that this means there is a mighty magnetism which draws us to each other, but unfortunately there is an equally forcible demanding that takes place? We are tremendously anxious that the other one fulfill us. That also means that unless we know Jesus Christ as Lord and Savior, we will demand too much. Again, death of self in Jesus Christ on the cross is the key to life.

Here we want to point out one of the most basic things we see in counseling. If a husband does not have his own direct relation with Jesus, so that the Lord fulfills and satisfies him, in some ways he will have to play God. But in other ways he will subconsciously ask his wife to do for him what only God can do. That is too much for the wife to bear. He expects his wife to extend to him the comfort, solace, and fulness only the Holy Spirit can give. It works the other way too. The wife expects, if she doesn't know the Lord, that her husband will act as God to her. The paradox is then that if we need something desperately from our mate, that is the last thing we will receive. If we don't "desperately need it," if we have found abundant life in Jesus Christ, then the husband or wife may be able to give what we do need humanly. Jesus said, "Seek ye first the kingdom of God and his righteousness; and all these things shall be added unto you" (Matt. 6:33). Conversely, if we don't seek God first, all these things will be taken away from us. The law is inexorable. We have too much fire in us for each other, too much claim from our incomplete being to be completed. Until we allow the Lord Jesus Christ to fill that God-shaped space in us, we will demand our mate to fill it. The Lord is the only whole one, who can complete both sides of our being. He is the only one who has fully expressed both sides of the being in balance, who could weep for Lazarus in his anima and in the same minute command in the power of the animus, "Lazarus, come forth" (John 11:35, 43). Our Lord is the only one who perfectly expresses authority and tenderness, judgment and mercy, discipline and forgiveness, principle and flexibility, philosophy and spontaneity, common sense and high mysticism, logic and creativity. He only is balance and wholeness. If we do not find our balance in Him, we will not achieve it in our relationship with our mate. If we fail to obtain wholeness from Him, we will try to "use" our mate. But if we find abundant life in Him, He blesses us with a sweet fulness through our mate's presence. "For to him who has will more be given. . ." (Matt. 13:12 RSV). *Has* what? Fulness of life in Jesus Christ.

Now let us speak more directly concerning communication. A man lives in the workaday world that is dominated by the animus. Business is controlled by principle, logic, structure, and authority. In that realm a man must not say the obvious thing nor speak repetitiously. If he repeats or says the obvious thing too often, he will soon earn disrespect. Others will make jokes about "that dumb guy." A man must sense the economy of what is needed, and say that and only that. Now he comes home, having been in that kind of world all day. His wife has prepared a delicious meal and has dressed especially for him. She knows already with logic that it's a nice meal, and she knows she looks good. Concerning those facts she couldn't care less about logic or repetition. It doesn't matter at all to her that he complimented her or liked the meal last week or yesterday. This moment is all-important and she needs to hear, "Gee, it's nice. This is a good meal. And I think you're pretty, honey."

84

Something, anything—a word is needed.

The husband notices that she looks nice. Usually he appreciates her appearance and is grateful that it's a well-prepared meal. But he sits down and just grunts. The longer he sits in silence and eats, the angrier she becomes. Maybe he remembers he should have given her a compliment. But he said that yesterday. He doesn't want to repeat himself, and men don't say the obvious things. He thinks, "I like the meal but she knows that, and I'm eating it, aren't I?" He cannot bring himself to make small talk.

I (John) used to come home and be amazed after a while that Paula was angry. Totally bemused, I would think, "What does this lovely creature want now?" Pulling my hair out in mystery, I would finally say to her, "This isn't fair. You have to tell me. What *do* you want?"

"Well, if I tell you, that'll spoil it. You should know." Needing a compliment, it took all the virtue out of it for her if she had to say, "Tell me you appreciate me." So I learned to compliment her, twice a week, whether she needed it or not, because logic and duty said to! I didn't really feel it until the Lord opened my heart. So men miss women.

A man lives by logic. In logic, one puts everything in a box and gets it running efficiently so as to leave it alone and do something else. Unconsciously a man wants to program his wife that way. He wants to establish their life together as a smoothly running machine, keep the house running efficiently, and thus be free to leave her alone and do whatever else comes to mind. Which is of course the very antithesis of what woman is. Woman says, "Don't put me in a box." Spontaneity not only keeps romance alive, it is the spice which flavors all of life. By it a wife says, "Need me. Meet me. Be real." We have even had women present to us what would seem to be the opposite. "The trouble with my husband is he compliments me for *every* meal." Though that seems right, the problem is that he caught the idea, the principle that he should compliment; now he does it out of duty, and she perceives that it is only that. The complimenting has lost its spontaneity, it has no real emotional base, and she feels somehow only polished like a thing. She wishes that sometimes he would say, "Throw that hash away!" Anything—if only it were real. Some women would rather their husbands would explode than live behind such a wall of philosophy. Often a wife purposefully starts a fight, just to break out of the boxes of boredom and into his heart.

Another more vitiating example of the breakdown of communication by not understanding the difference between animus and anima is what happens to women whose husbands never show any emotion. Both by childhood trauma and continual conditioning at work a husband often becomes an Alan Ladd, the face that never shows any true feelings. Whether he knows it or not, the husband's heart has been hurting again and again all day. Either he suffers empathically for others, and/or others are not affirmative to him, or work becomes tedious and tense, or deadly boring and impersonal, and so on. So he comes home drained. The moment he steps in the house, the wife senses it. She can feel it because she is identified with his anima.

"Something the matter, honey?"

"Nothin'."

"No, I know there's something wrong."

"Get off my back. There's nothin' wrong with me." Now she feels entirely rejected, not aware that she could have refreshed his heart by simple touch and affection without enlisting the mental defenses of the animus. So many, many times we fail to hear each other. We don't understand.

Quite often what happens in the family of an Alan Ladd type is that the wife suffers all manner of physical disorders. One after another, or sometimes all at once, she has ulcers, high blood pressure, migraine headaches, female dysfunctions, diverticulitis, etc. Bills accumulate. She has had so many things taken out surgically there's nothing left she can do without! Her husband never has any physical disabilities. He is the cool, philosophical type. He always remains calm and collected. Because she has become continually more high strung, nervous, and overemotional, he thinks he has an immature wife. Lacking awareness of the interrelationships of the animus and anima, there is no way he could see the actual fact in a thousand years of pondering. The truth is that because he is so philosophical, he has suppressed his anima and is unaware of his feelings. Because he does not face any of his emotions, they boil inside him like a house internally afire with all the doors and windows sealed. But he is married to a warm, loving, affectionate wife. Whenever he is present she bears empathically everything he has not faced. All his tensions, anxieties, and hurts become hers, and they roll like storm clouds and lightning inside her. He will never talk to her about it because there is never anything wrong with him. So now what she feels has no name. It boils up psychosomatically. She thinks something is wrong with her, and so does he. All the doctor's tests seem to prove it. No way can she understand that the very real physical fact of her problems has its base in his nature. It is amazing how often we have seen instances in which such a husband died or for one reason or another was gone from the home, and that woman's health returned. She was no longer forced to bear his unfaced tensions.

Before the Lord taught us these things, I (John) used to become overburdened and uptight, studying in seminary what my spirit did not want to receive. I would return home emotionally disturbed but unable to cry or even admit my unsettledness, picking on Paula with unintended insults, slights and demands until finally she would cry. The moment her tears appeared, I was released. Her crying accomplished what I couldn't. That is one reason men, becoming inebriated, beat on their wives. Consciously they are unaware that they need their wives' emotions. Women should never be ashamed of their tears. Men sometimes say to their wives, "Aw, dry up!" But they don't really mean it. Tears actually bless and release men. But since that also begins to crack open the feeling center a man has fought to suppress, part of him desperately wants her to weep, whereas the other part is frightened by it. If she continues, and he allows her heart to warm his, he will become sensitive, vulnerable, and appropriately emotional. That is the very blessing he is most afraid to receive. His reactions are therefore totally ambivalent and equally confusing to his wife. A wife needs to have so much security and freedom in the Lord Jesus Christ that she can continue to be herself until her man can become himself.

A woman returns to self-control mainly by relating to the man of her life. For example, when I (Paula) would struggle with the children all day, becoming more and more distraught, what I wanted when John came home was for him to share my frustrations. If John would just listen, empathize with me, hug me, and say very little, his strength would restore my own animus, enabling me to do my own thinking with more detachment, restoring my self-control. I wanted to return to balance by relating to John. But John did not know that then. Men attempt to establish self-control by thinking a thing through. The more a man thinks, the angrier he may become, or the calmer. Primarily he reasons his way into an emotion, or turns it off. Having fought as a child to control his emotions, he has a built-in automatic capacity. Unfortunately that practice is not so much something he controls as something that controls him and denies him access to himself and his wife. Normally a woman apprehends life through the more intuitive faculties of her inner being. She feels or senses rather than analyzes first. A man talks himself into something, usually unaware that his supposedly objective rationales actually justify decisions he also has arrived at subliminally. Women have been allowed in our culture to be more naturally free to sense and feel as a base for decision. When I would pour out my frustrations to John, he would feel the burden of them, but then he would immediately translate the task into a demand for logical responses. He would feel betrayed because he had wanted to come home to rest, to avoid making more decisions, and he would take my need as another demand for decisions. Actually my emotions could have refreshed him and brought him back to balance. But he thought my behavior meant I was immature. "She can't control her emotions like I can, poor creature." So he would say, "Well now, look, Paula, if you would just organize your day: step one, step two, step three . . ."—and then he would become befuddled when I would go through the roof! When John missed me so completely I thought, "You dummy, why can't you hear me?" All I needed was for John merely to be there for me, but instead he gave advice. He tried to settle things logically because that's where he was, but that's not where I was. His logic did not appear logical to me at all. To me it would have been logical for him to have recognized the need and given appropriate sympathetic comfort.

Husbands must learn to shift gears. A man has two worlds whereas the wife confines her priorities mainly to one. However many activities occupy a woman's time, her life centers in her home, her man, and her children. Her feelings revolve around that basic position and task. It blows her mind and fills her with jealousy that her husband loses his simple, basic roots and becomes pulled by two worlds. His world at work establishes priorities which often conflict with those of the home. She thinks it ought to be simple to keep the true priority of the home at the center. But for the man it is not that simple. His need to contribute to society (which he identifies as the creative urge of his life), his ambitions and loyalties at work override his family priorities and create for him a second world which he thinks of as being apart from his family. A wife thinks the family should not only nurture him to do his job, but that his experiences at work should enrich the life of the family. She, therefore, often wants him to share what he wants to forget. He so tends to separate home and work that in effect he uses the family to energize him and so to further his ambitions. It surprises and wounds him that she cannot see and readily agree that he should be allowed to have a separate world at work. He usually perceives her need for him to put his family first as a compelling demand, and that robs him of his freedom to choose her and the children. He begins to feel like a "kept" man if he submits, whereas she feels that he just doesn't love her and the children.

A man feels confident at work; he knows how to handle things. His logic is appropriate and honored there. But when he comes home, none of those ways work. A wife and children can't be pushed, pulled, organized, and manipulated. They refuse to be run like machines. Therefore, he feels ill at ease, awkward, and out of his element. The familiarity and manageableness of his work become seductive to him, a place to flee to where he knows how to be himself and how to make things happen.

Sometimes a man thinks, "I ought to keep the romance going." "Honey," he says, "let's go out to dinner and a show."

She says, "We can't afford it," but since our lips seldom manage to say what the heart means, that usually translates, "Now that you mention it, I'd better be worth more than money." But men are trained in the business world to "say what you mean and mean what you say"—logic!

"Okay, honey, we'll stay home." Now the wife is disappointed and more hurt than if he had said nothing. He failed to understand the female world again.

Or he brings home a gift.

"Oh, honey, you shouldn't have." Translation: "I am thrilled. You're affirming me. Tell me again I'm worth more than money." But Christian logic tells him to be humble, so he responds, "Oh, it wasn't anything," which was exactly the wrong thing to say! It was everything. Again his principled mind failed to read her heart language. But she misses him as often because she listens to his words and fails to read his heart's intent. The gift was the intent; never mind that his mind blew it! How we wish that every couple would learn by the grace of Jesus to believe the best behind every mate's worst. We ought not to listen to each other's words, but to listen to each other's hearts. We don't say what we mean. If it seems delusive to trust that our mate means well when actions and words appear to say the opposite, it's the happiest delusion going, and we will soon learn that what we choose to believe becomes a reality.

Language seldom carries the meaning of what actually is transpiring. Let's imagine a man on his knees replacing a flat tire as you are walking along the road. You say, "Hi, mister. Whatcha doin'? Fixin' a tire?"

"No, I'm milking a cow."

But "Fixin' a tire?" wasn't what you really wanted to say. Translated it means, "I see you are in trouble; show me you're a nice guy and I might offer to help you, or I might at least visit with you." Or you come up to somebody and say, "How are you?" and he makes the mistake of telling you! That was what you said but that wasn't what you asked. In marriage we most desperately need to learn how to hear what is really being said. Understanding the difference between context and content, and between animus and anima, can grant us protection from failure. We may then not be so apt to charge *at* each other. "Wisdom is a fountain of life to him who has it, but folly is the chastisement of fools" (Prov. 16:22 RSV).

What are we saying about communication? Learn to understand how your mate feels and thinks. You don't have to think alike to agree. All you have to do is to be willing to grant the other the right to live from a different base.

What usually happens when a man and wife argue is that the wife has an idea which she probably sensed and felt but could not tell where it came from. She just knows that she knows that she knows—from deep inside. So the husband says, "Where did you get *that* idea? You know you gotta have things figured out. You oughta know where you started from, and how you got there, and stuff like that. So what's your first principle?"

"Well, I don't know that."

"Why don't you? You ought to."

"I don't have to know."

"Yes, you do." And around they go. All that is needed is, "All right. I understand what you feel." Or, "I don't understand. But I don't have to. I trust you." Let the other one be free to be what he is. You might have a different opinion. Okay, you can agree to disagree. Unity is not uniformity, but forbearance and forgiveness. Forbearing is based on acceptance and trust of the Lord in others, not condescension, compromise or toleration of the other guy, who you are sure is quite wrong. Forbearing is willingness to wait humbly for time to validate opinion, without grudge-holding or grievances and "I told you so's." If you can't understand, you can't understand. It is absolutely essential to learn to grant to the other the right to be what he is.

The single root cause of failure in every marriage is selfishness. People commonly think selfishness means stinginess, but the most generous man in the world may be completely selfish. Selfish means "*self*-ish," to be wrapped up in one's own self-images and definitions, requiring that everyone else see life as you do. Seemingly altruistic, self-sacrificing servants of the Lord may be totally selfish by being self-centered, compelling all around to fit into their scheme of things. In just this way, our very strengths may hide our deepest weaknesses.

Jesus said, "If any man would come after me, let him deny *himself* and take up his cross and follow me" (Matt. 16:24). We think that means to "deny his stingy desires and give to others" or "deny his ambitions and become a missionary" or "deny his pleasures and go to work," and so on. It won't hurt to make such applications, but that is not what He said. The call is to deny our *self*. The self is all our practices, habits, philosophies, and images by which we control our own life and others. That is why "deny himself" is followed by "take up *his* cross." Not Jesus' cross but that cross which crucifies our own flesh (Gal. 2:20). "Oh, what a cross I have to bear" is the exact antithesis of "take up *his* cross." By the former we exalt our picture of ourselves as martyrs—and usually insist that all around join us in our idolatry. Only those truly dead to self can allow the other to be free.

Only by the grace of Jesus Christ can we give the other one the right to think and feel, and be what he is. We don't have to push each other into our own molds to be happy—quite the opposite. But we are basically insecure and lonely in our differentnesses. Because we are afraid, we want to make everybody be just like us, ". . . who through fear of death were subject to lifelong bondage" (Heb. 2:15b RSV). In addition to fear of physical death we also fear the death of our self-control. The way we think may be a prison, but at least we are familiar with it. Those families succeed where individual members develop such a life of worship and prayer that God's grace can grant them courage to die to the self-centered "I" and develop an ability to become corporate in their outlook. In Christ our differentnesses are the spice of life, but without Him they become the fright of it.

We heard someone say that God's angels are filled with logic, structure and principle, but that they cannot feel what human beings do. If so, perhaps a part of God's purpose in creating mankind in the flesh on earth is to create male and female, to bring forth a new order of sons of God who, whether male or female, hold both poles in one being. Did the reader ever notice that there are no women angels spoken of in the Bible? Woman is not a temporary creation, nor is woman-ness in man-ness something temporary, nor man-ness in woman-ness a passing thing; we are to become an eternal wholeness. If we don't have Jesus Christ, we can't hold together the many opposites of our being, let alone the male and female poles. And so we fall off into one pole or the other. We are either tyrannized by feelings run amok, or we become unfeeling philosophers.

Men have said to us when they have heard this teaching, "Good grief, how am I ever going to know what my wife really thinks or feels? She's a mystery." Of course! You are not supposed to understand women fully! If you did, that would rob woman of a basic part of her essence; part of her grace is mystery. To completely understand would reduce woman's life to logic and thus become the very loss of what she is. But whereas women don't want to be understood completely, men do want to know, "How can I understand that woman more?" Jesus Christ imparts courage to men to live with mystery. If a man will relate to Jesus not religiously or as an idea, but person-to-person, Jesus will establish in him His balanced, loving nature. Only then can a man truly revere his wife.

Man's logic without woman's sensitivity is like a flying carpet which has no place to touch down upon reality, not anchored to the true facts of the body and heart. So the woman is suspect of the man's logical world, whereas the man thinks, "You have the right feeling, I'm sure, but you missed the whole principle of the thing." So the blessings of our strengths become the dividing walls of our competitions, and only in Jesus is resolution, "For he is our peace, who has made us both one, and has broken down the dividing wall of hostility" (Eph. 2:14 RSV)—spoken of Jew and Gentile, but applicable to our inner beings as well.

The best counsel for communication is therefore to pray together aloud, honestly, practically, and factually about what you truly feel and actually think, asking God to continually keep you open to each other. You may then begin to identify with each other sympathetically, and hear from within each other's points of view. Then your differences will become complementary and complimentary. That is real communication, real sharing, and real marriage.

5

FATHERS, SONS AND DAUGHTERS

And a woman who held a babe against her bosom said, "Speak to us of children" and he said: "Your children are not your children. They are the sons and daughters of life's longing for itself. They come through you but not from you. And though they are with you, yet they belong not to you. You may give them your love but not your thoughts, for they have their own thoughts. You may house their bodies but not their souls. For their souls dwell in the house of tomorrow, which you cannot visit; not even in your dreams. You may strive to be like them, but seek not to make them like you. For life goes not backward nor tarries with yesterday. You are the bows from which your children as living arrows are sent forth. The archer sees the mark upon the path of the infinite, and he bends you with his might that his arrows may go swift and far. Let your bending in the archer's hand be for gladness; for even as he loves the arrow that flies, so he loves the bow that is stable." (Kahlil Gibran, *The Prophet*, "On Children" pp. 17, 18)

God holds us responsible to present to our children an environment in which He can cause their souls to thrive. Therefore our basic text for fathers is: "Children, obey your parents in the Lord, for this is right. 'Honor your father and your mother' (this is the first commandment with a promise), 'that it may be well with you and that you may live long on the earth.' Fathers, do not provoke your children to anger, but bring them up in the discipline and instruction of the Lord'' (Eph. 6:1-4 RSV).

We rejoice that we have Sunday schools and public schools to which fathers can delegate authority for the teaching of their children. But we have surrendered too much. Fathers have almost abdicated the pilgrim concept given throughout Deuteronomy and Proverbs that it is their task to teach their own children. Sharing in Bible times was done in the cool of the evenings as the family fell asleep, talking of the things of God. During the children's first six years much of the job was assigned to the mothers, who taught them prayers, songs, and Scriptures. From six on, it became the father's task to nurture and instruct the boys till manhood. Fathers and mothers were therefore literally in bed with the children, and considered that time as inviolate, not to be interfered with, as we read, "Trouble me not: the door is now shut, and my children are with me in bed; I *cannot* rise and give thee'' (Luke 11:7). How often do we sacrifice our children's time with us for more "worthy" causes? Is it not a commentary on our common abdication that we do not now say, "I cannot give you my children's time!" In Proverbs again and again we hear the counsel of fathers: "My son, do not forget my teachings, but let your heart keep my commandments; for length of days and years of life and abundant welfare will they give you'' (Prov. 3:1, 2 RSV). "My son, do not despise the Lord's discipline or be weary of his reproof; for the Lord reproves him whom He loves, as a father the son in whom he delights'' (Prov. 3:11, 12 RSV). "Hear, O sons, a father's instruction, and be attentive, that you may gain insight; for I give you good precepts; do not forsake my teaching. When I was a son with my father, tender, the only one in the sight of my mother, he taught me and said to me, 'Let your heart hold fast my words; keep my commandments, and live; do not forget, and do not turn away from the words of my mouth' '' (Prov. 4:1-5a RSV). Such are only a few of the many passages a good concordance will reveal.

We began this book by saying that in our culture families have been corrupted by materialism. Fathers' minds and hearts have been robbed by Satan until all too many think of themselves only as bacon-bringers. The culture causes the society to value only what is concrete and visible. The predominant group model of education which forms our mentality tends to confine teaching solely to mental exercises performed by trained teachers in Sunday and public schools. Consequently, fathers see little parental value in what they believe and what their hearts feel. We do retain in our spirits the nagging hunch that we ought to be doing something more than just providing financially for our families. We know we ought to be teaching about the Lord, but we are too much satisfied that the Bible is taught in Sunday and parochial schools. And besides, even for most dedicated Christian fathers, the Bible has become a book of mystery, gathering dust on the shelves. Anti-Christ culture has stolen from fathers their daily attentiveness to the life of their own spirits and souls, and therefore fathers' awareness of their task of nurturing their families has been stolen. Fathers nurture children by and in everything they do—embraces, discussions at the table, the way they relate to their wives, how they settle problems, how they forgive and cherish, how they discipline, the way they play games, what language they use, and so on. Everything a father does in the presence of a son or daughter is an implantation of what the father is to the children. A child does not become what the father says; he becomes what the father is.

I (John) watched my father discipline when I was a child. Actually his was a good way. But I didn't like it. So I created in my mind a picture of myself disciplining my children quite differently. But how *do* I discipline? Just like my father! What he is was written into me. Again and again we meet people in counseling who were raised in broken homes in which the way the father treated the family became what was written on the heart of the child. Those children thought, and were determined, "I'll never treat my wife and children like that!" They constructed a glorious fantasy of themselves being ideal husbands and fathers, but became humiliated and broken-hearted, and sat down to cry with Elijah, ". . . O Lord, take away my life; for I am no better than my fathers" (1 Kings 19:4b RSV). We do what we have become as a result of living with our parents. A corollary of the golden rule is, "You will do to others what has been done to you." Real teaching is accomplished by what we are every moment of our lives with our children. The medium is the message. We *are* the teaching.

When Jesus said, "I *am* the way, the truth, and the life" (John 14:6a RSV), He meant that He embodies truth. He has lived truth for us. He himself is the teaching and the life. By living with Him we become what He is. We may search the Scriptures as He warned that the Pharisees do (John 5:39), thinking to find something mentally, and "yet you refuse to come to me that you may have life" (v. 40 RSV). Real coming to Jesus is a momentary walking and talking with Him as our constant companion and best friend. All our life needs to be lived hand in hand with Christ. Only so do we become what He is. And that is exactly God's plan for sons with their fathers. If the father has truly lived the Way in Christ, it is easy for a son to do the same; if the father has not, our Lord will first have to overcome and bring to death in the son what the father was.

Regrettably, in our nonspiritual culture, a father tends to think that once he has begotten a child he has nothing more to do and is of no importance to it until the baby comes out of the womb. He feels disenfranchised, as though in some solely feminine mystery a baby is formed quite apart from him irrelevant of what he thinks and feels. But that is not so. Some primitive societies possess more of a sense of reality than ours. In some primitive cultures, when a wife discovers her pregnancy, she continues to work in the fields, but the father retires to a hut in seclusion. There he believes he is to build his child's temperament through meditation and prayer. Our society scoffs at that as a comical and superstitious practice. But now psychologists, some psychiatrists, and many Christian counselors concur that a fetus is very really affected by the absence or presence of its father. A father's voice near the mother, his cruelty or kindnesses, sexual advances, insensitivity or tendernesses already affect the baby's spirit. It has often been the case that women coming to us for counsel concerning fear of sex were little helped until the Holy Spirit revealed that not only was their fear buttressed by molestations and remembrances of the father's actions, but that those fears began when the father was violent and insensitive to the mother in sex while the child was in the womb. When we have prayed aloud with such counselees, asking the Lord to find and minister to the inner child, comforting the unborn spirit and enabling them to forgive their fathers (and thus all men), sexual ease and freedom have been the result. The reference quoted earlier about John the Baptist leaping in the womb of Elizabeth demonstrates, according to the Word of God, that our spirits understand what transpires outside the womb and react with intelligence and emotion. Thus the father's presence with the mother is already basic to the formation of a child's character before birth. Let each father meditate concerning what he should be doing to help form his child in his wife's womb—such as expressions of gentleness, appreciation and tenderness toward the mother, and the life of prayer. Our son Loren, having learned from us, placed his hand each night upon his wife, Beth, and said a prayer of blessing for his unborn child.

As we have said before, when a child is born, he has already been wounded. A fetus has been encased in the darkness of the womb for nine months, accustomed to the warmth and rocking motion of the mother's body. Then it is cast out into the trauma of pain and blood, into shocking light and cold in which the first breath is often caused by a spanking. All too many fathers still think their child is the mother's business. We are grateful that now many obstetricians not only allow, but encourage, fathers to be present in the delivery room, urging them to receive training in natural childbirth methods so that birth can become a cooperative effort on the part of both parents. One Christian father related to us with a glow on his face how he had been allowed to catch the baby in his own hands and place his child on his wife's abdomen. Imagine what a blessing of love to that child's spirit to be greeted with delight in the spirit and hands of his own father! Praise God that today even "secular" medicine is discovering that fathers should not be excluded.

Many fathers feel embarrassed and awkward in the presence of a baby. Afraid of the tininess and fragility of the child, feeling clumsy and terrified of dropping the baby, they have been glad to relegate child care exclusively to their wives. That is a tragedy. A baby needs its father's arms. In its first few weeks, a baby learns to come to rest in the nurturing strength of the father's presence. Even in the first weeks, a baby girl is learning to nestle in and come to rest, trusting herself to let go in what a man is.

I (Paula) was born with an enlarged thymus which the doctors in those days mistakenly treated with x-ray. My dad was a traveling salesman out on the road for two weeks at a time, and my frequent crying was a constant source of concern to my anxious and inexperienced mother. It seemed the more she would try to comfort, the louder I would cry. My Uncle Henry tells laughingly, and I think with some residue of painful memory, of his attempts to quiet the tiny, squalling redhead.

His efforts yielded little more result than exercised self-control in checking the impulse to throw me out the window. But the moment my father would return home and pick me up, my crying would cease. I was fortunate, for what many learn is the terror of a huge face looming in anger over the crib shouting obscenities.

Trust beyond reason, or unreasoning fear, seat themselves by experience in the first few weeks with a father. A baby boy begins to learn in deep levels what it is to be a man by the way his father walks with him, pats his back, and sings to him in the dark hours of the night. As a father sacrifices his sleep in love for his child, or fails to, a father's compassion and patience, or lack of it, already create a freedom for the child to be himself, and a trust that he will be received, or a fear to venture. Every baby *needs* its own father's presence. Babies need their fathers to feed them, change their diapers, and hold them long hours in their laps.

Likewise the first twelve months are as much a father's concern as a mother's. It is not that she will teach him to walk and talk and then hand daddy a son to play with. Except for breast-feeding, there is no function of child care which is not as much the father's as the mother's. Infants sometimes need to sit on their daddy's lap at the table and be fed by him. Since they take a lot of falls in their first year, the way the daddy patiently picks them up prepares them to expect the Father God to restore them when they venture later. They learn more than can be told as they are enfolded in the hug a father and mother share. Likewise they feel and act out tensions between their parents. Fathers who are inordinately proud of precocious children and make them perform for guests sometimes create a sense of fear and striving in the child which remain throughout life. A son senses his father's pride and feels the fear of performing. A father who is caught up in his own self-centered pride may sacrifice his child to his own image, becoming embarrassed and angry, creating fears in his son which may ricochet through many areas—fear of insensitive authority, nervousness in public, feelings of inadequacy, etc. On the other hand, fathers who overcomfort their children for each bruise may teach their children how to use their wounds to control others. Since the countless daily events of life are what form children rather than what we consciously teach, one can see that only a life lived continuously in Jesus is a proper formation for a child. How important it is for the father to be the head of the house by giving his life in surrender to Jesus Christ.

Anyone can see by inference how a father's life influences his children, not only in infancy but throughout life. As a child begins to encounter painful experiences with his brothers or among his peer group, if his father is there to comfort, educate, and discipline, the son is made strong. But if the father is harsh and insensitive, brutal and undisciplined emotionally and mentally, he shatters his son's capacities. It is vital to the children for the father to exhibit gentleness and strength in the Lord Jesus Christ.

Let us now speak of the next age. The age between six and twelve is the gang age, especially for boys. Boys undergo a "pilgrimage." They commence to move out from the home, to test themselves against other people. Their gang becomes important. For the first time a son is gripped by pressing, sometimes compelling, belongings and loyalties which often contrast or conflict with his home. For the first time he suffers great tensions, the gang on one side and the father on the other. A boy's loyalties and concepts of who he is will be tested. What his father and mother have said is right will be challenged. He will have to make decisions. Sometimes he will go along with the gang, filled with fear and guilt, and sometimes he will decide to stand by his parents' principles. If he does decide to do as the father and mother have said, sometimes that is merely conformity out of fear. But sometimes it means he has achieved real strength from his life with his father. But if he says no to the parents, and does wrong, that child comes home needing a father who has both the understanding to know that his son must experiment, must differentiate, and become his own person, but who will also discipline firmly and strongly, so that the son knows both that he is free to make his own mistakes, and not free to escape their consequences. At this time especially, sons need to have seen loyalties and principles operating *in* their fathers, not merely shouted at them. Fathers who spend hours after work at beer halls or elsewhere have no forum to require their sons to come home and do chores. Not only is it necessary for sons to see their fathers living what is noble, they need understanding. They need fathers who remember their own childhood, who can give them freedom to stumble long enough to learn on their own, coupled with necessary discipline, forgiveness, and affection.

Suppose a father is stopped by a policeman, and says, "Yes, sir; yes, sir; yes, sir," in the presence of his son. But as they drive on, the father curses and says, "Man, I told him where to get off. He had no right to pull me over." That father has shot down his own authority with his son. Now his verbal teaching will come across as something different than what he is. Multiply this instance by a thousand experiences in the home and one comprehends the necessity for the life of Jesus Christ to be the father's life every moment.

Suppose a boy goes out with a gang and throws a rock through Tom Jones's grocery store window. He comes running home filled with apprehension and blurts out, "Daddy, daddy, I did something awful."

A wise father says, "Oh, what did you do?"

"I did something awful. I did something awful."

The father persists in asking for details, "*What* did you do?"

Finally the boy says, "I threw a rock through Jones's grocery window." Now a decision is upon the father. If he reacts to the wounding of his own image as a father and blows up at him, he demonstrates his self-centered inability to be concerned for his son's sake. His son's inner spirit will know it, and perhaps his mind as well. That is not Christian discipline. It tells the son, "My concern for you is really only my own concern for myself; you are only an extension of me, not a person in your own right, and how could you have dared to act as though you were your own person?" But the father can make other choices which demonstrate Christian discipline and understanding. He can talk *with* his son, and by his manner and inflections, convey to him both that he knows that he is guilty and that he understands and forgives. And then say, "All right now, let's go and talk with the man." Together they go and talk with Mr. Jones and arrange for restitution to be made. When they return, he may have to apply further discipline if he deems it necessary, but his son knows his father has faced something *with* him. A bridge has been built. It is sad how often we hear from counselees, "Oh, I would never tell my father anything. He just never understands." Understanding comes naturally when a father's heart is set right for his children.

We want to plead the case for physical discipline. Some psychologists have said that if a father spanks a child he will give him a complex. Nonsense. Christian fathers need to be guided by the Word of God and the love of our Lord Jesus Christ, not by man's mistaken notions. The Word of God is as psychologically up-to-date as tomorrow's newspaper. When a child comes home having done something wrong, he suffers anxiety, fear, and guilt. If his father is determined to be only sweetly reasonable, he is actually repressing his feelings. He is not being honest with his son. When the son comes into his father's presence, he senses and feels the hurt and anger in his father, no matter what he says. Children react to what they sense behind our words rather than our logic. A guilty son hears the big abstract words of a sweetly reasonable father and thinks, "I don't get it. But boy, he sure is angry!" Anxiety now smolders in him; it cannot come to a resolution because it could not be objectified to his conscious mind and dealt with appropriately. Physical discipline brings things to objective, "measurable" pain. Physical pain focuses fear and guilt in a measurable justice. Unnamed and unfaced anxiety cannot be dealt with. Unresolved guilt erodes security. As sin separates God and man, so guilt prevents fellowship between fathers and sons. Physical pain tells the inner being that punishment has been accomplished. Guilt is over and done with. The Bible expressly calls for physical discipline. The Bible is God's handbook. We will append to this chapter a list of Scriptures concerning discipline which we suggest that all parents take the time to read.

When our first son, Loren, was a little boy, he used to stare at what he wanted to do, knowing it was wrong, and then look at us. We could see him measuring the pain. If it was worth it, he did it. And he got his spanking. But it was objective. It could be dealt with. He was happy and confident and took his spanking as a matter of course. One person we find it difficult to help in counseling is a counselee whose father never disciplined physically. His feelings will not come clear. His father seemed so good that the counselee never realized he had any bad feelings toward his father. Confused feelings were suppressed in each instance. He could not forgive his father, because he didn't know he was mad at him. On the other hand, counselees who had severe disciplinarians for fathers are more readily able to forgive than those whose fathers failed to discipline at all because the counselees' feelings toward their fathers are easily identifiable and can be dealt with. But sons of wishy-washy fathers lack real banks for the rivers of their feelings. My (John's) father was very tender-hearted, but he had a temper, and hands like the side of a ham. I remember seeing the flash of his hand and watching my brother reeling across the living room and under the dining room table. But dad could never keep his anger very long. We could almost calculate how soon we would hear his steps coming up the stairs. He would come into the bedroom where we had been sent, take us on his lap, and say, "You know, that hurt me more than it did you."

And we would think, "Oh, yeah?" But we knew what he meant. We knew his heart really did care.

And then he would hold and hug us and say, "I love you guys, and I forgive you; do you forgive me?" And it was all healed. Life was more fun for the making up. All discipline needs to be enveloped in love. None of us can discipline perfectly. But "Love covers a multitude of sins" (1 Pet. 4:8b RSV).

Not only in the gang age but in every year of his life, a child needs to see his father bowing his head. Fathers should say the grace or be the one to delegate to some other member of the family. Fathers should say a prayer at night over the children. They should go with them to church, not leave them there. Seeing a father humbling himself before God writes faith upon the child's heart. The exact moment frustrations, hurts, and disappointments occur is the moment of learning for a child. A father who prays often but curses and expresses resentment at people and events may in fact innoculate his children against ever getting true faith. I (John) remember seeing my father smash his thumb with a hammer or drop something on his toe and dance about holding the injured member, whistling or exclaiming, "Ooh—ooh—ooh!" But I almost never heard him utter a curse word or express anger at what could not be helped. Paula's father always said, "Dagnabit," and quickly returned to good humor. Since children become what their fathers are, it is nothing of pride and only gratitude that neither of us curses or flies off the handle emotionally.

As counselors we hear parents say too frequently when their

children get into trouble, "I don't understand. We gave them everything." But when we check to see *what* they gave their children, we discover that they did truly give them every *thing*, and nearly nothing else. The children seldom saw them in church or in prayer. They didn't hear them reading the Bible. They didn't receive real affection and discipline. They did see their parents lose their tempers, insult each other, swear, get drunk occasionally, and live for their own egos rather than for the Lord. What was needed for the soul the children didn't get at all. And the parents can't understand what went wrong with them! The truth usually comes out that the parents do know what's wrong, and have been unwilling and afraid to admit it. We all would like Christian nurture to be some detached thing we can do on Sunday morning or in five minutes at the dinner table. It is frightening to learn that it happens in every moment.

As young people enter their teen-age years they must learn to internalize. Whatever parents teach is something handed *to* children. No matter how much parental teachings have become a part of us, each of us must make whatever has been given to us our own. That requires a process of examining, testing, wrestling, and sometimes rebelling. The struggle is called internalization because until parental teachings become our own by our own mature conscious decision, they remain external to us, much as an animal reacts by external conditioning rather than by personal choice. The struggle is usually more intense for boys, though girls must also internalize. In a boy's pilgrimage, he begins life enfolded in his mother's womb, totally dependent. His first breath declares independence from the mother's organic system. One by one, bodily functions become dissociated from the parents' care as he is weaned and diaper changing stops. Emotional dependence continues but it wanes throughout childhood. In teen-age years, internalization completes the process of individuation. Now he must examine whatever knowledges, morals, and precepts have been taught to him from outside himself. He must stand over against everything that has formed him, wrestle with it, and discover the why's of it for himself. Then it belongs to him. It has become his own. Perhaps such internalization can happen without rebellion, but in all our years of counseling, though we have seen many subtle forms of rebellion, we cannot remember encountering a single instance of a healthy adult who did not undergo some form of teen-age rebellion. Boys particularly need time and room to rebel.

Parents who understand teen-agers know that such rebellion does not mean rejection of them even if one form of that rebellion expresses itself in rejection. The stronger the love and nurture he receives, the more it may take for a teen-ager to distinguish himself from his parents. Mothers and fathers whose security is in Jesus Christ rather than in their own pictures of themselves as parents can and do allow their children to stand over against them. Unfortunately, most parents do not understand, try too hard, and make matters worse.

Parents must learn to step out of the way. Wise parents will have so instructed and disciplined that their child has been assuming responsibility more and more all along. But now there comes a transfer point in which a young person must take full responsibility for himself—though he is in no way capable of maintaining himself consistently. If a father still preempts this initiative as though the child were ten years old, a teen-ager's own budding life is crimped. For example, suppose a young man, because he wants to, is about to pick up the water bucket to wash the car, but the father says, "Son, go wash the car!" That has now become the last thing the son wants to do; the initiative has been taken from him. We're not speaking of manners only. It may help to ask, "Son, would you please wash the car?" but courtesy is not the main point. What is important is the ability of a parent to respect a teen-ager's need to see and do for himself what should be done. The contrary cry of parents is, "But if I didn't tell him, he would never see it." Dutiful and sensitive children, who have been thoughtful and attentive, often do an about face in their teen-age years. The tensions of internalization and individuation often turn the most lovingly outgoing children into self-centered, selfish and insensitive teen-agers. That is as normal as apple pie in America, not a matter for condemnation. The problem for every parent is to learn how to remind a teen-ager of his duties without condemning him, putting him down, or robbing him of his own enterprise.

To some extent it simply can't be done. No matter how sensitive, we are doomed to fail simply because we are the parents from whom he must cut free. Teen-agers flip-flop. One day they are wise, free and strong, resisting courteously all our overdoings. And the next day they regress to wanting to be told what to do, or shout harsh words at us for trying to. There are no longer any safe predictabilities. Each day requires that we meet our teen-ager as a new person, in the grace of our Lord Jesus Christ. The most important lesson for parents of teen-agers is to learn the capacity in Christ to set our half-mature fledglings free to fall!

True authority has never meant that a father has the right to protect his own fatherhood by controlling his family. Rather it means that one is put in the same type of position as the Father God. Though He has all the power in the universe, in whatever degree any action would impair our learning for ourselves or deprive us of our free will, He cannot do it. Though He loves and weeps over us as He casts us into the earth (Ps. 126:6 and Matt. 13:37), He must let us fall until we have learned. Just so an earthly father is called upon to restrain himself, be embarrassed, and hurt by and for his teen-agers, until they regain by trial and error their own balance and common sense. Notice in the Parable of the Prodigal Son that the father did not go after the prodigal. Nor did he send a Pinkerton detective. He sat at home and waited (Luke 15:11-31). Trusting in God to protect his son, and praying for him continually, a father is therefore saying to his son in one way or another, "I know you are going to stumble and burn your fingers and hurt your heart and ours; nevertheless I trust the Lord in you, and I know you will learn what you have to, and come out of it on your own. I know you are going to have to make mistakes, but you will learn by trial and error, and I set you free to do so." The primary task of a father of teen-agers is to undergird them with that kind of trust. Such trust is not naiveté. It is not blind, excusing, or permissive. It is an ability to believe in the Father's redeeming grace. It is a capacity to endure godly grief until the other has found himself.

Our son Loren, now a competent ordained minister, says, "I can now be trusted because my parents trusted me when I couldn't be trusted." The rule is simple. The more a father understands and sets his son free to err, the less the son has to rebel to find himself. The tighter the father holds the reins, the more he continues to demand that his son live the same as he has been taught, the more sinfully his son must rebel in order to become his own person. A young tree set under the branches of an older one can find no room to grow. Parents who have taken up all the space of moral righteousness should not be surprised when their sons find their only space by living in immorality. Again, death of self in Christ, and God's love alive in each for the other is the key to successful family living. Some people think they have succeeded if their children always obey and do what is pleasing to them and to society. In fact what may have been accomplished is the destruction of their children. Often we counsel adults who failed to find themselves because they dared not rebel in their teen-age years.

Parents tend to fall to either extreme with teen-agers, either hyper-control or permissiveness. Neither is the answer. Rules must still be maintained. But at this stage, the teen-ager should be invited into the process. We have sat down with our children to discuss with them what they think might be fair hours and rules around the house. Together we set penalties. These became the rules of the game. We made it clear that rules were not intended to cramp anyone's enjoyment of life, but rather to establish a structure of mutual consideration so that each member of the family might be given a restful, secure place of experiencing and growing with a minimum of pushing and pulling. With each child such conferences had to be handled differently. With some it was easier than with others. Since Loren at fourteen wanted to talk about everything, it was much easier than with Johnny who at that age seldom wanted to talk about anything. But once the rules had been set, our discipline became more detached in manner than it had been previously. When they were younger, our insistence and discipline had as its base our responsibility before God to build the structure of morality. Now it was time to believe even when the teen-ager stood over against us that that task had in fact been accomplished in the deep heart. We became more like referees in a game then, who blew the whistle when the rules of the game had been broken. Our teen-agers knew we still had to insist that the rules be kept, but the base was now different. They had freely chosen; now they must pay the penalty. But it was not that we were maintaining our life style in them. They were choosing and learning.

Teen-agers need the approval of their fathers. Approval is not backslapping or condoning or falsehood. It is not really predicated upon behavior, but, rather, a sense a teen-ager has that his father likes him and loves him just because he is. This sets him free to try his own wings. If he must so have his father's approval that he must compulsively appear to do or be as his father wishes, he cannot venture to become his own person. But if he knows his father wants him to be his own person and will be proud of him that he has tried, whatever the result, he can risk failure. He does not have to become a star football player because that would earn him a place with his father. He can enter whatever enterprise appeals to him for his own sake whether his father would be pleased or not. The question of approval has already been settled.

Boys who have been given sensitive, loving natures find it most difficult to achieve their place in the teen-age world. Loren was a good athlete until in his teen-age years he could not countenance the ways of the "jocks." Now he faced the question, "How can I be part of my teen-age culture and society?" He came to us, wanting to become a rock-and-roll band leader. At the time we were pastoring the leading church in Wallace, Idaho, when rock-and-roll was even more disreputable than it is today, especially among evangelical church people. We knew that Loren would be exposed to the worst elements of society, tempted by drugs and drink, and by girls who would be only too willing to throw themselves at a rock-and-roll hero. We could not believe that Loren could keep himself totally free from these influences. Yet we felt that the counsel of the Lord was not only to give permission, but to back him all the way, financially and by our presence as chaperones, and by loaning our car and/or driving them all over the Northwest to perform. Night after night we would pray into the wee hours of the morning. Twice there were wrecks on snowy roads. Some nights as chaperones we would feel the urge to run outside periodically to let all of the sound out of our ears. We eventually were backing "The Long Awaited" band as countersigners until their equipment (which they paid for) amounted to over ten thousand dollars and they had become so successful as to win third place in a contest of over 150 bands. By being on stage Loren managed not only to be accepted among his peers, but also to be counted a leader, while in fact their long practice hours kept the entire group out of the scrapes of the rest of their society. They, themselves, refused the worst songs of the time. Loren did tell us later that he tried "pot" a few times, and he nearly wrecked the voice he needed as a music major in college, but he came through his teen-age years with valuable experiences, knowing that his parents had paid the cost to be with him, not against him.

Johnny rebelled more openly and vociferously than the others, putting us to the test in everything we teach other parents. And we failed gloriously. We got angry, demanded behavior, scolded and shouted—and learned all over again what failures we are as parents, and how only God can give the grace to allow a son freedom to learn the hard way. Twice the Lord warned us that Johnny was about to be killed in a car wreck unless we prayed fervently. Both times he was in spectacular wrecks which totally demolished the cars in which he was riding. Both times he was unhurt except for minor scratches and a sprained ankle. Through it all Johnny matured strong and free. Parents must walk so closely to the Lord that He can call them, whether or not they have learned to hear directly, to protect their children while they venture forth. The life of prayer is essential. Teen-agers are out of our control, but not out of our responsibility. We are reduced to prayer, talks, groundings, scoldings, the help of friends and often do nothing more than add fuel to the fire.

Mark was, on the other hand, so straight we wished he *would* do something. But rebellion was proceeding quietly, within, in his own subtle ways. Every child is different, and Mark surely was! Each youth must be met as a totally different individual. What works for one will not work for another. Not one of our four sons has approached the teen-age period anything like his brothers. As the Father allows each of us to become what we are, so must parents allow their children to learn to become themselves. Hard and fast rules are therefore good things to use as a springboard for doing something different! Only prayer allows the Holy Spirit so to soften our hearts as to allow us to do something unique, even spontaneous, in each instance.

In the following section, Paula writes concerning daughters. Many things we have said concerning fathers and sons in the first six years apply also to girls. Particularly from her father a daughter derives her inner structure, those unconscious practices and devices in her nature which will operate throughout her life. From him come self-discipline, security, strength, and the real nature of her life with the Father God. But some fathers react to their daughters with awkwardness, afraid of their own feelings. Someone so defenseless, so beautiful, so lovely as to melt a heart, they love like a "little doll," from a safe distance. Not knowing that it is his unique privilege and responsibility to hold and comfort his daughter, and that by so doing he will awaken her capacity to relate to a man as an adult, too often the father abdicates and leaves her in the crib or solely to the mother's care. This prevents her from developing the capacity to relate rightly to a man. Her soul remains undeveloped in that area. We have counseled with many women who had much worse experiences. Their fathers were loud, insensitive, drunken, and violent. Such daughters have been so inwardly destroyed that now they can neither give to their husbands, nor open up to receive from them. They are like some potatoes, round and beautiful on the outside, but blighted on the inside. But for a daughter of the King it is never too late. Prayer for inner transformation and restoration can set such women free and empower them to live an abundant life.

Girls undergo the same kind of pilgrimage from dependence to independence, but in a different way. While boys are traveling in gangs, girls are gathering in clubs and cliques. Girls' groups are usually not so obviously set to mischief, but they tend to become more traumatic for girls because of their exclusiveness. Parents who have enjoyed warm, relaxed sharing with their daughter may suddenly find it difficult to accept this "stranger" who has become secretive and at times snippy. Even at this age girls have a greater desire to please than boys normally do. Inability to be pleasing and acceptable to others can become far more wounding to them. They need the security of their father's love openly and consistently expressed. As boys need to view their fathers with some degree of hero worship, girls need far more to have a crush on their daddies. Such admiration is a sacred trust never to be violated.

As hormones begin to introduce a girl to puberty, she commences to practice feeling what it is to be a woman. She begins to feel differently about being dressed up for Sunday school. A comb becomes an indispensable part of the paraphernalia she carries to school. "What shall I wear?" becomes the number-one decision of each day. I (John) used to err by my continual lack of awareness. Andrea would pirouette before me in a pretty new dress and say with her heart in her throat, "How do I look?" I would look up from reading something long enough to toss off an absent minded, "Yeah, okay, fine." She needed to hear, "You look wonderful—beautiful!" I was unaware that my response was affecting Andrea's confidence in herself, and building expectations in her unconscious about men and their inattentiveness. She was four then, and now that she is eleven she is still learning the same lessons. By the grace of God, the Lord has now opened my heart and made me aware, so that I actually am delighted with her and pleased by her appearance and can say so. A girl has a tremendous need to feel she is a delight to her father. She needs to try out on him her ability to allure men. If she can cause his eyes to sparkle with pride, she gains confidence in her power to attract a man. She needs to flirt with her dad, snuggle up to him, and even imagine that she is winning a contest with her mother for him. Both the father and the mother should be aware of this game and allow it; it is innocuous and beautiful, and by it she will acquire confidence to know herself as a lovely and desirable person.

A woman came to us who was in fact a beauty queen. I (John)

asked her, "Are you beautiful?"

She said, "No."

"Are you lovely?"

"No."

"Pretty?"

"No, I'm ugly!"

"Desirable?"

"No!"

Then a woman came who was, physically speaking, ugly as a mud fence. "Are you beautiful?"

"Yes."

"Are you lovely?"

"Yes." Because she thought she was beautiful, she was; beauty radiated from her. What was the difference? The beauty queen could never feel that her father appreciated her, no matter how hard she tried to win his approval. The lady who thought she was beautiful had a father who doted on her and complimented her often. A woman needs to know her own beauty. If she does not know, she will continually ask her husband to prove it to her and be unable to receive it even if he tries. It puts a constant burden on a husband, and strains the relationship. Paradoxically, if a woman so knows her beauty without conceit, she does not need her husband to tell her; he is then free to do so, and may quite often. Her inner expectancy from her life with her father may either prevent or enable. A woman who knows her own beauty is a great blessing to her husband because out of that sense of beauty and worth she feeds him. A wife should know that the self she presents to her husband is not a wet dishrag but a lovely rose. Her opinion of herself will make all the difference as to whether she pours loveliness into him or acts as a drain on his energies. It is a father's primary task to create that sense of beauty and value in his daughters.

Tragically, all too frequently when girls becoming women

have practiced their natural allurements before the men of their family, men have acted like ignorant beasts. In one town, as we counseled, five women, one after the other, confessed that their fathers, grandfathers, brothers, or uncles had molested them. Rachel Johnson, child protection counselor and wife of William Johnson, head of the psychology and sociology departments of Whitworth College, Spokane, Washington, informed us that recent statistics show that one out of every five women have been molested. The greatest tragedy created by such betrayal of trust is the message conveyed to the growing woman's heart. The fright and shame tell her that it is not all right and safe for her to be the woman she is becoming, for that will somehow get out of hand and result in nastiness. It is then as though the sepals of the bud can never open to allow the glorious bloom of the flower. Women molested as girls often have difficulty letting go in the proper fulness of sex with their husbands. Very often molested girls become locked into secrecy for fear of destroying their mother's relation with their father or stepfather and then develop long-lasting confused angers and guilts toward their mothers.

A father's hugs and kisses need to be given generously to daughters in a clean, clearly defined and understood father-role with absolutely no sexual undertones or overtones. His little girl is blossoming into womanhood, and he is the gardener who protects her as he admires and nurtures. The mother needs to contribute to the healthy quality of that process by not reacting in fear or jealousy.

A girl in her teens goes through her own kind of revolt; it is usually more subtle than a boy's. Inside herself she dreams, thinks, ponders, fantasizes, and then expresses outwardly in little dramas which test the reality of who and what she imagines herself to be. She is a little girl one day, sweet and innocent and wanting very much to please. The next day she may be relishing the role of a scarlet woman of the world. At the deep feeling level, she may throw herself intensely into a variety of roles without any intention of acting upon the emotion or settling into the role as a life style. She is simply experimenting in order to discover for herself who she really is. It is vital for her to have a father who can stand in gentle strength for her, understanding and affirming her until she can come to maturity and rest. If he or her mother attach too much significance to her expression of a mood or phase, they may lock her into it by her need to defend where she is. She will feel misunderstood, judged, and rejected, and may be unwilling or unable to move on until she is assured of unqualified love and acceptance.

Worse, suppose a daughter feels guilty about something she has been involved in with her peer group, or simply wants to share a guilt for a feeling she has entertained. She tells her father about it and he responds, "Now listen, no daughter of mine is going to act like that! Now you straighten yourself out, and I don't want to hear of your doing a thing like that again!" Proud of himself, he thinks he has been a dutiful father. What he has done is to allow a panic dynamic to invade the relationship, and that causes an immediate and automatic slamming of the door of communication. It is not likely that he *will* hear of her doing a thing like that again. He has in effect said to her, "I am not going to be with you; I am going to be over against you. You can't tell me anything because I'm not going to hear you. I will put you down. I am only going to hear my own need." He has also said to her that she is not by any means to attempt to become her own person. A father must be made sensitive by the Lord Jesus Christ to *hear* the daughter, because she needs to be able to unburden herself to him and then hug him. His manner needs to tell her that he can let her experience, find out, trust her not to go too far, and then love her and forgive her when she stumbles.

We used to give a nickname to our daughter, Ami, who is now twenty-six. We called her the "love boat." She would hug her dad awhile, go on her way, then as if she had run out of gas, come back for a refueling. She knew he was there for her, and that if she needed a hauling up short, he would do it without condemnation. Girls are different from boys in this respect. By her manner, Ami would ask that a behavioral line be drawn, and when it was, she could relax, and say no to a boy friend who was getting out of line. Christian sensitivity rules Christian discipline. For the teen, physical discipline is no longer appropriate. Discipline needs to be in terms of, "Look, here is the line. You're on your own, but you know if you step over the line you're the one who made the choice. Here are the penalties. They have to be observed but I love you no matter what." A girl really wants to test against her dad her ability to twist men around her finger. There are battles she must not win, for if she does, she will operate that way with her husband later in the form of unconscious manipulation. A father must be strong in the discipline of the Lord, but sensitive to his daughter.

Do we see that there is no palming off the teaching ministry of a father to his children? He *will* teach them, by who and what he is. Every man must make his own peace with God, or his children will feel the lack in every area of their formation. That is why the Old Testament closes with such powerful words. "Behold, I will send you Elijah the prophet before the coming of the great and dreadful day of the Lord: And he shall turn the heart of the fathers to the children and the heart of the children to their fathers, lest I come and smite the earth with a curse" (Mal. 4:5, 6).

DISCIPLINE:
Deuteronomy 8:5, 6
Proverbs 5: especially verses 11, 12, and 23
　　　　13:24
　　　　19:18
　　　　22:15

        23:13, 14
        25:28
        26:3
        29:15, 17
Ephesians 6:1-4
Hebrews 12

HOW TO GIVE REPROOF:
Luke 17:3
Galatians 6:1
1 Timothy 5:1
        5:19, 20
2 Timothy 4:1-5
Titus 1:7-13
     2:15
Ephesians 4:25-27 and 29-32
Matthew 7:1-5
        18:15-22

*CONCERNING REPROOF AND CORRECTION AND THOSE
WHO REFUSE IT:*

Proverbs 3:11, 12	15:22, 23
5:23	15:32
6:23	
9:7-9	Proverbs 17:9-14
10:17	18:1
12:1	23:9
13:1	24:24, 25
14:29, 30	26:3-5
15:1, 2	27:5, 6
15:4, 5	27:15-17
15:10	28:23
15:12	29:1
15:18	29:9, 11, 15, 17

6

MOTHERS, SONS AND DAUGHTERS

Our materialistic culture has also done much to destroy what mothers should know themselves to be. Since we have spoken concerning how the culture deprives fathers, and much of that applies to mothers, we will teach here more about what can be done to restore mothers' roles. The premier Scripture is Proverbs 31, the tenth verse and following:

A good wife who can find? She is far more precious than jewels. The heart of her husband trusts in her, and he will have no lack of gain. She does him good, and not harm, all the days of her life. She seeks wool and flax, and works with willing hands. She is like the ships of the merchant, she brings her food from afar. She rises while it is yet night and provides food for her household and tasks for her maidens. She considers a field and buys it; with the fruit of her hands she plants a vineyard. She girds her loins with strength and makes her arms strong. She perceives that her merchandise is profitable. Her lamp does not go out at night. She puts her hands to the distaff, and her hands hold the spindle. She opens her hand to the poor, and reaches out her hands to the needy. She is not afraid of snow for her household, for all her household are clothed in scarlet. She makes herself coverings; her clothing is fine linen and purple. Her husband is known in the gates, when he sits among the elders of the land. She makes linen garments and sells them; she delivers girdles to the merchant. Strength and dignity are her clothing, and she laughs at the time to come. She opens her mouth with wisdom, and the teaching of kindness is on her tongue. She looks well to the ways of her household, and does not eat the bread of idleness. Her children rise up and call her blessed; her husband also, and he praises her: "Many women have done excellently, but you surpass them all." Charm is deceitful, and beauty is vain, but a woman who fears the Lord is to be praised. Give her of the fruit of her hands, and let her works praise her in the gates. (RSV)

One cannot help seeing that most of the things listed here are menial, time-consuming tasks that must be done again and again day after day—sewing, marketing, and running the household in multitudes of little details. A woman's work is never finished. Life seems unfair and unglamorous to many women now, and it appears to have been more so in the biblical society which had no modern appliances. But there was then a basically different way of viewing life. The Bible expresses that culture our Lord was establishing upon earth in which He said, "But he that is greatest among you shall be your servant" (Matt. 23:11). As we explained in chapter two, people in the Bible believed that the Spirit of God flows through everything a woman touches. They understood that what she does with her hands is spiritual. Her work, however tedious, is not solely an earthly, physical thing. God's Spirit flows through everything she is and does. Mothers today need to regain that sense of not being alone as they move about the house doing what seems to them routine monotony. They need to comprehend that the Spirit of God witnesses the life of Christ to all in and around her home as she does those tasks which seem so meaningless. As with fathers, what she is forms her children. Mothers also are the medium; they are the teaching.

In the beginning, as the Lord first began to work upon the conscience of men, women were regarded as little more than chattel in a male-dominated culture. Throughout the Bible one can trace a progression of respect and emancipation of women, from Sarah's embarrassed laughter (Gen. 18:9-15) to Rebecca's wisdom (Gen. 27) to Deborah's rule (Judg. 4 & 5) and Jael's faithfulness (Judg. 4 & 5). It is no coincidence that the Word carefully records the descent of the Davidic line through Ruth the Moabitess. By the time Proverbs is written we hear that a good wife is a gift of God (Prov. 12:4; 18:22; 19:14; 31:10) and "She will do him good and not evil all the days of her life" (Prov. 31:12). By the time of the New Testament Elizabeth and Mary are both visited by the angel of God and exalted among men forever (Luke 1, especially v. 48). Jesus honored His mother, even from the cross (John 19:26) and declared that no man could put his wife away (Matt. 5:31, 32). St. Paul made a most astounding statement for those days, that husbands and wives should be subject *to one another* (Eph. 5:21) and that a husband does not rule over his own body but the wife does (1 Cor. 7:4). Historically, it can be shown that geographically wherever Hebraic or Christian faith has appeared, respect for and emancipation of women from the dominance of men have been consequences.

Therefore when we write concerning the menial tasks of motherhood we are not continuing the supposed chauvinistic suppression of women to slavery. Rather we are celebrating that division of labor by which God has exalted women to the highest position by giving them the place of greatest service.

We do not see how any Christian mother can be satisfied and fulfilled so long as her eyes are dazzled by the seeming importance of grandiose things done outside the home, such as missionary work, evangelism, healing the sick, etc. Until I (Paula) became content and saw myself fulfilled as a homemaker and mother and knew the glory of God to be in the tedium of everyday life as much as anywhere else, the Lord did not release me to the teamwork of ministry we now share. Satan cometh but to rob, steal, kill, and destroy (John 10:10). Perhaps his greatest theft from women has been their spiritual awareness of the unique glory of their position and tasks as mothers. Right there in the constant repetitions of daily unnoticed chores, in the midst of the drudgery, sparkles the radiance of God's presence, incarnating the life of Jesus Christ among men. How easy it is to slide over thirty years of carpentry to identify the witness of Jesus solely with three years of speaking, healing, and dying. And it is just as easy to identify being Christian with church attendance, prayer meetings, and various activities while failing to see that worship and prayer meetings are to refuel the spirit for the main life of Christianity, which is in the home. Every mother's heart is the place of the Lord's visitation upon her, where the Holy Spirit breaks from the page to reality in daily living. When worship experiences, however glorious, rather than the home, become identified as the glory of our life in Christ, they have become a seduction and an idolatry. A worship service, however good, is only a small part of our life in the Spirit, a gathering and a retreat in the midst of the natural flow of human events where God is. The home is the primary meeting place of God and man. And that meeting is in words across the dinner table, or hands sharing dish towels, or games of checkers or picnics at the park. It is there that God sparkles in reality. Rushing through housework, hurrying the children to the baby-sitter's in order to get out to do something "important" for God demonstrates that a wife has things exactly backwards. Her home is her first calling. Her family is her primary ministry. And that is not a reduction from the great things she could have done, but an elevation to the highest.

In Episcopal Bishop William Frey's home in Denver, where sometimes as many as twenty-one people live in community as an extended family, no one is assigned a menial job to do. But someone is given a kitchen ministry, the bishop himself has a furnace-room ministry, another the bathroom ministry. And as Bishop Frey says, "If the bathroom ministry is neglected, the ministry at the cathedral suffers." So it is in every family. If the home is not in order, there is no place of security from which to minister effectively anywhere else.

During the nine months in which the spirit of a child dwells within the womb of a mother, the vessel that she is, her body, her emotions, her life with Christ or lack of it, influence the spirit and the formation of the soul of her child. The Word of God indicates in several places the ability of our spirits to know things while we are being formed in the womb. We have already spoken of Luke 1:39-45 in which John the Baptist leaped in Elizabeth's womb when Mary entered the room. In Jeremiah 1:5 God says, "Before I formed you in the womb I knew you, and before you were born I consecrated you; I appointed you a prophet of the nations" (RSV). Notice the words, "I formed you in the womb." Is He speaking merely of the natural body? Or also of the formation of character? The context concerns his appointment and anointing to be a prophet. Aidan MacFarlane, a British pediatrician, writing in his book, *The Psychology of Childbirth*, states, "Unborn children, long before the full term of pregnancy, develop senses of taste, hearing, touch, perhaps even sight. *They respond to the emotional states of their mothers* and are probably susceptible to rudimentary learning" (*Logos Journal* editorial, page 45, Nov. 1977). So we see how important it is for a child to be held in the womb of a mother whose spirit, body, and soul are being made into a clean vessel through the Lord Jesus Christ. It is frightening to realize that old hatreds and fears harbored within her soul affect her child. But we can testify to hundreds of counseling cases in which hatreds, fears, and anxieties were traceable directly to the womb.

To carry such a realization too far and so fear that everything in a mother becomes part of her child is to reduce it to absurdity. Some of us who are older can remember the superstitious fears of some mothers who were sure they had marked their children. We need to guard against such fears, while on the other hand we need to rediscover the necessity for ensuring good wholesome experiences for women in pregnancy. Biblical women considered the first three to five months of pregnancy as being crucial to the formation of their child. "And after these days his wife Elizabeth conceived, and for five months she hid herself saying, 'Thus the Lord has done to me in the days when he looked on me to take away my reproach among men.' "

Some have wondered why Elizabeth hid herself, and some have erroneously concluded she was ashamed to be pregnant. Not at all. Elizabeth had been ashamed *not* to be pregnant. In that day a woman was under reproach if she could not bring forth sons. Therefore, when she became pregnant, she called people to see, "Look what I have accomplished for my husband!" She made sure everyone who had been taunting her would see that she was bearing a child. Both Rachel and Elizabeth exclaimed, "God hath taken away my reproach . . ." (Gen. 30:23; Luke 1:25). But why, if she was not a-shamed, did Elizabeth hide herself? Luke 1:39 says, "In those days Mary arose and went with haste into the hill country, to a city of Judah and she entered the house of Zechariah, and greeted Elizabeth." We can understand her haste because Gabriel had said that Elizabeth's pregnancy would be a sign to Mary. But observe what follows, "Mary remained with her *about three months*." Why a stay of three months? Why did she not quickly return to Joseph? Bishop K.C. Pillai, a man from the East, explained to us that in the biblical society when a woman knew that she had conceived, she secreted herself from her husband and from her family and from all other involvements.

She would retire to the home of a dear friend or relative who could be counted on to protect her seclusion. During that time she would pray, read Scripture, sing praises, and meditate about God in order to bless her child with a beautifully formed soul.

But why remove themselves from their husbands? They also believed that in those first three months it was not good to continue in sexual intercourse, and though the husband could be asked to restrain himself for that time, wifely duties in all the family would also beckon and tempt unless some distance allowed rest and privacy. Obstetricians have recently discovered that if a mother engages in sexual intercourse in the first three months, that can sometimes deprive the baby of oxygen during the approach to climax, which can affect the brain. Why should it surprise us that people guided by the Holy Spirit should follow practices which modern science now validates?

Since we have thought in our anti-Christ culture that our spirit is something different and apart from our body, we have considered the growth of a fetus as merely a physical thing. And so we have allowed a pregnant woman to return to work, be exposed to all manner of noise and hassle, smoke, drink, gossip, think harsh thoughts—and then we wonder why the newborn baby is colicky and nervous, cries so much, and develops a personality and character full of problems. We no longer live the wisdom that is in the Bible. Having counseled thousands of people, we firmly believe that if a pregnant mother prays and meditates, her baby will be blessed accordingly. While we were teaching with a prominent Christian psychiatrist,* someone asked him, "Can what the mother thinks and feels really affect the baby in the womb?" He replied, "We know that the mother's emotions affect the rate of blood coming to the baby, affect the supply of oxygen, and generally influence many things physically." He went on to comment that we do not know how much the baby may be

*Dr. Lee Griffin—School of Pastoral Care, Pilgrim Firs, Washington, 1969

affected emotionally and spiritually because we cannot measure that scientifically, but it is certainly reasonable to infer that the same stimuli affect the child in every other part of its being.

Paula became pregnant with Andrea at the same time that Millie Suhr, a member of our prayer group, conceived their son Mike. We were surprised to discover later that the Holy Spirit had spoken very similarly to both, in their own guidance apart from each other, pulling them back from all intercessory burdens and from all works in the church. Both were told to retreat into their homes, to meditate and pray, and to enjoy wholesome family living. It seemed especially important that both, who were burden-bearers for the Lord, carry no intercessory burdens at all during their pregnancies. Hidden wisdom within them received that word with a sigh of recognition and relief, and their pregnancies became a time of blessing and refreshment—and both children show it, in their security and loving natures.

If a negative thing has happened which could introduce fear or hurt through the mother into the child's nature, then we should simply pray for that thing to be healed and turned to blessing. That is one reason our Lord came to earth through a mother's womb, so that because He has experienced human life, He is able to heal those who suffer and are tempted (Heb. 2:18).

Obviously we are against the new abortion laws which permit abortion simply because the mother doesn't want to have a child. No fetus is an "it" which can be discarded as an inconvenience. A baby in the womb is a living spirit and abortion is murder. When we encourage a woman to have an abortion, we are accomplices with her in that crime. Some months ago a woman came to us whose husband was pressuring her to have an abortion. Because the new laws seemed designed to soothe the conscience, and her husband persisted, she consented to him, despite her misgivings. We listened to the woman in silence while she confessed her feelings and then watched in compassion as she sat and sobbed and sobbed. She knew she had killed the life God had given to her, and she was unconsolable. How we wish that lawmakers could sit with us to experience the heartbreak of such women as they are overwhelmed by a guilty conscience after the fact. Forgiveness lifts away the weight of guilt, but it is more difficult to fill the sense of loss.

Too often men think if society passes a law, that makes a thing all right. But laws contrary to God's law never make anything all right with God. Murder remains murder no matter what men declare. We are *not* saying that there are not times when the Lord might himself allow a life to be taken. That is out of our province. But we do know that giving a carte blanche to kill all babies we don't want is horrendous in the sight of God. Many times, in calling us to pray about this, the Lord has called to mind Scriptures concerning the sacrifice of infants to false gods (Ps. 106:38; Isa. 57:5; Jer. 19:5; Ezek. 16:20). When human comfort and pleasures become more important than human life, we are verily sacrificing our children to idols, and drawing upon this nation the wrath of God.

Some time ago our parental technology reached the nadir of its captivity to the split mentality which has been its philosophical base. Whatever was natural became suspect. Mothers' milk was no longer thought to be as valuable as substitutes. Then came that most destructive of all parental teachings—"four hours in the crib, awaken and feed, back in the crib four hours, awaken and feed; don't hold the child too much, you'll spoil him." Today women are discovering again the value of breast-feeding, and of holding the child in the arms. Breast-feeding not only physically conveys antibodies needed by the infant to ward off disease, but more importantly, the mother's spirit enfolds the child and flows through her breast and nipples to sustain and bless the baby in the wellspring of its inner life. A baby drinks more than milk from its mother. No bottle can copy or replace in any way who she is.

Time-Life Films has produced a movie entitled *Rock-a-Bye Baby–Life Around Us* in which the theme is again and again stated, through the reporting of scientific experiments and studies made of animal and human mothering, that infants require stimulation of all their senses. The need to be touched and moved is as undeniable as the need to be fed; the baby craves and needs to be rocked. If the child is denied mothering and rocking, an abnormal functioning of the cerebellum results which adversely affects social and emotional behavior and often manifests itself in serious mental retardation.

The movie reports that Dr. Mary Neil conducted experiments in several New York hospitals with incubators designed to rock. Some premature infants were placed in these and rocked for several weeks for half-hour periods three times a day. They were then tested for rate of growth and development against premature infants kept in conventional, stationary incubators. Inquiry and testing concerned such questions as strength of hand grasp. How long did it take a baby to raise his head enough to lift the nose from the mattress? What changes took place in coordination? The infants who were rocked showed higher development in all these areas, plus greater weight gain and increased responses to sight and sound stimuli.

Dr. Harry Harlow of the University of Wisconsin conducted extensive experiments with monkeys. They were taken from their natural mothers and given two types of substitutes; one was made of wire and the other was cloth-covered. The baby monkeys would spend as much as fifteen hours a day for as long as two years clinging to their cloth-covered substitutes. The wire substitutes seemed to offer no excitement or comfort even when they were equipped with a bottle. The infants would invariably run to the foodless cloth mothers particularly when they were startled to fear. Dr. Harlow then provided two types of fur-covered mother substitutes. They were identical except that one was stationary while the other was constantly moving and rocking. The monkey raised with the moving mother indulged in some thumb sucking, but was generally bold and friendly. The one raised with the stationary mother was extremely timid and unsociable, afraid of changes made in his environment. Moreover, he exhibited the repeated pattern of rocking back and forth that had been observed by Dr. Rene Spitz in retarded, institutionalized children who were seldom held and loved.

At Hazelton Laboratories, Dr. James Prescott observed that monkeys who were raised by their natural mothers were healthy and reacted happily to one another in play. Touch was so important to them that when attempts were made to separate them, they resisted, clinging to one another to maintain body contact. On the other hand, monkeys raised in isolation did not know how to play when put together. They were at best indifferent to touch, and sometimes reacted to touch as if it were something extremely unpleasant. When held, they would exhibit great stress to the point of screeching.

We have found in counseling that it is easier to bring a person to wholeness, even if he has experienced the abuse of overdiscipline from the parents, if he has also received physical affection from those parents. Affection has called to life in him the capacity to open, to forgive, to risk, to love and be loved. But to minister to a person who has never been hugged to life in the beginning and to bring him to the point of sharing really and lovingly in any sort of relationship requires a miracle of God through consistent, persistent offering of someone affectionately as friend and mother-father substitute. It is not a learning and transformation that can be accomplished with the recognition and understanding of the intellect and setting of the will alone.

The demonstrated love of a mother for her child throughout the early years is so important that we have often wondered how the course of history might have been changed had the Hitlers of the world been nurtured in the loving arms of Christian mothers.

A mother, perhaps more than a father, finds her identity as a person in her role as a parent. Though she may pursue many avenues of creativity, finding success in whatever opportunities are presented to make use of her unique talents, her primary sense of being fulfilled may yet come in the rewards of watching her children grow into the fulness of their own lives. It is a part of her nature to bring forth life, and she has within her a natural inclination to nurture and protect. Much of the depth of herself is poured into the helpless infant she nurses, an immeasurable amount of time and energy is spent rescuing toddlers at the point of takeoff at the top of staircases, in washing dirty hands and wiping runny noses, bandaging skinned knees, and comforting tummy aches and hurt feelings. For a number of years her schedule revolves around the needs and activities of her children. It is difficult to let the children go then when they need to cut free. She is emotionally invested and involved in a risk relationship with them, and to achieve the appropriate degree of detachment involves a deliberate choosing to die to her self-images, hopes, dreams and fears in order to trust. Her head says (with Kahlil Gibran) that her children are not her own, that they have been entrusted to her by God, that they are as arrows shot forth from the home and that God himself will direct them to their mark. But in her heart she ties a rope to the end of each arrow, hangs on tightly and follows, flying through the air with her mouth going sixty miles a minute, "Don't forget what I told you!"–"Remember when"–"Watch out!"–"Be careful!" She tells herself she has taught her children the basics of how to live the very best she knew how, but there is always the nagging question in the face of what lies beyond the door of the home, "Is it enough?" If she believes with all her heart the promise, "Train up a child in the way he should go and when he is old he will not depart from it" (Prov. 22:6), her cry from the heart level is, "But not *too* old. Lord, please?"

It was easy for me (Paula) to see that to give my teen-age children too much warning and advice was to communicate mistrust to them, and might often have the same effect as telling a child not to put beans up his nose (he hadn't thought of it, but it is suddenly attractive). But for a time I, like many other responsible Christian mothers, took on the terribly intense and serious task of yearning, interceding, protecting with devoted hours of standing as a prayer warrior, weeping, repenting, hanging onto every little word and action to measure the success of my effort. Johnny gave me a firmly kind and liberating word one day when he said, "Mom, you're trying too hard." Had he said, "Get off my case," I could have received it as ingratitude, rebellion, and rejection, and settled into a noble martyr role. But there was only mildly irritated compassion in his tone. That caused me to become aware that he was sensitive to me on a deep feeling level, and that my lack of rest and peace and trust of him in the Lord's hands was compounding his difficulty in dealing with the tension that already existed between his two worlds—the value systems of home and the peer group. There was no way I knew *how* to let go, but I repented sincerely for having put judgment and pressure on him, told him I was sorry, and asked the Lord to slay the part of me that wanted to be the savior of my son. I had been unconsciously demanding that he fill my image, live out my expectations, and save himself and me pain. The Lord heard, again slew my overmothering, and created that kind of space between us in which His own Spirit of grace could operate to release old tensions, enable real forgiveness and establish us in freedom to communicate with one another trustingly, no longer having to defend ourselves. That was the immediate beginning of a new level of maturity for Johnny. I knew the breakthrough was real when he light-heartedly introduced me to his buddies at work as his "girl friend." I continue to pray for him, but my prayers affirm that the Lord is on the throne of our lives, and ask Him to fill my almost-grown children with their own strength and might in the inner man that they might have power from within to discern and choose wisely.

We say we believe in a God who is an all-knowing, ever-present, loving, caring Father whose faithfulness is never lacking. We may sing a lusty, "I know whom I have believed, and am persuaded that He is able to keep that which I have committed unto Him. . ."; the test of our faith comes again and again in terms of the genuineness of our relinquishment of our teen-age children to Him. Do we really believe that if we give up our control, God will be there to protect, discipline, defend, and nurture? Giving up control is not coterminous with permissiveness. We may still draw firm lines, but if our heart is free, our children will sense it.

Our second son, Mark, was from the beginning gifted and creative. For most of his young life he was out of step with the rest of the world. For him time stood still while he kicked leaves from one end of the block to the other, and the school day wore on without him. Friends along the school route watched for him, so as to direct him to flow with the school traffic. In the first grade his practices in penmanship would proceed normally to a point of boredom, and then there would appear little hanging vines from the base of the letters, with elves swinging from the curlycues. Such creativity was viewed by others as a mixture of delightfulness and wierdness. The entire process of coming into the more inhibited disciplines of our educational system succeeded in communicating to him that somehow it was not all right to be himself, and resulted in some pain of awkwardness and loneliness for him as he grew older. On a hike through the woods he would be left far behind by those who could not comprehend what possible value there could be in pursuing friendship with a bug on the underside of a leaf of trillium. His sensitive and imaginative faculties enabled him to experience life in perceptions his peers could little see and hardly understand, and he tended to interpret a great deal of their rambunctious joking and jostling as rejection of him personally. It seemed to him to be a phony sort of game they played. It remained foreign to his nature to "get with it," and of questionable value at best. He learned to function in the world by sharing very little out of his inner guarded treasure, while growing in depth in his own spirit, and yet manifesting an unnerving sort of naiveté in relation to what other people were thinking and doing. A significant interchange while he was still in grade school went something like this: (out of the blue, no prelude) "I was telling you the truth then."

"When, Mark?"

"When I first came to you." End of conversation. I particularly, with all my mother hen instincts, wanted to protect him, and found it very difficult to believe that this young man who could spend a half hour putting his socks on could function successfully at college without our scheduling and constant practical direction. But Mark chose a university that was four hundred miles away from home, and the Lord said clearly, "Let go." We have since then lived in growing awe of how much better a parent our Lord God has been than we have been! Mark secured a grant and a job through the work-study program, and has made his own way financially with only occasional help from us (rarely solicited), and has bought a car. He has made the dean's list almost every semester through five years of college (a number of times with a perfect 4.0). Disciplining himself to a program of weight lifting, he has grown into manhood looking like a young Greek god. He earnestly sought Christian fellowship and found it. The art work he has produced is magnificent. He has worked through personal relationships to become compassionate, understanding, and outgoing, has come into an appreciative acceptance of himself, and is planning to work for a year so he can enroll at a seminary to study for the ministry. We shudder to think how we might have prevented his life, thinking to preserve it, had we given in to what our anxiety-ridden senses told us.

Several years ago a woman came to John for counsel. She was in great distress, complaining that her son was rebelling, beginning to go astray, and giving way to fits of anger. She was at a loss to know how to control him. The woman was well enough along in years that as she talked, John was beginning to wonder if she could be a Sarah. And then the son appeared at the door—a thirty-seven year old, still walking with the toddling step of a three year old, his middle-aged spread filling his summer shorts like baby fat. He left, following at mommy's heels.

Recently we have talked with a series of wives who have found themselves married to little boys who constantly run to mama for aid and comfort. When the wife complains that responsibilities at home are being neglected, or that they as husband and wife can never talk things through, she suddenly becomes the enemy. No man likes to be told that he is still dragging his umbilical cord. His defense becomes, "You're jealous—I'm just helping out—after all, think of all my parents have done for me—I don't know why you can't get along with my mother." On the other hand, there are wives who still run to mama for approval and advice and support that should come from the husband. He feels aced out, an intruder in the family, rejected, forced into a position of competing for his place.

If a mother has given enough physical affection to her child in all of the formative years, and then has let go in the heart while continuing to express affection to her teen-ager, she will find herself with an adult child who is free to grow into his own destiny and take adult responsibility for his own life with his family. He will also be free to give his love and attention to his parents in appropriate ways and measure without being driven and drawn by unsatisfied hungers and insecurities and demands upon his inner being. Mother is a blessing. "Smother" is a bane. 138

PART II

7

THE POSITION OF A HUSBAND

In Part I we spoke about how our carnal natures are formed and deformed in the family, in the first years especially. This second part explores what kind of corrupt dynamics arise in adult life from our early malformations, and what we can do to overcome and restore them. We, therefore, feel it is necessary to clarify what is meant, and not meant, by the healing of the inner man, sometimes called the healing of memories.

In 1961, I (John) began to work with Agnes Sanford, who had entered into pioneering what was then called "the healing of memories." Together we spoke in quite a few places across the country, teaching about and elaborating on the concept of the healing of the inner man. Agnes never liked the term, "healing of memories," nor did I. That handle somehow became attached to the work, and remained. She always insisted that what actually transpires is nothing other than the confessional, the revealing and confession of long-forgotten sins. Imbedded guilts and resultant behavior patterns rob Christians of their promised abundant life, and so Agnes taught that common, everyday Christians could and should pray for forgiveness à la James 5:16. I came along to insist continually that all our understandings of this ministry be rooted and grounded in the Word and in solid doctrine and theology. It has been a grief to both Agnes and me that throughout the succeeding years we have seen many enter the field who had neither her long rootage in solid church doctrine nor my grounding in the Word and evangelical theology. Consequently we have lamented the incursion of many unbiblical approaches and practices, which often blasphemed the ministry to the very people who need it most. I have many times found it necessary to defend the ministry from misunderstandings and projections upon it. Clarification is long overdue. Many abuses and misunderstandings need to be reproved and corrected.

In one sense there is no healing of the inner man. The Lord does not want to put new wine into old wineskins (Matt. 9:17; Mark 2:22; Luke 5:37, 38). He does not want to heal what needs to come to death in Him. Many idealistic people, not grounded biblically, have heard of the healing of the inner man and have rushed in to pour water on a fire God is building.

A psychologist has his eyes on the capacity to function. He wants to restore people to function normally. If he can do that, he thinks he has succeeded. A Christian counselor has no such primary intent. He knows, as Bob Mumford has said, that if he fixes the fix God has fixed to fix a man, God will have to fix another fix to fix him.

A Christian counselor knows that when a man has received Jesus, all that man's sins have already been forgiven, and positionally that man's sin nature has died, but that not all of the person's mind, heart, and spirit has received that blessed fact. Consequently, the counselor's work is to bring into full effect that conversion, death, and resurrection which has already happened. A Christian counselor is involved in helping Christians reckon their sin as dead in Christ (Rom. 4) in order to claim the new life.

Christ did not come to improve us. He did not come to make us better people. Nor does He want committed people, or devoted, or good, gentle, kind or wise people. He wants dead ones, that the life of Christ may shine through us (Gal. 2:16-21, Phil. 3:9). He does not want to repair our righteousness. He wants to slay it, so that His righteousness may clothe us anew (1 Cor. 1:26-31, Gal. 2 and 3, 1 Cor. 15:47-58). We become better people not by healing our broken places so that we can function better, but by dying to self so that His righteousness may be expressed in and through us. He will then be that devotion, kindness, and gentleness in us that He wants us to be.

Healing seems to connote that something was once good and "done got broke," so we fix it up in order for it to work again. There never was anything good in human life which could be repaired! (Ps. 14, Rom. 3). It has been a continuing grief to me that many Christians who did not understand the radical nature of sin and the centrality of the cross, and therefore the necessity for death and rebirth, have rushed into the healing of memories and have in fact postponed the fulness of death and rebirth! Because of this serious error on the part of a few, there has been negative reaction from some quarters to all who pray for inner healing. Hear this: We are not servants of mammon, trying idealistically to restore people to the good life so they can be happy. We are servants of Jesus who depart from Him the moment we forget that every counseling encounter has as its base the necessity to evangelize unbelieving hearts.

Our task is to reveal hidden sins that they may be forgiven. Our task is then to help the counselee reckon as dead on the cross whatever practices in the old man resulted from sin (Col. 3:3-10). And then to stand by in faith as the Lord resurrects the other in newness of life (1 Cor. 15:42, 43).

Transformation of the inner man is most desperately needed for the restoration of families. But as the Lord restores such a powerful ministry into fragile human hands, we can stumble into countless pitfalls. Our sinful propensity is to turn every blessing God has given into bane. For instance, the sacrament of communion given for unity is changed into something to quarrel about doctrinally, or sex given for blessed fulfillment into pornography and prostitution. Just so, we manage to turn great insights for healing the inner man into perversions and corruptions. We list, then, the many pitfalls and corrections, not necessarily in their order of importance.

Many who have entered into the ministry to the inner man have become problem-centered, both counselors and counselees. Life is not a series of problems. Problems are not the issue of life. Life is not an overcoming of problems, one after another. We are not navel contemplators. Life is sonship in the Lord Jesus Christ, living to bless the Father God. It is celebration and wonder, human laughter and fun, growth and mystery, procreation and labor, and so on, defying definition. The only reason one looks at problems is to discover, like a good mechanic, what is keeping the machine from running—not merely to restore to function, but to enable that death and rebirth which is essential to maturity into sonship. Many problems do not have to be seen. We simply grow out of them. To this date, some sixteen years into this ministry, I cannot tell why some things must be known consciously, and others not. Not knowing, we are left with simple dependence on the Holy Spirit, rather than human control.

Becoming problem-centered is part of what causes some in this ministry to elevate the conscious mind too high. It is then as if we must know and understand a great many things in order to be saved. That is the basic heresy of Gnosticism, that we are only saved by right knowledge. It is not by right knowledge that we are saved, but by the person of our Lord Jesus Christ. To what degree He wants us to understand in the process of salvation and growth to maturity, to that degree let us be open to hear, but when He leads us to freedom to live and love without ever understanding what blocked us, blind to the process of healing (Isa. 42:19), let us be willing not to see.

Becoming Gnostics, who insist that our counselees see in

order to be saved, makes us idolaters. We have hacked out a position whereby counselees must have us guide them, or the dear souls will be lost. Just as the deluded soul will no longer do anything without consulting his diviner or astrologer, so many will no longer act without consulting their counselor, fearful lest they not have the right bit of insight.

Once we have established knowledge and insight on the throne, it is a simple step to install psychology rather than the Word of God as our guide. I personally was well-trained in psychology, having a minor in social psychology in college, and a major in the religion and personality department at seminary. But having entered this field of ministry, I renounced psychology. I want no ministry or thoughts other than the Word of God. This does not mean that I reject all insights of psychology. It means rather that all my mind is captive to the Word of God that I may be free (2 Cor. 10:5), so that the Holy Spirit in balance may reach in to use any psychological insight, but no psychological insight can use me. I weep for a number of my brothers who started out in the Lord dancing with psychology and now, unbeknownst to them, are out of the Lord while psychology dances with them.

It is a frightful thing to mess around with the insides of another! For this reason many have said that we have no business whatsoever in the field. But the Word is clear. "Counsel in the heart of man is like deep water, but a man of understanding will draw it out" (Prov. 20:5). "If you find a man of wisdom, let your foot wear out his threshold" (Sirach or Ecclesiasticus 6:36). "Every purpose is established by counsel: and with good advice make war" (Prov. 20:18). "In a multitude of counselors there is safety" (Prov. 11:14). And of course, James 5:13-16.

No one should ever be allowed to "mess around" inside another. There is risk enough for those who are determined to die to self so much as never to interfere in another's life, without ever thinking we have license to change another. It has come to my attention that there are counselors and writers who, upon hearing of something traumatic in childhood, have advised the counselee to change the memory. For example, having had a violent, critical father, to go back and paint a vivid picture in the mind of that father being loving and gentle and kind. That is terribly fallacious counseling! Such treatment is a lie. It is a veneer which the inner honesty of the Spirit will someday throw off. It participates in auto-suggestive techniques akin to hypnotism. And worst of all, it avoids the simple power of the cross. Nothing must supplant forgiveness, death, and rebirth.

Healing of the inner man never erases or changes a memory. That would invalidate our purpose for living through whatever it was. We lie when we repeat that old saw, "Well, if you haven't forgotten, you haven't forgiven." Nonsense. Romans 8:28 is His purpose, "All things work together for good to them that love God, to them who are the called according to his purpose." Healing is the transformation of the mind and heart (Rom. 12:2) whereby we remember what happened as it happened, but with a changed attitude. What once was crushing becomes blessing. What once was the lizard on our backs becomes our steed. Healing is not complete, nor the purpose fulfilled for which God allowed a given thing to happen, until in retrospect we are even grateful it happened. By going through it, we have become more sure of His grace and sweetness, more humble and compassionate, more able to minister to others. As with Jesus, so it is with us: "For in that he himself hath suffered being tempted, he is able to succour them that are tempted" (Heb. 2:18).

Many evangelically minded people think there is no need for the healing of the inner man. They charge that this undoes our conversion experience. They maintain that all the problems of the inner nature died with us on the cross, and that we simply need to believe that and walk on in faith. How heartily we agree that when we received Jesus, all that inner nature, the "old man," our carnal self, died. It *is* dead. We do no new work. Herein is the most fundamental correction we make upon all who enter this field not soundly based in evangelical faith: We are not adding to or changing what Jesus has done on the cross. Nor are we mending an old self-image that needed to die, and did. What we *are* doing is extending the application of that death once died to every area of the heart and mind. In short, not every area of our inner being believes or has received that good news we claimed. We are actually converting anew the already converted.

What has been lacking in Christianity is a proper theology of sanctification. In the vacuum, many have stepped in to try to build Christian character. Transformation of the inner man is not the healing or building of good character. Many groups in Christ have erred by trying to build Christian character. But ". . . other foundation can no man lay than that is laid, which is Jesus Christ" (1 Cor. 3:11). Jesus has already become our character, and He is writing it into us. Christian growth is a matter of growth in faith. Maturity is a matter of rest in Jesus. Whoever seeks to build character returns to the flesh and manifests the circumcision party anew. Sanctification is simply an entrance into the fulness of death and rebirth.

Psychology has persuaded all too many to accept the lie that we need a good self-image. Therefore, many in the counseling field have set out to make people feel better, to find some area in the person that works so that the person can find confidence and stand on that area. In Christian counseling we point out that Christians have died to self. Our attempt to build an acceptable self-image is what died when we received Jesus, that He might build us anew. We do need to cherish and give thanks for the new creature we are in Christ Jesus. But that is not a self-image which gives glory to our own flesh (1 Cor. 1:29). That is to love what God is building in us and to praise God continually for new and joyous life in Him. Thus we live for Christ, crucified, dead, and new in Him. Our only self-image is, "I am a sinner, redeemed and new in Jesus Christ." "For we are the circumcision, which worship God in the spirit, and rejoice in Christ Jesus, and *have no confidence in the flesh*" (Phil. 3:3). "There is therefore now no condemnation to them which are in Christ Jesus, *who walk not after the flesh,* but after the Spirit" (Rom. 8:1). Trying to find and support a good self-image is a direct seeking after and supporting of the carnal nature to find some righteousness in ourselves on which to stand. Its opposite is what we work for:

> For ye see your calling, brethren, how that not many wise men after the flesh, not many mighty, not many noble, are called: But God hath chosen the foolish things of the world to confound the wise; and God hath chosen the weak things of the world to confound the things which are mighty: And base things of the world, and things which are despised, hath God chosen, yea, and things which are not, to bring to nought things that are: That no flesh should glory in his presence. But of him are ye in Christ Jesus, who of God is made unto us wisdom and righteousness, and sanctification, and redemption: That, according as it is written, He that glorieth, let him glory in the Lord. (1 Cor. 1:26-31)

And that results in Philippians 4:13, "I can do all things through Christ which strengtheneth me." That is a Christian's image, that God can and will accomplish all good things in and through Him.

Sanctification does not mean, therefore, that we strive by healing the inner man to build a better self which will be more acceptable. It means that we reveal the hidden works of darkness in the human heart because Jesus came to destroy the works of darkness (1 John 3:8). We pray so that the Christian may claim more of that death he has already died so that more of that life which is already in him by the indwelling Christ may shine out.

The Christian counselor is necessary because the human heart is deceptive. The counselor works by the gifts of perception and knowledge to expose what areas of the flesh yet operate to block the expression of the life of Christ. His aim is to witness how the Holy Spirit shall convict and release the other in the mercy of the Lord Jesus Christ.

But pitfalls abound. Counselors often buttress pity parties. Many, not grounded in the Word as they ought to be, have rushed in to comfort people whose parents ostensibly failed them, and then wondered why their counselees continued weak and faltering. The more comfort given, the more self-pitying the person, if we do not understand God's Word. Let every counselor hear: look behind every wound for sinful reactions. The Lord Jesus Christ came to bear our sorrows and carry our griefs (Isa. 53:4, 5). But if that is the extent of our ministry, the other will not get well. For we react to wounds sinfully. The response to hurt or neglect is anger and resentment. Resentment becomes hate, most often repressed and forgotten, but lividly active, like a land mine waiting to be stepped on. A counselor's task is to help people to see and confess resentment, else we only buttress self-pitying.

Counselors are tempted to probe around in people soulishly. Counselees want (unconsciously) to "run numbers" on their counselors. They often want to tell a counselor their list of gripes and confusions so that they can confirm their errors if only the counselor will listen and agree. Telling someone else who agrees seats that thing in the mind. Counselors who are not dead to their techniques put people in boxes and try to turn out people as carbon copies of their own style of life. "Love does not insist on its own way" (1 Cor. 13:5 RSV). A counselor's task is to lay down his life so that the counselee may come into his own life in Christ.

Counselors may usurp the position of others—pastor, husband, father, wife, or mother. Counselors and counselees may fall into soulish transferences, by which the counselee thinks she or he is in love with the counselor. Counselors may fail to keep confidences. Counselees may "use" what the counselor has said to "whip" others, or quite often put words in the counselor's mouth which he in no way intended or said.

Sexual confusions can and do abound so profusely in and about counseling that many avoid the healing of the inner man altogether when they ought to risk it—and some ought to flee out of it and don't!

Pitfalls are as endless as the capacity of human nature to find varieties of ways to sin. Nevertheless, our Lord has called us to minister to one another, and we must. What we see so repentantly is that men have so fallen from walking in the Lord according to His Word that more and more fathers and mothers are failing or abandoning their children. Because children react sinfully and are formed in sin, because we must be loved to life in order to become human, we see that these children of sin are producing children less human than they, and the others worse than the first, so that we are rapidly heading into the curse of Sodom and Gomorrah. Inner cities are now ravaged by groups of youth who fulfill St. Paul's prophecy:

This know also, that in the last days perilous times shall come. For men shall be lovers of their own selves, covetous, boasters, proud, blasphemers, disobedient to parents, unthankful, unholy, Without natural affection, trucebreakers, false accusers, incontinent, fierce, despisers of those that are good, Traitors, heady, highminded, lovers of pleasures more than lovers of God; Having a form of godliness, but denying the power thereof:

from such turn away. (2 Tim. 3:1-5)

But when the enemy pours in as a flood, the Lord raises up His ensign to stand in the gap (Isa. 59:19). And we have the promise of Malachi 4:5, 6, "Behold, I will send you Elijah the prophet *before* the coming of the great and dreadful day of the Lord: And he shall turn the heart of the fathers to the children, and the heart of the children to their fathers, lest I come and smite the earth with a curse."

Therefore the call is upon the Lord's own. We must learn how to ". . . build the old waste places: thou shalt raise up the foundations of many generations; and thou shalt be called, The repairer of the breach, The restorer of paths to dwell in" (Isa. 58:12). We must learn how to heal and restore broken lives so that our Lord may turn this very history of denigration and degradation into the glory out of which the redeemed minister. We must restore the individuals of families, else we cannot restore the Christian family. And we must proceed apace with the preventive medicine of solid teaching. How many have said to us, "Oh, had we only known this when we were young, and still had our children with us! God forgive us!"

We believe that restoration of the Christian family must begin with return to the lordship of Jesus Christ. Some Christians have never really known Him. They may have received Him as Savior, but they still do not know who He really is and what that means to Christian family life. Some, knowing, have forgotten or been distracted. Knowing who Jesus is is essential to family living, "For where jealousy and selfish ambition exist, there will be disorder and every vile practice" (James 3:16 RSV). Jealousy and selfish ambition manifest wherever men, women, and children have not subjected their unruly passions of the flesh to the lordship of Jesus Christ.

We are called to "Be subject to one another out of reverence for Christ'' (Eph. 5:21 RSV). That is not a nice exhortation but a statement of principle for family (or any other) living. Its inverse corollary is: "If we are not subject to the Lord Jesus Christ out of reverence for Him, in no way can we be subject to one another." "Subject" does not mean "controlled by" or "dominated." "Subject to one another" means voluntarily surrendering our prideful self-wills in love for the other to bless and bring happiness to the other. But we cannot do that, we cannot escape the demands of the flesh, we cannot overcome what we are, short of Jesus' lordship. Families who try, not knowing full surrender to Him, fail in ratio to their determination to succeed, for the strength of sin is the law (1 Cor. 15:56). Put more simply, when we try to live like Jesus without His grace to do it, the harder we try the more we enlist the strivings and ambitions of our prideful and jealous flesh, and so the sooner we fail.

Who then is Jesus? He is not just a man, nor only God. He is the God-man, fully God and fully man (John 1:14), who created us (John 1:1-3; Col. 1:15, 16) and who redeemed us by His blood (Eph. 1:7). But more than that, He is our ever-present Lord and ruler (Matt. 28:18; Acts 2:36; Matt. 28:20). Throughout the New Testament the apostles referred to Jesus by His full name and title, "the Lord Jesus Christ" (Rom. 1:4; 1 Cor. 1:2; 7-9; 2 Cor. 1:2, 3; Gal. 1:3; Eph. 1:2, 3; Phil. 1:2; Col. 1:3; 1 Thess. 1:1, 3; 2 Thess. 1:2; 2:1; 3:6; etc. in Paul's letters, and in James 1:1; 2:1; and in 1 Pet. 1:3, and 2 Pet. 1:2; Jude 4, and throughout 1, 2, and 3 John and the Revelation). Such naming is not simply a verbal issue. It is crucial to family life (and all our life) that we know and recognize Jesus for who He is. He is not merely the Savior who did that wonderful thing for us way back there in the past. He is the Alpha and Omega (Rev. 1:8; 21:6; 22:13), the beginning blueprint and finished product of all we are. He is the fully human, fully spiritual person like whom we are becoming. And He is presently reigning as Lord, not merely sometime in the future when He returns.

We do not come into the fulness of salvation until we know Him as Lord. We did not say, "know *about* Him as Lord." The word "know" in the Greek comes from the marriage word, as "Adam *knew* Eve his wife; and she conceived" (Gen. 4:1). It means "to meet, apprehend, experience and embrace." Salvation does not mean only justification and redemption but the fulness of life in Christ as He intended (Eph. 2:10). Only as we invite Jesus to express in us the fulness of His lordship does He have permission to humble us and crush us (Matt. 21:44) as He must to bring us into that meekness by which, and only by which, we can live together as families in blessedness.

The flesh must be conquered. All of human love, which we honor as so noble and wonderful, is in fact shot through with use, manipulation, exploitation, and demand. Every person, whether he knows it or not, is seeking to build and establish his own image, his own self, his own empire. The most naturally loving and kind are yet fully "self-ish." From that proclivity to build our own kingdom arises every sort of vile jealousy and disorder. Therefore, outside of the lordship of the Lord Jesus Christ, the flesh *will* rule and destroy.

It is not safe for us to live with each other as we are. What is in us will come out, no matter how we try to suppress, sublimate, or control. Human flesh is by nature self-and-other-destructive. "Let *every* one beware of his neighbor, and put no trust in *any* brother; for *every* brother is a supplanter, and *every* neighbor goes about as a slanderer" (Jer.9:4 RSV).

The church must regain awareness of the radical nature of sin. Not sins. Sins are deeds done. Sin is our very nature, what we are. And with that awareness, we must return to complete daily momentary dependence upon the lordship of Jesus. "Then Jesus told his disciples, 'If any man would come after me, let him deny himself and take up his cross and follow me. For whoever would save his life will lose it, and whoever loses his life for my sake will find it" (Matt. 16:24, 25 RSV).

Our Christian families are falling apart because we think that having accepted Jesus as Savior, we ought now to be able to treat each other rightly. And so we become furious with each other, insistent and jealous, blaming and condemning because we think the other ought to have done better because he *could* have. Nonsense! We cannot. Compassion begins to develop when we join hands at the foot of the cross, realizing we are all shot through with sin, no one better than any other, and all dependent momentarily upon the flow of Christ's love through us to bring forth anything good at all. We have too much lost sight of the fact that the flesh profits nothing (Gal. 5:17; 6:8; 1 Cor. 13:3) and "Without me, ye can do *nothing*" (John 15:5). Thinking that Jesus has washed us clean, we think we ought to be able to live like Him, and so pastors exhort and parents scold. But absolutely no one in himself can be or express the fruits of the Spirit. Only the Holy Spirit can express the fruits *of the Spirit*.

Husbands are created in God to make first surrender to Jesus that all the family may find that life style by example, not coercion. Leadership means taking initiative and responsibility in presenting the family under the lordship of Jesus. The husband is head of the family (Eph. 5:23, 24). We will speak later of what can be done if the husband abdicates, but for now let us see what headship really is.

Headship is actually responsibility to serve. ". . . but whosoever will be great among you, let him be your minister; And whosoever will be chief among you, let him be your servant" (Matt. 20:26, 27). Too many Christian husbands have heard the call to headship, only to translate the world's concepts of authority into the home. That has brought control, dominance, and exaltation of the flesh, not blessing.

Christian headship means responsibility to lay down the life for the other (John 15:13). In the world and in the flesh, those in authority aggrandize, direct, and control those under them, reducing others in the end to extensions of the leader's thoughts and way of life. But the Christian in authority exists to set those under him free to become their own persons. That means that whereas the world's authority uses force, threat, or manipulation to extract behavior from the other, with or without free consent, the Christian authority never insists on his own way (1 Cor. 13:5). He must not resort to force or any device to insist that the other do what he thinks is right. He may command, but behind that command is only the free covenant of the other's will by which he has granted to the leader the right to give him an order. Even though the husband's position may grant him the right to demand and insist, he may not protect himself from hurt and disappointment by "causing" his wife to obey. He wins agreement by pure love and willingness, or not at all. As Jesus rules by ". . . the power which enables him to subject all things to himself" (Phil. 3:21 RSV), and that power is simple love, so the Christian husband must earn his right to command by so having laid down his life in loving service for his wife that obedience is willingly given.

This does not make the Christian head a "wheedler," who must yet be a manipulator, "using" love to get things done. Sometimes he must scold and bark, rebuke and exhort, yet all such is restrained by the necessity to invite the giving of the other's will. And his work is to execute what the family (or group) has revealed and covenanted as its will, not his own. .

A husband is given to bless and fulfill his wife's life. Husbands who want to quit the marriage because they "can't find happiness with that woman" reveal that they never understood the first concept of husbandship. Their intent was never to give but to get. Failure came therefore not as the result but at the very inception. The attempt to fulfill her life does not make him a martyr who never receives anything from her. Part of fulfilling her is learning how to let her love him, which can be more humbling than giving all the time.

Husbands are given to take leadership in prayer—not to do all of it or to control it. In day-to-day life, that means the husband should take the responsibility to say table graces or delegate this privilege to a family member. He should pray aloud for his wife if she is ill, or say a blessing if she is to take a trip or speak before a group or minister somewhere. He should establish and maintain family prayer times. His reading of the Word and meditating upon the law of God provides the context and style of the family's life.

As the children experience the openness and humility of a father's carrying the family problems and concerns to the Father in prayer, as they hear him praise the Lord for His faithfulness in all things, as they sit beside him in church in shared devotion, they will receive his structure of godliness as a natural part of the fabric of their lives. If the head of the household is in tune with the joys and the sorrows of those in his charge, and meets them where they are, he will call forth from them an ability to respond to authority throughout their lives without fear and guile.

The husband is the first comforter of a child, not the laggard, nagged-at one who finally sees and does because his wife gave him no peace—"Jim, can't you see how your daughter is hurting and needs you?"

A Christian head of a household is one who knows his position is a God-given privilege, an opportunity to express and experience the creative nurturing grace of the Father, not a burden to be endured in the spaces between the times he calls his own. He is refreshed on the golf course, and by national championship ball games, no more than he is by finding quiet joy in shared thoughts and adventures with his wife and children.

The mantle of protection that a Christian husband extends over his family is made of the substance of his belonging and trusting in God. A wife is bone of her husband's bones and flesh of his flesh (Gen. 2:23). As he is rooted and grounded in love

(Eph. 3:17) and as he walks obediently in God's wisdom, his house is built upon a rock, and his wife and children dwell restfully within that house. A man is not God to his wife. The Lord will shelter her, defend her, guide her, correct her, and refresh her directly as she stands in her own relationship with Him. But there is a special quality of security and restfulness that God provides through the husband who knows who he is in the Lord.

Some, learning that cover should come through the husband, have rushed into religious practices which "fail to sanctify the nature of God" (Num. 20:12), and result in subjecting wives and children to bondage. One husband we know would not let his wife go anywhere without first obtaining his permission and informing exactly where she would be, when and with whom. Such practices reduce wives to a ten-year-old status. The Lord would never so disrespect the common sense judgment of any adult.

Some time ago I (John) visited in the home of a couple in California. They showed me their new home with delight. When we arrived in the master bedroom, the husband said, "You know, it's strange; this is the one room I have never liked."

I said, "Who decorated this room?"

"I did," he responded.

"That's the problem. The wife is the nest-builder. Give her whatever money is required, and let her decorate it, and then see how you like it." They did. And several months later when I returned, they reported that the room was now a delight.

Subsequently, this lovely couple entered into a prevalent teaching in the area which attempted to restore husbands to headship and cover. In this teaching, husbands were to make all the decisions, and wives should submit to whatever they decided, filling out the husband's picture of what life should be. For a wife to express her opinion was considered rebellious. She was to be docile, sweet, and a perfect expression of her husband's wishes. The teaching went so far as to say that when the couple went out to eat, he should sense what his wife might like, and order without consulting her.

About a year later, Paula and I came again to California, and that young wife, hearing we had come, called me in tears. "My husband has just gone to spend a week with another woman and tells me that being a submissive wife means that I should let him do this so he can find out if he really wants to choose me or her!" I was furious at that delusion so wounding to my friends and prayed, binding those spirits and loosing my friend to return to his home. That night he came to his senses and drove home. The next morning they called me for counsel.

His complaint was, "There is nothing to her. I don't like her any more." What had happened was that she had tried to do everything that teaching required. She asked his permission for everything—the result being that he no longer wanted to make love to a child. He wanted a woman beside him. She tried to become everything he wanted her to be—and now, just like the bedroom, he didn't like what he had created. She was no longer God's gift to him, a unique person, a counterfoil over against him; she was only an extension of him—and he was lonely.

Cover and protection are not a matter of religious practices. We do not need to return to Old Testament ways. True cover never causes a man to usurp God's place with his wife.

When I am home, Paula feels more secure. When my heart is right with God, her own devotions are not invaded by demonic powers or distractions. Paula is one with me, but at the same time she is distinct from me. We do not meet as complete husband to incomplete wife, nor do we come together as two halves to become one whole. We two are identified with one another so He can bless and reform us through the other while He brings each of us to wholeness individually by the Lord Jesus Christ. He perfects each of us according to our need to grow up into salvation. At the same time, He nurtures those qualities in each of us that He in His wisdom knows will add just the right depth and dimension to the team (corporate life) He has called us to be.

Many husbands cannot present themselves so vulnerably in the marriage relationship that individual death and rebirth into corporate life can happen. They are still too bound up in fear of the mother's critical tongue or controlling spirit to let the wife into their hearts. Unconsciously they want to *have* a wife, but do not want true corporate life *with* a wife. This prevents real sexual union, for nowhere is the man more vulnerable than in the marriage bed. Not uncommon is the husband who, succeeding in arousing his wife sexually, is deathly afraid of any responsive, aggressive action she might take, for fear of being controlled, or dominated, or less than a man. More frequently, however, the husband has been taught by society that he must perform aggressively and competently in sex, and his sense of manhood is too closely knit with this. His wife's responses to his advances tell him how well he has "succeeded" or how miserably he has "failed." He has no understanding of sexual union as giving, meeting, and sharing physically, emotionally, and spiritually. Consequently, he fails to "meet her," to cherish her as a person for her sake, and so uses her that she eventually flees into frigidity.

Too often he proceeds ignorant of the basic male-female differences. He may not know (1) that her natural desire for him (even if she is free from inhibitions) is subject to her menstrual cycle; (2) that her desire for him is enhanced or limited by what has gone on during the day, particularly in relation to his choosing to appreciate and share positively with her; (3) that her passions are more slowly aroused and often require some tender, sensitive stimulation; and (4) that she sometimes needs a long period of quiet embrace and sharing of life in simple chit-chat before her inner being finds its place of belonging in him so that her triggering mechanism is ready to stimulate sexual organs and feelings. Accustomed to treating objects as "its," unaware of the sensitive life of the human spirit, he comes on like a freight train and soon finds himself with no more track to run on, derailed, frustrated, rejected, and angry. Innerly he feels guilty and insecure, but men are supposed to be strong and controlled. So he accuses her of being frigid, uncaring, not wanting to be a wife to him, playing games. He may then begin to look elsewhere for relationships that, however shallow or temporary, build his ego. He may exchange natural conjugal sex for girly magazines and masturbation. He may even go to such extremes as complete sublimation of sexual drive out of fear of risking, or on the other hand he may force the issue to the point of raping his own wife for self-gratification.

The Christian husband participates in the sexual relationship as his wife's Christian lover. A lover is one who cherishes the life of the other, to give joy to the other. Men who think to "get" in marital sex have never entered the arena of true love. True marital happiness in sex is found when a husband lays down his life to bring joy and fulfillment to his wife. The more he can restrain his own desire for immediate fulfillment to cherish her into a sense of blessedness and happiness, the greater his own joy will be.

"Love is patient and kind; love is not jealous or boastful; it is not arrogant or rude. Love does not insist on its own way; it is not irritable or resentful; it does not rejoice at wrong, but rejoices in the right. Love bears all things, believes all things, hopes all things, endures all things. Love never ends . . ." (1 Cor. 13:4-8 RSV). If the Christian husband finds it difficult to enter into true corporate life and fulfillment of his partner in sex because of past woundings, disappointments, and fears, he should read further in 1 Corinthians 13. "When I was a child, I spoke like a child, I thought like a child, I reasoned like a child; when I became a man I gave up childish ways" (v. 11 RSV).

Giving up the attitudes that were formed in him from his childhood may mean he will have to sit down with a friend or counselor to lift out the root causes of his negative expectations, fears, resentments, and self-centeredness so that they may be confessed as sin, and brought to death on the cross. It may mean a deep humbling which counters what his culture has taught him about the real man handling everything himself, taking care of his own problems. But he will then be free to learn to relate to his wife as a mature husband and lover. He will then be able to bring her to life, which in turn enables her to meet and nurture him.

Few husbands, trained in our shallow, materialistic culture, discover the true glory of the marriage bed. "Let thy fountain be blessed: and rejoice with the wife of thy youth. Let her be as the loving hind and pleasant roe; let her breasts satisfy thee at all times; and be thou ravished always with her love" (Prov. 5:18, 19). A man who finds the true reality of meeting his wife spirit to spirit through the embrace of their bodies will be "ravished always with her love." He will know intuitively that no other woman, however beautiful of face or figure, or personality, can have for him what his wife has. No other woman's spirit has been attuned by God through the wedding ceremony, and by their daily life, to complete him and fulfill him in his spirit. What ravishes him is the glory of her being, singing into the very cells of his body who and what he is as a man. If sex becomes delimited to physical release, a husband has failed, however long or adequately he may perform physically. Through a woman's body, and especially through her breasts, an energy of love flows like a river into a man. Blessed is the man whose spirit is so alive by prayer that he can feel the song of his wife's spirit rising through him.

We have found in counseling that too few husbands know the virtue of nudity with their wives. Our spirits pour forth to one another much like electricity. We need the current of each other.

Clothes tend to insulate. A husband needs the power of his wife's body against his, quite apart from sexual union.

All too few husbands and wives understand that verse, "Let her breasts satisfy thee at all times." During the day, husbands need to hug their wives long enough to let that current which flows from her pierce the heart to refresh and strengthen. Woman was taken from the rib of man. Man protects woman by his strength and logic, but woman protects the heart area of man. Her breasts satisfy him when held against his chest. Her energy fills and warms all his thinking with wisdom and gentleness. In sexual embrace, husbands most often fail to touch, hold, and kiss the breasts enough. Men need to feed, sensitively and quietly, a long time upon their wives' breasts. The command is to "*let* her breasts satisfy thee at *all* times." It is fulfilling and satisfying to both partners. A man who is fully satisfied in his wife's embrace, who truly feeds upon her love, is not easily tempted to another. Who would take a bologna sandwich to a banquet? Only his own wife is a fully satisfying banquet to his heart and soul and spirit and body. Let husbands pray that God will reveal to them the true gift and power of their wives' love for them. It is not that we are too sexual, but not sexual enough, because we do not discover how to meet and nourish, cherish, embrace, and feed upon one another's love as we ought.

Although we have been speaking mainly of husbands' sexual confusions and ignorances because in this chapter we seek to restore the position of a husband, many marital, sexual difficulties arise from a lie taught to both partners by our nineteenth century, Victorian culture. Still today, movies, TV, novels, and romance literature tend to perpetuate in our minds that men are the sexual chasers and women the reluctant givers. Nothing could be further from fact or biblical precedent! The fact is that it is women who want far more than men will give. "Your desire shall be for your husband" (Gen. 3:16 RSV). For one man who complains to Paula or me that his wife will not give enough sex, fifty women complain that their husbands will not. "The husband should give to his wife her conjugal rights, and likewise the wife to her husband" (1 Cor. 7:3 RSV). Leah bargained with Rachel, and having bought Jacob's services for the night, ran gleefully to meet him crying, "I get you tonight" (Gen. 30:14-16, authors' paraphrase). The command had to be given to men again and again to "love your wives" (Eph. 5:25, 28; Col. 3:19) but only once to wives (Titus 2:4), though wives had to be told again and again to be submissive and to respect (Eph. 5:22, 24, 33; Titus 2:5; and 1 Pet. 3:1, 5).

As a result of that confusion, the husband feels burdened as the pursuer, as an imposition to whom a wife grants favors. And wives have thought it unladylike to be aggressive. Both are frustrated by such attitudes. The desire of either for the other should be an opportunity to bless. "Do not refuse one another except perhaps by agreement for a season" (1 Cor. 7:5 RSV). We have rightly understood that to mean that whichever wants, the other should give, but notice the inference. St. Paul did not say, "Do not refuse the husband . . ." as though only husbands asked for sex. Obviously wives in Bible times were free to ask their husbands to make love to them. Husbands need to feel sought after and claimed, even as Leah bargained precious mandrakes for a chance to lie with Jacob. How healthy it is that in more recent trends women are being given more freedom to be expressive and aggressive sexually and to seduce their husbands wholesomely. Husbands need to be chased by their wives.

The popular "Wedding Song" lyric sings, "Woman draws her life from man, and gives it back again." Nowhere is this more true than in the meeting of their minds. Though a wife has a mind of her own, her desire is to find and complement and nurture that structure of life which is his philosophy, his understanding, his picture of what life is all about. Though a couple must work through many hidden psychological quirks in their natures, and that is accomplished by experience, they must thresh the wheat of each other's minds by discussion. Wives are given as the gift of God (Prov. 18:22) and by that their natural desire is to support and be loyal to their husbands' thought—but to do that they hunger to know his thought. The consistent cry of wives is, "Talk to me." In counseling, we find few husbands who freely share their thinking with their wives as much as they should. "Iron sharpens iron, and one man sharpens another" (Prov. 27:17 RSV).

Many husbands learned in childhood that whatever was revealed to mama "can and will be used against you in a court of law." They have painfully experienced that mothers have elephantine memories which preserve acute details men have long forgotten. This leaves them afraid as husbands to reveal to their wives all they think or feel. They fear being controlled, censored, castrated, or all of the above. They feel unequipped in verbal battles because wives' memories put them at a disadvantage. But husbands who have learned to share with their wives find their own balance and wisdom, restraint, and self-discipline. Only as husbands have learned to find trust and willingness to risk themselves in Jesus can they impute that quality into their marital discussions and so find grace to open their minds to the full scrutiny of the wife's mind and heart.

A wife finds herself insecure and confused if she cannot know whether what she thinks and does is in accord with her husband's thought. She finds her mental security in the teamwork of sharing. If a husband's philosophy is too narrow or shallow for her commitment to Christ, she feels lonely and exposed, uncovered and endangered. She is shocked and feels betrayed if she overhears some new idea shared first with a friend or acquaintance at a party. If he presents that new idea as if it represents both of them, she feels railroaded or swallowed up in him, and is hurt.

One of the most striking, probably purposeful, omissions in

the Bible is found in Genesis 2 and 3. When the command was given not to eat of the tree of the knowledge of good and evil, Eve had not yet been formed from Adam's rib (Gen. 2:15-25). When Satan talked with Eve in Genesis 3:1-6, Eve revealed great confusion. She thought they were never to eat of the tree *"in the midst of the garden,"* whereas there was no proscription not to eat of the tree *in the midst*, which was the tree of life (Gen. 2:9); and she thought they were not to "touch it" (Gen. 3:3), though nothing had been said about touch. Obviously either Adam failed to communicate accurately, or she misunderstood or forgot. How wise of God not to compound the battle of the sexes by telling us which was which! Still today marital confusions abound because men fail to share and/or wives do not comprehend or retain. Perhaps no greater restoration is needed than the capacity of husbands and wives to share their minds amicably and fully. A wife who finds herself living with a stranger cannot unlock the deep gates of sexual sharing. *Her mind must find where her threads knit to his to form the one garment which is the plaid of their clan.* Christian husbands must discipline themselves to the regular habit of sharing—else, as of old, Satan finds a playfield.

Where was Adam when Eve was talking to that serpent?

8

THE IMPORTANCE OF A
FATHER'S LOVE

*Behold, I will send you Elijah the prophet before the
coming of the great and dreadful day of the Lord: And he
shall turn the heart of the fathers to the children, and the
heart of the children to their fathers, lest I come and smite
the earth with a curse.* (Mal. 4:5, 6)

Fathers' love for their children is so important that without it a
curse comes upon the land. The word is not to turn the heart of
parents, or mothers, to their children, but *fathers*. The word is
not to turn the minds, or attention, of fathers to their children,
but to turn their hearts. Men can give lip service to an idea, or set
their wills to accomplish something, but only the Lord can give
grace to change and set the heart. We call men by this chapter
not to set their teeth to try, but to set their knees to cry. God will
hear, but only God-given repentance can accomplish the change
that is required.

When Paula and I were in seminary, and my major was in the
religion and personality department, we were required in those
days to write a major book-sized thesis to qualify for
graduation. I chose to try to develop a test to reveal what the
Sunday schools of various denominations had actually taught.
We chose representative denominations, two liturgical, two

fundamental, and two liberal, and asked for six students from each, having composed a long and exacting test, from which we wrote a thesis entitled *Testing Young People's Grasp of Christianity.** We discovered, as we expected, that the liturgical and fundamental young people knew the Word far better than the liberal students sampled, and the liberal ones seemed to have a better attitude about love and service. But what shocked us was an unlooked-for revelation. In the test was a semantic space test which revealed attitudes towards fathers and mothers, pastors, churches, our bodies, sex, and many other things. Across the board, no matter in which Sunday school, those students who rated their fathers and mothers as worthless, distasteful, weak, shallow, and sinful revealed trouble in every other area, especially in their ability to meet trying interpersonal life situations and in what they thought of their bodies and sex.

The revelation was so unexpected and so incise, it became one of the major considerations which propelled our ministry into the restoration of families. We saw unequivocally that unless the hearts of fathers were turned to their children and the hearts of children to their fathers, it mattered little what else we taught or did in our churches! We saw beyond doubt that right head knowledge of the faith produced nothing in terms of ability to express the fruits of the Spirit unless what was lodged in the heart relative to parents was met by effective grace in Jesus on the cross. We saw that conversion by itself failed to affect what had become engrammic in the sin nature, without full sanctification by confession and daily self-death. The test revealed to us that in dreadful, actual fact a curse does lie upon all who dishonor their parents (Mark 7:10). It is to the lifting of that curse that the church must move, posthaste, through fathers.

Note that the promise of God is to send Elijah the prophet *before* the great and terrible day of the Lord comes, and that he

*Available only in the Chicago Theological Seminary library, Chicago, Ill.

will in fact turn the hearts of fathers and children. The promise of God is positive. He *will* accomplish what He says. It remains only to be seen by whom. Who will say, "Here am I, send me"? (Isa. 6:8).

Some time ago, Mr. Carl Foss, whose ministry through the organization called "The Vision" is to men in prison, came to visit in our town. He calls for men to volunteer to accept prisoners on a one-to-one basis as sons in Christ, to whom they are to be as fathers. He reported that between 90 and 95% of those in prison have never known the love of a father and referred simply to prisoners as "the fatherless." In a visit to a reformatory, speaking to more than forty young people, he discovered that not one could claim the love of a father. Offering to sit in private with whomever would come to be with a father for fifteen minutes, he was overwhelmed with the response, and with the tears of supposedly hardened tough juveniles. He reported that on McNeil Island, in that prison, a man who had become a prison lawyer, an extremely intelligent man and a competent artist, had prepared a handsome, hand-done Father's Day card, which he offered for sale to his fellow inmates for $4.00. Finding no takers, he reduced the offer to $2.00. Finally he tried giving the card away. Not one would take a Father's Day card! Stunned, he came to Carl, who said, "Have you spent twenty years in this prison, and you still don't know that not one of these 1280 prisoners has a father who loves him?"

He reported that studies done by him and others have revealed that children raised without fathers commonly lack strength of character, lack "backbone," tend more to have sexually-deviant behavior, and fall more easily into crime. He informed us that in 1965 in America 3,000,000 mothers were raising children without fathers, but that by 1975, 10,000,000 were without fathers. And that the crime rate is not doubling but tripling. He predicted that by the 1980s if the hearts of fathers have not turned to their children, our cities' streets will erupt in holocausts of violence, by gangs of fatherless children. Shades of 2 Timothy 3!

Why are fathers that important? Simply because God so created them. We could reiterate chapters one and five, embellishing endlessly, and not exhaust the single fact that God created children to drink their life from their father's spirit. The greatest tragedy of our silly, materialistic culture is that men have been demeaned of their status as sons of God. Not knowing they have spirits and souls, they have little or no awareness of what they are to their children. Truly Satan came to rob and to steal. Fathers' identities have been stolen from them!

We are created in the image of God. As we must drink our life from our Father in heaven, so must our children from us. Wherever a father hugs his son, or takes him fishing, or binds a wound, or hears a complaint or administers discipline, there the Word of God is made flesh (1 John 4:2). We confess Him in the flesh by more than lips, for if we shout His glory from the hilltops but fail to say a kind word to our little ones, the Word of God has not become flesh, no matter what we say. And God says to us,

When ye come to appear before me, who hath required this at your hand, to tread my courts? Bring no more vain oblations; incense is an abomination unto me; the new moons and sabbaths, the calling of assemblies, I cannot away with; it is iniquity, even the solemn meeting. Your new moons and your appointed feasts my soul hateth: they are a trouble unto me; I am weary to bear them. And when ye spread forth your hands, I will hide mine eyes from you: yea, when ye make many prayers, I will not hear: your hands are full of blood. Wash you, make you clean; put away the evil of your doings from before mine eyes; cease to do evil; Learn to do well; seek judgment, relieve the

oppressed, judge the fatherless, plead for the widow. (Isa.
1:12-17)

If a father fails to be with his child, that child's spirit withers.
Jesus told us that unless we abide in Him, we are as a branch
apart that withers (John 15:5, 6). So must a child abide in his
father's favor and love. Affection is effective transfer of energy.
Without strength of spirit, we cannot withstand. Fathers impart
that strength. Their love is not a nice addition; it is the *sine qua
non,* the essential necessity of a child's life.

If fathers fail, substitutes can be provided. The Father "left
not himself without witness" (Acts 14:17). But no substitute
can ever discover to a child the identity that calls from his genes
to be realized. Every failure in life can be traced sooner or later
to the breaking of the one command, "Honor thy father and thy
mother . . . that it may go well with thee" (Deut. 5:16). That is
root and trunk to the leaf of every blessing and problem in all of
life. Girls who are raised with violent, drunken fathers almost
invariably marry violent, drunken men. Dominant, brutal
fathers breed dominant, brutal sons and daughters whose
husbands become dominant and brutal—unless the cross of
Christ intervenes.

Mankind is infinitely varied. But the equations of the heart
are as easy to figure as fractions. We all have one common
denominator—our life with or without our fathers and mothers.
Upon that base, numerators vary to infinite varieties. Satan has
no new game; only variations on a theme.

Every Christian is a counselor, professional or not. The Holy
Spirit is the Counselor. And He would heal families through
every child of God. Therefore, every servant must know the
basic rudiments of hearing and understanding. And of
intercessory prayer.

God has built an orderly universe. All things operate on
principles, whether we are aware of them or not. When God

commanded that we honor our parents "that it may go well with thee," that was a description of the operation of a specific law of the universe. If a child judges his father for lying, by that law of Deuteronomy 5:16 (plus Matt. 7:1 and Rom. 2:1), he dooms himself to become a liar. When a daughter hates her father for not sharing himself, being too quiet and withdrawing from her, that dooms her by law (unless the cross intervenes) to reap the same from her husband and/or her children. If a child rebels against a father's judgmental, hateful ways, he will struggle against his own predilection to judge others until he repents of his judgment of his father. If we see that each judgment of our parents as children must be reaped in our own lives, we see the reality of the curse which brings death, of which Jesus spoke (Matt. 15:4, Mark 7:10). This death is not a physical one, but it is death to abundant life and happiness.

If we agree that each sowing of sin reaps trouble, then conversely we can see that each present trouble has its roots in our early life with our parents. Every Christian who counsels another should therefore not heal lightly, touching only the present surface events, but track from leaf to branch to root in those early years, and apply forgiveness through the cross of Christ.

The following are the questions we have used for years when setting out to locate the roots of evil in any human heart. "Did your father give you affection? Could you run and jump in his lap? Did he ever rough and tumble with you?" Since children are loyal, adults frequently remember the best and repress the worst. Therefore questions must often be rephrased more specifically, such as: "Would he ever take the initiative, and seeing your need, come over and take you on his lap? Or did you have to come to him first? If you had a problem, would you feel free to tell him all? Would he understand, or jump to a conclusion? How did he discipline? Was he fair? What kind of job did he have? Was he gone a lot? If you did some work around the house, would he notice, not notice, affirm or criticize? Did you feel that you pleased him? Did he approve of you? Would you say he was a kind man, or cruel? Which would be closer to the truth? Was he a drinker? Did he have any other vices? What about his faith? Did he believe in God? Did he take you to church with him? How did he get along with your mother? Did he show her affection? Did he respect her? Do you know whether he was a faithful husband?''

Behind every answer lie gratitudes and resentments. In countless moments of living with our parents as little children, we have formed judgments. Our spirits sense when parents act wrongly or fail to do good. Emotionally, we react. Sometimes the mind loyally refuses to acknowledge anger, or excuses the parents. But that hurt remains in the heart. If the same hurtful thing happens repeatedly, our inner mind forms a bitter judgment, even if we successfully rationalize and control feelings on the surface. Conscious judgments and grudges are more easily remembered and recognized but are not more vitiating in effect than what is stored in the unconscious. In both cases seeds sown will have to be reaped either by us or by the Lord for us in merciful deliverance. Since the person may be vastly unaware of what is lodged in the heart, know by faith what is there. Jesus said, ''Ye shall know them by their fruits. Do men gather grapes of thorns, or figs of thistles? Even so every good tree bringeth forth good fruit; but a corrupt tree bringeth forth evil fruit. A good tree cannot bring forth evil fruit, neither can a corrupt tree bring forth good fruit'' (Matt. 7:16-18). If a problem exists in our nature, that is bad fruit. That bad fruit cannot exist unless there is a bad tree somewhere in our nature. Nor can good fruit exist outside of grace unless a good tree has been planted in the nature by the father's (and/or mother's) life.

No one else is primary. This is the importance of a father's love, that if a father's love is sufficient, whatever else is done to us by whomever else will only add to his good root, or if evil, will be overcome by the father's more basic example. If whatever else happens finds a lodging place in the heart, it has to have a congruent root in the child's life with the father, else it could not endure.

We see that principle in the case of Adam and Eve. Eve was deluded and ate of the forbidden fruit. But nothing happened! She gave to Adam and he did eat, "and the eyes *of them both* were opened" (Gen. 3:7). The principle of husband and wife is true for parents. In the natural, the influence of the father is primary to the influence of the mother. Praise God, in grace the power of the Father says that ". . . the unbelieving husband is sanctified by the wife, and the unbelieving wife is sanctified by the husband: else were your children unclean; but now they are holy" (1 Cor. 7:14). Here, we trace the impact of the sin nature. Let counselors remember that given equal presence of both parents, the father's nature takes precedence.

A Christian friend's task is to track the present bad fruit to past experience, like stopping a leak by shutting off the water at the source. Dike pluggers who forget this become like little saviors who run out of fingers.

Once whatever the problem is finds its root in parental experience, the hearer is involved in the confessional. Repentance does not have to be felt to be effective. Feelings are delusory. We minister by faith, and faith comes by hearing. A Christian having seen by faith that the presence of a bad fruit indicates the presence of a bad tree, and having seen by counsel or insight that the root lies in hidden resentments and judgments, can and should repent by faith, no matter what he feels or doesn't feel.

No one can reach in to change his heart. Can a leopard change his spots? (Jer. 13:23). We are not merely involved in forgiveness. Sins of judgment and bitterness can be forgiven easily. The blood washes clean of *all* unrighteousness (1 John 1:9). But far more important are the structures that are built into the nature. Woundings and resentments cause adaptive behavior patterns, called by St. Paul "the old nature with its practices" (Col. 3:9 RSV). Countless such "practices" form our sin nature, the shape of the "old man" or carnal self. Our sin nature can only be dealt with by the cross. The blood of Jesus dismantles or transforms nothing. It only washes clean. Solely the cross breaks the engram of our nature and sets us free from the inner prisons of our habits. For this reason St. Paul writes, "Put to death therefore what is earthly in you: immorality, impurity, passion, evil desire, and covetousness, which is idolatry. On account of these the wrath of God is coming. In these you once walked, when you lived in them. But now put them all away: anger, wrath, malice, slander, and foul talk from your mouth. Do not lie to one another, seeing that you have put off the *old nature with its practices* and have put on the new nature, which is being renewed in knowledge after the image of its creator" (Col. 3:5-9 RSV). And Jesus said, "If any man will come after me, let him deny himself, and take up his cross, and follow me" (Matt. 16:24).

Therein is the battle. Any Christian can easily claim the forgiveness of God according to the Word in prayer with any other, or by himself alone. But to overcome the results of sin in the nature is a matter of daily struggle to let Jesus bring that aspect of our sinful nature to its death on His cross.

We do not need therefore to blame or criticize or be unthankful for our fathers. What they have done, however wicked or wholesome, gives us the context of our struggle in life. That is the basic importance of a father's life with his child. His genes, his example, his presence, his touch and absence form the context of our soul's struggle with God. In the shape of his track with us, we will wrestle with our own nature before God. His blessings will be ours. But the merciful providence of

God is that whatever we formed in negative reaction to him will be so transformed by His grace that in the end we shall be empowered to minister to the degree of our trouble and sinful reaction. "Because he himself has suffered and been tempted, he is able . . ." (Heb. 2:18 RSV) also refers to our own life with our fathers. Whatever our father has been to us will become that much more sweet and blessed by the life of the Father God in us, as we allow His shaping hand to increase and purge every good inheritance, and turn every evil to good, according to His purpose (Rom. 8:28).

9

THE PLACE OF A WIFE

A good wife who can find? She is far more precious than jewels. The heart of her husband trusts in her, and he will have no lack of gain. She does him good, and not harm, all the days of her life. (Prov. 31:10-12 RSV)

From the beginning (Gen. 2:18) woman was conceived as the gift of God to man. That conception was first as companion and friend, an helpmeet, to do him good all the days of her life. I (John) cherish the beauty of each successive word in ". . . the *heart* of her husband doth *safely trust in her.*" She holds his heart *in* her. Becoming one flesh does not mean one body, but such a union that the woman does as St. Paul for the church at Philippi, ". . . because I have you in my heart" (Phil. 1:7). And the heart is hidden. What wife does not know her husband's heart far better than he? And "safely." Much assurance is held in that simple promise. It is security and rest to me that I never have to worry about Paula's heart for me. All her scolding and sharing, teasing and love-making has behind it that fact that God has locked her heart into mine, to do me good. Even if she errs, which is often, love covers a multitude of sins (James 5:20), and God turns her efforts to good for me. His Word is true, so that she truly does do me good *all* the days of her life, whether I

176

know it or not. Such is the grace and providence of God.

It is God who brings the woman to the man (Gen. 2:22). By whatever method of choosing or selection, by dating or arrangement, free will or shotgun, we believe that normally God by His providence manages to connect us to the right one for us. This is not to say that occasionally our sin may not fail the will of God and trap us into the wrong marriage, but that given normal sinfulness and confusion, God in the long wisdom of His foresight has managed so to plan within the confines of our free will and seeming chance that the child of God who was created to be ours becomes so.

Paula and I were fortunate. God spoke to me and said, "She's the one," and that settled it. But perhaps I was more of a Thomas, less blessed for having to be told so concretely what many discover by hindsight or happenstance. In any case, we believe God knows how to gift us with the one of His choice.

"And he shall have no lack of gain." We have found it to be a principle, as in Psalm 133, that where unity exists, God has commanded the blessing. Where husband and wife pull together in harness, prosperity, whether inner or outer or both, is soon manifested. Sometimes other things block the prosperity their unity should reap, but always disunity sooner or later fractures wealth. "It is not good that the man should be alone" (Gen. 2:18) referred perhaps not only to his loneliness, but to his capacity to gain and store prosperity in heart and land as well. A wife is given that man should prosper—as the rest of Proverbs 31 so amply lays out. However, the flesh being the weakness it is, union and unity have a way of merging into a thousand and one forms of possession and use of each other. Fearing that, men all too often flee connubial bliss into the silent divorce mentioned in chapter three. Or, as is regretfully the case, they protect themselves by reducing the wife to a servant or slave or manikin programed to give back only what is put in. Far too often men find justifications in the Scriptures for behavior which does not sanctify the Lord in relation to their wives. Men would reduce the gift to a machine, but God would wed us to a friend.

Paula is her own person, and I want her to be fully that. If Paula were to come to me for permission to go to a regular meeting, to go shopping, or whatever, I would say, "You are your own person. Make up your own mind." I want a full partner. We detest what Paula and I have heard around the country these last several years, which is that so glibly used cop-out phrase whenever a wife expresses her own opinion, "You're in rebellion." If Paula's voice is silenced, I have lost half of my wisdom. Submission and the docility of 1 Peter 3:1-4 is not an exterior silence. Those verses referred solely to how a wife should win an unbelieving husband, not to the regular day-to-day communicative practices of Christian husbands and wives. A wife whose heart is gentle and meek can and should open the full broadside of her wisdom against her husband's foolishness.

If either Paula or I face a major decision, neither should make it without consulting the other. That is being subject to one another as we ought. We are a team, not a man with a helper.

In Genesis 2:18 the Lord said, "It is not good that the man should be alone; I will make an help meet for him." Note that the word is not "helper." A help MEET is a full and equal partner, who stands alongside her mate in equal possession of their common purpose and destiny. "Henceforth I call you not servants; for the servant knoweth not what his lord doeth: but I have called you friends; for all things that I have heard of my Father I have made known unto you" (John 15:15). My wife is my friend, not my helper.

Before I met Paula, the Lord called me and gave to me the commission to serve Him. When I met Paula, and we began to be serious in our relationship, I told her, "Paula, I am given to the Lord. Whatever He calls me to do, I will do. If He calls me away from you, I will go. You need to understand that, and if you can still accept me on that basis, okay." Paula wisely just accepted me, not at all agreeing. I had no idea how arrogant I was and what a misunderstanding of the nature of God I had.

For years, therefore, I thought God had given me a ministry, and then brought Paula along to help. It was *my* ministry and she was *my* helper. The Lord was never content with that (nor Paula). That had never been His intent. Gradually He caused me to see that He had called her to a mission too. But I still thought of it as my mission, to which she had also lately been called. Through the years He humbled my arrogance and opened me to Proverbs 31:10 following. At last He caused me to see that from the ground plan of creation He had created Paula and me as one team. It had never been *my* ministry but always *ours*. As with Adam in Genesis 2, He gave me the description of the calling first, but that was only a matter of His speaking to the head first, not of His creation and ordination. Paula felt that call on her life years before she met me.

Immediately after the fall of Adam and Eve, the relation of husband and wife reverted from full and equal partnership to dominance. God said to Eve, ". . . and thy desire shall be to thy husband, and he shall rule over thee" (Gen. 3:16b). Eve's desire already by creation was unto her husband. The Word is not redundant. The inference is plain that He meant that natural desire would become inordinate. Wives often tend to develop great insecurity for fear of not being pleasing to their husbands. Wives, more than husbands, tend to idolize their mates, seeking from them what only God can give. As love scorned becomes hate, so we tend to disrespect those we have idolized when their faults grieve us. For this reason wives become so frustrated and disillusioned with their husbands—they expected them to act like gods, and they didn't. For that reason the Word had to be given so many times to wives to respect their husbands. Sin created disorder, a desiring of the man more than God, perhaps as a reaping for the fact that Adam, not deluded as Eve was, knowingly chose Eve before God; so idolatry sown reaped idolatry.

"And he shall rule over thee." God's principles that the first-born shall rule and that the man shall have headship were already the facts of their existence, whether consciously known by Eve or not. The Word means then that sin fractures easy cooperation of hearts and minds so that the natural flow of direction and command in love is broken, and rule becomes oppressive rather than liberating. We see this in the Lord's explaining to Cain that had he done well, Abel's natural desire would have been unto Cain; Abel would easily and joyously have welcomed Cain's rule over him (Gen. 4:7). Had Adam and Eve kept the order of God, his headship would have rested lightly, as blessing, upon her. But wherever men have fallen, and to that degree, women have become suppressed and controlled. Most heresies bear the distinctive mark of suppressing women. Jesus would restore women to the glory of their creation as full and equal partners in life; Satan would rob and suppress. Never should a husband allow himself to get between God and his wife. "The husband is the head of the wife" (Eph. 5:23a), but the Lord is her Lord. The husband is her companion.

"Wives, be subject to your husbands, as to the Lord" (Eph. 5:22 RSV). I (Paula) am subject to the Lord because I love Him, because something is not complete in me without Him, because I want to bless Him with the gift of myself so that His mission to restore me to the Father might be fulfilled in joy. I *give* myself to the Lord because it is not His nature to force, and without that voluntary submission of my life I would never be partaker with Him, co-partner with Him, co-heir with Him of all that God gives. I know that if I seek to save my life, tenaciously hanging on to the control of me, defending my position, measuring costs and benefits of giving according to my ambition for self-advantage and advancement, I will lose my life, for that would be to spend my energies counter to the plan of my Creator. But if I risk myself and submit every area of my life to the Lord in identification with Him for who He is, out of love for Him for His sake, I will gain my life, for that is the way God has provided for me to become all that I am. I will listen and learn from Him with a teachable and respectful spirit. I will share with Him in all His sufferings. I will rejoice with Him in His victories. I will rest in Him as the structure of my being and walk in His protective cover.

My husband is not my Lord. But I will relate to him *as* to the Lord, voluntarily and lovingly giving, self-sacrificing, trusting, risking all that I am in the faith that life is a gift to those who live within the plan of the Creator.

In the early years of our marriage, I rebelled at the idea of living in submission to another person. My husband was obviously not the perfect one I knew my Lord Jesus to be. I was capable of making enough mistakes on my own without risking participation in the rewards of my husband's errors. He was the sort of person who would plunge headlong into whatever task or opportunity lay ahead. He was searching for truth with a vigor, not yet having come to rest in the truth who is Jesus. I followed him down many tangents with black skidmarks, becoming ever more afraid to trust. I did not know then that while we are warned to "put no trust in any brother" (Jer. 9:4 RSV), we are to trust the Lord to relate to us faithfully through those to whom we are joined by Him. The faithfulness of God is greater than anyone's inadequacy or sinful nature. "If we are faithless (do not believe and are untrue to Him), He remains true (faithful to His Word and His righteous character), for He cannot deny Himself" (2 Tim. 2:13 TAB). He is large enough to overcome all error and bring good out of every circumstance (Rom. 8:28; 2 Thess. 5:23). A second cause of my reticence to submit had to do with the fear of being somehow diminished or swallowed up in my husband's life and ministry. He had a specific call to serve. So did I. He was gifted with a multitude of talents. So was I. He is a strong personality. So am I. My delusion was that I had something to protect. My arrogance was that I could defend me better than the Lord or my husband could. Light began to seep into my mind and heart when I realized fully that abundant life is promised to *all* of God's children (John 10:10), that in the kingdom there is neither male nor female (Gal. 3:28), and that submitting my life to my husband does not mean being wiped out as an individual but being offered the privilege of complementing another in a unique way that enables the Lord to bring a new dimension of life to both. I began to see that flaws and imperfections in him were appropriate to the areas in me which needed revealing and refining, that it was for that reason as much as any that the Lord had brought us to one another. We needed the kind of struggle our coming together would create in order for us both to be broken and prepared for a growing depth and expansion of service to Him. Without that polishing in a close human risk-relationship we could neither of us have come into our own. I began to accept the realization that the pain that might develop was well worth the joy that would result, and began to pray in repentance for my lack of trust in God and my husband, for the spirit of control that I had developed, and for the load of negative judgment and expectation that I had dumped on him to help him go off course. Then I began to realize the reality and practicality of seed planting. I had been reaping where and what I had sown. As I began to give more wholly and freely of myself in every area to John, I was not diminished. I was set free to receive abundantly more than I had thought or asked.

Proverbs 31 began to come alive to me. I became aware that in being submitted and committed to her husband to do him good all the days of his life, a woman fills a very important variety of roles—enough to keep any woman hopping if she were faithful to them all! The ''wonder woman'' of Proverbs 31 is engaged in planting and harvesting (vv. 13, 16), providing food (vv. 14, 15), making clothing for her family (v. 22), preparing food for a household which she also manages (v. 27), buying land (v. 16), and delivering handcrafted goods to the merchants (v. 24). Besides all this, she ministers to the poor and the needy (v. 20). She is strong, courageous, wise, kind, honorable (vv. 17, 25, 26), and blessed by her children (v. 28) whom (apparently) she has not neglected while she has been doing all these other things. To me that sounds like a terribly exciting life with a potential for expression in unlimited directions. And to top it all, the good wife is not simply an extension of her husband, for the Scripture says, ''Give her of the fruit of her hands; and let *her own* works praise her in the gates'' (v. 31). All this is for the woman who fears the Lord (v. 30), which I believe means to be in awe and respect of and obedience to the perfect order of almighty Father God. Real freedom has never meant license to do as one pleases, but, rather, it means complete freedom to express *within* the operating principles of the universe. Those principles manifest solely the nature of Jesus, who calls us to give as He gave himself, that in dying to self to lose our life, we might find it (Luke 9:24).

10

THE IMPORTANCE OF A MOTHER'S LOVE

"She stretcheth out her hand to the poor; yea, she reacheth forth her hands to the needy" (Prov. 31:20). One of the most liberating revelations of my life was the realization that the "poor and needy" in my life are those lives entrusted to me especially—my husband and my children. I always cared deeply for them, and knew a measure of the importance of expressed love in their lives and mine. I had some awareness of the unique position I have to feed and nurture them. But for a time the depth of that awareness was blocked by my own lack of mature insight, and the rich excitement of motherhood was well hidden beneath a pile of dirty diapers and the repeated accumulation of "same-old-mess" associated with small children. I wanted to hurry past these to get on with the "important things" of life. Like thousands of other young mothers I was blind to the fact that the ordering and reordering of my home in an attitude of blessedness was in itself designed to teach invaluable lessons to my children which they could learn in no other place. And so I defeated myself and wasted a part of my calling for a time by chafing against what I had judged to be interruptions and blocks to my more creative urges. I sometimes envied my husband who seemed to be so much freer than I to minister to the hungry and the naked and the lame in a significant way—out there in the world.

It was not that I was confined to home duties by any means. As a pastor's wife I was busy with a round of meetings—choir practices, women's fellowship, youth activities, Sunday school, prayer groups, community service—running here and there wherever an overdeveloped sense of responsibility and a need to perform well called me to respond. The more I did, the harder it was to hold it all together, and the more irritated I became with clothes tossed carelessly on the floor, messes left in the kitchen sink, and splatters on the bathroom mirror. My martyr's mind asked, "Why am I the only one in the household who knows how to put a new roll of toilet paper on the spindle?" I felt more and more heavily the pressure of conflicting demands on my time and energies, the confusion of undefined priorities, and the apparent ingratitudes of people for whom I alone seemed to be working so hard. My mother worried that I might work myself into a nervous breakdown. My children expressed the pressured driving pace of my life by their busy cluttering, and my husband, who seemed always to be bringing one more task for me to do, wasn't much help when he said, "Sometimes I wish I'd married a dumb blonde who didn't know how to do anything!" The Lord caught me mercifully in the midst of a spluttering response, opened my eyes to see my husband and children as needing *me* infinitely more than all I could possibly *do* for them, and He began to reorder my priorities.

Again and again in my devotional time the Lord called my attention to the Scriptures in Matthew 14 and Mark 8 about the loaves and fishes. I began to identify with that little boy who offered so simply the little that he had for the immediate feeding of those close at hand. I realized that I *am* those loaves and fishes, and that it is my calling to offer myself simply where the Lord has placed me. It is the Lord's job to do the breaking and multiplying and distributing. I had been trying to do it all. Succeeding in the breaking and distributing, I had spread my resources too thin to feed anyone well, because only the Lord has the power to multiply. And He has established a holy order which works for multiplying and distributing blessing through families. Every other order works temporarily and with diminishing effect. Perhaps the best way I can represent the vision of order He has shown me is in the diagram below. I have found to my great joy and relief that in this order my energies flow without my striving, as every endeavor is empowered by the Lord as I do what I see my Father doing (John 5:19).

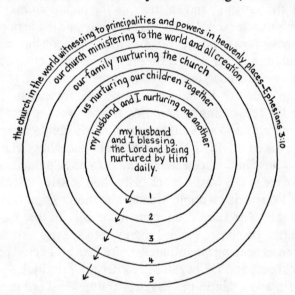

I look at this diagram as I would peer into a basket. The Lord will multiply the offering of my life to overflow the basket. But my offering is not hung on the top rim of the basket; it is given first into the depth of the center.

Practically, and specifically for me, this means that though the Lord has called me to receive people for counseling during the day, I will be free to greet my children when they come home from school. My listening ear must be sensitively tuned to the confessions of counselees; my heart must be in established rapport with my own children, else my not being there for them when they want to talk will create problems for some other counselor to deal with in them someday. I must not allow myself to become so poured out for others that I come to my husband drained and limp, or so full of the concerns of others that that is all I have to share with him. The appointments John and I make to counsel with individuals or address assemblies are to be held no more inviolate than the plans we make with our family for playing games together or sharing a picnic or attending a ball game or band concert in which our children have a part. It used to be very difficult for me to turn anyone away or put them off for fear that I would be failing both them and God. The Lord has set me free from that bondage to self-importance and unfaith by teaching me that He does not call me to answer every need and trouble I see around me, that He is quite capable of providing for all His creation (". . . God is able of these stones to raise up children. . ." [Matt. 3:9]) through the caring and sharing of many. But I am the only wife He has provided for my husband, and the only mother He has given to my children. I am uniquely and irreplaceably important to these few.

Every mother must examine her own life to determine decisions about loyalties and expenditures of time and energies. I suggest some common sense questions as guidelines:

Is this activity I want to become involved in contributing to or competing with the goals to which our family is committed? (Hopefully you as a family have considered these together.)

Is this activity so timed that my participation will not put an unhealthy strain on my family? Is God calling me to do this thing NOW?

Does my husband put his blessing on my involvement in

this activity? If not, are his objections valid? If they are not, and he perceives my giving to some other project as a rejection of him (or perhaps even the church or the Lord as a rival for my affection), then how am I failing to love and nurture him in a satisfying way so he is secure enough to bless my going?

While I am investing myself outside the home, do I maintain our home in the sort of relaxed orderliness that enables my husband and children to bring friends home to visit comfortably and yet without apology? Is there enough of my skill and artistry reflected in the meals I set on the table to say consistently to my family, "I love you and want the best for you"? Or are special colorful culinary efforts always a signal to the children that company is coming or that mom is taking her pride to the church dinner?

Does my attitude set up invisible images and demands that my family must live up to so that I can be free to "do my thing," or am I meeting others where they are, and adjusting my desire to express freely with their needs to be themselves? Do I communicate to my children that they reside in *my* house, and must live according to *my* rules, or do I communicate that *we* live in a home in which the Lord rules by love and invitation to share? Do I communicate that necessary behavioral rules are a guide to considerate living together? Or my defense of my own image as a "good mother"?

If I decide to take employment outside the home to add to the family income, are the tangible benefits worth the possible cost of the loss of intangibles?

The most important question is always, for everyone, "Is this the perfect will of the Father God for my life today?" Answers will not always come clearly. We may not be sure that our expressions of love are motivated purely. But if we are choosing consistently to lay down our lives for others, to walk in the paths God has prepared for us, if we are making ourselves available to His leading by prayer and study of the Word, and family discussions, the Lord will have ample access to direct our decisions. Only He can effect balance in our lives, give grace to correct error, and create good in all circumstances.

Real love may sometimes mean sacrificing for a time those very personal adult relationships which have taught and supported us as parents. One young couple was concerned over their son's bed wetting problem and the fact that their daughter's grades had been slipping. Prayerfully examining their lives, they saw that they were going in too many directions with adult friends, leaving the children alone too much and thus scattering their children's base of security. It was difficult to determine where to retreat from activities which were meaningful and enriching, but they determined for a time that there would be at least one parent at home as anchor man every night of the week. This bore good fruit.

Children need to know that there is a home base to touch which doesn't move. It is important for mother to be "there," available, providing continuity for all the coming and going. Our son John was independent at age five, and eager to begin kindergarten. I had already gone through the experience of releasing three babies into the scholastic world, so I was not really clinging to my fledgling when the first day of school rolled around. But I naturally expected that I would walk to school that one time with him.

"You don't have to come. I know the way."

"I know that, John, but there might be papers to sign—and it would make me feel good to go with you once. Mothers are like that."

He agreed, but I had to follow at some distance behind him, all the way! Several weeks later, I was shocked to find this super-independent, well-adjusted young man sitting in a dejected heap outside the door when I returned home fifteen minutes late.

"What's the matter, John?"

"I didn't know where you were."

Thirteen years later he manages excellently for himself—but still wants to know where I will be, how long I will be gone, and when I will be home.

A mother is a nurse ready to supply tender love and first aid to bind wounds, with enough detachment not to bind her children to their wounds.

She is interpreter to inform in the gaps which cannot be avoided between children and their father as he travels between two worlds. She is not to defend, nor to get into the middle position which prevents direct communication; she is not to choose sides. But she often is the connecting link through a simple word:

"Susie's feeling low today. She had a falling out with her boy friend."

"Be careful what you say to Joey. He didn't make the team."

"Be sure to notice your daughter's new hairdo."

Her prompting in love should communicate to him and to the children a considerate affirmation of his caring, not an accusation for his not noticing.

If a mother finds herself in the position of referee in the outcropping of sibling rivalries or heated interchange among playmates, she must know she is there to draw lines and enforce rules, not to fight battles for her children and rob them of the lessons to be learned in the struggle. One mother we know is continually in the midst of her children's quarrels. Rather than learning to settle differences themselves, they seem to be learning that to quarrel, to tattle, to complain loudly is a sure way to attract mama's attention. Her willingness to be manipulated in that way sets the children up for a continual wail. There is no peace in that household. If that mother does not learn to stand back and quietly suffer childish outbursts and check her impulse to control, the wail of the children will become such habit patterns that as adults, they will be their society's malcontents, the stirrers of trouble, the blamers, the self-pitiers. Real love does not rob a child of the enterprise of his own growth in skills needed to live peaceably among men.

Every mother cherishes a close relationship with her children where dreams and joys and sorrows can be shared, but a wise mother will always remember she wears a parental mantle which cannot be taken off. In her sharing, she must preserve her supportive role for her growing child, regardless of her own need; she never should allow the relationship to become inverted by dumping a load of care, hurt, fear, or frustration on a child who will respond in loving sympathy, but will in no way be prepared by maturity to carry what she lays on him. All too often John and I have ministered to over-serious, joyless, striving individuals borne down with the weight of the world's problems to the point of rage or depression. The root is then revealed to be that at a too early age the child assumed the role of confidante or counselor to a widowed mother, or a mother in marital difficulty, or one who was divorced. The burden is too much to bear. Loyalty to a loved parent prevents rejection of the load. The child has the functions of a mate except the marriage bed, and so the child grows into adulthood trapped by a confusion of roles, unable later to come to rest and relate freely in the loving gift of self with a mate.

Often, because mother is available when questions arise, she becomes the child's instructor in sex education more than the father. If she answers questions frankly, openly, without embarrassment or anxiety, sexual being and functions will be communicated as a natural part of everyday life—wholesome, clean, and comfortable. In that context, proper warnings and restrictions can be presented and they will not be interpreted as negative taboos to be rebelliously violated. Neither will they register as "nasties." Regarding such matters as being "nasty" prevents the uninhibited nurturing sexual relationship between married couples.

"How much detail should I share in answer to my child's inquiries?" Many mothers have asked that question, and the answer is simple: "As much as the individual child is asking for, qualified only by that child's maturity level to receive with understanding." Our friend Maria Bates tells of an experience she had with a curious preschooler who was her neighbor. Maria had just given birth to a baby boy, and obviously there had been some discussion about the exciting event among the neighborhood children. A little boy came into her home one afternoon and carefully and admiringly examined the baby sleeping in the basket. Then after a few moments of thoughtful staring at Maria's midsection, he ventured,

"Mrs. Bates, that baby used to be in your tummy, didn't he?"

"Yes, Tommy, he did. I went to the hospital so the doctor could help when it was time for him to come out into the world."

"Did it hurt when the baby came out?"

"Well, yes, it hurt some. But mothers forget that hurt very quickly because they are so happy to see a beautiful healthy baby."

"Oh,"—long silence—"Mrs. Bates, can I ask you another question?"

"Yes, Tommy."

"Promise you won't tell my dad?" Maria summoned her poise and prepared herself for the next question.

"What is your question, Tommy?"

"Mrs. Bates—can I have a banana?"

The whole picture need not be spelled out for a preschooler, but if a parent wants his child to know the facts of life within a Christian context before he has been significantly influenced by the misinformation of his peers, before he has been colored by the amoral influence of the media, he had best do some carefully accurate and sensitively communicated teaching before the child reaches the junior high level. If the parent who wants to teach the spiritual values of the sexual relationship feels inadequate to accurately describe the physical functions of the male and female in sexual union, then it is a simple matter to enlist the aid of an illustrated encyclopedia. But it is unreasonable and irresponsible to abdicate this most important aspect of a child's education to someone in the public school system and then accuse and blame the schools for failing to teach morality and spirituality. That is not their primary job. A teacher, a nurse, or a doctor in the public school system will be prepared with the encyclopedic presentation, but cannot present the moral and spiritual as parents can and should. We welcome sex education in the schools, but we urge Christian parents to give their children early a basic structure of understanding in which to receive clinical sexual information, that such might come to them as a tool for living life, and not as an awkward weapon which can be used destructively.

In the earliest stages of sex instruction a parent needs to realize that every God-given organ of the body deserves the respectful use of its proper name. If a parent finds it more difficult to pronounce aloud the words "breast" or "buttocks" or "penis" than he does "nose" or "elbow," and finds it necessary to substitute some cute slang expression to cover his own embarrassment, that parent has a problem to face in himself or herself. The Lord would like to deal with that before it is passed on to a child with compounded confusion. A mother who accepts her own sexuality as a God-given gift and grace and knows what it is to meet her husband sexually with a sense of wonder and thankfulness that the Creator has given such a beautiful plan, will not be shocked and devastated to find her small child stripping before the giggles and applause of neighborhood children. She will be able lovingly and firmly to stop the show and explain to the child in a way that does not lay a burden of condemnation on him. The meanings of the words "modest" and "private" (which have nothing to do with shameful), "inappropriate" (which does not mean bad), "mysterious" (unrelated to perverted), "naked" (not at all connected with pornographic), will be conveyed to the child as much by her relaxed manner as by what she says. Mothers need to know that experimentation and voyeurism are natural outbursts from childish curiosity. Most importantly, a relaxed mother will by her attitude invite her children to grow up looking to her as a reliable, understanding, and sympathetic source of accurate and valuable information. We have counseled many whose later sexual life was fraught with fear and tension because mother came down with oppressive, fearful, condemning hands and words instead of laughing and easy teaching.

Finally, mother is a launcher. When parents think of a wedding of a daughter, father gets all misty-eyed at the thought of walking down the aisle with his little girl by his side. Mother dreams of flowers and showers and dressmaking and music. Papa dreads the bills. But seldom do both realize that on their part the most important thing they do is contained in that short response to the simple question, "Who giveth this woman to this man?" When the father says, "Her mother and I do" and takes his seat beside the mother, a dramatic role change is effected, a most necessary relinquishment of responsibility for that child. From that moment on motherhood will mean a quiet and "distant" supporting of the relationship of the bride and groom. In no way does she have position to control or manage her children's marriage, or even to instruct, except by express invitation, and then with reticence. Many a young marriage has been prevented because the sharing of confidence was never transferred from parent to mate. The young couple were never given a chance to work things out for themselves. Parents continued to dominate, control, or to do too much for one or both of the marriage partners. Some counselors maintain that parents are among the most significant causes for most divorces, and some would place most of the fault on parental interference.

One of the most beautiful examples of healthy mother-in-lawing we have ever seen was in the home of some friends of ours. There, a lovely lady, visiting in her son's home from overseas, managed by the grace of the Lord to live sensitively with her children and grandchildren, participating but never interfering, working alongside her daughter-in-law, never criticizing, offering who and what she was freely but never in a spirit of competition. If she saw error, she kept silence and went to the Lord with it; she never chose sides. Her contribution to the home was significant enough to cause them to miss her deeply when she left, but in no way were any of them dependent on her so as to throw the household into imbalance in her absence. She knew who she was and gave of herself to them as she maturely related to their need. She was not driven by any insecurity of unaffirmed love or confusion of roles to push, pull, demand, manipulate, or compete in any way. Her daughter-in-law wept great tears of sorrow when she returned to her own country. Never had she been a burden to her, but only a blessing.

Let it be the earnest prayer of every mother, mother-in-law, and grandmother that she can so rest in who she is in the Lord, that in all her attempts to love there might eventually be accomplished that same sort of transition that happened between Jesus and His disciples (John 15:15) as He loved them to freedom to become His friends. A mother must relinquish. She must die to her role as mother, and let her child go, in order to receive again a friend and companion.

11

GETTING AT ROOTS OF BITTERNESS

See to it that no one fail to obtain the grace of God; that no "root of bitterness" spring up and cause trouble, and by it the many become defiled. (Heb. 12:15 RSV)

A lady came to us complaining bitterly. Her father had forced her to work on the farm like a hired hand. When she came in from the fields, he would drunkenly accuse her falsely of all manner of alleged evil doings, including fornication. Having endured the drunken father all of her youth, she married a man who for eighteen years forced her to go to work while he drank, and when she returned from work, reviled and accused her falsely of all manner of evils, including adultery. Finally she divorced him, and shortly remarried. Within a few months that man made her get a job, stayed home and got drunk, and each evening reviled her and accused her of all manner of vices, including adultery. After two years she divorced him. Being both attractive and determined, she sought carefully for a husband with whom she could be happy. At last she found a Christian man who had money in the bank and real estate holdings. One month after they married, he sent her to work while he stayed home to drink, and he began to revile her each evening after work, accusing her of adultery!

What was doing it? Did she have that kind of psychic power to control men's lives? Of course not. But the law of God does have such power. "Judge not, lest ye be judged" (Matt. 7:1). Not psychic power but the law of God swings inexorably to retribution. An old proverb says, "He who gossips is like him who throws mud straight up." Another simply says, "Expressing hate is like spitting in the wind." As what goes up must come down, so what is said must return. Unfortunately, the law of judgment is effective not only for what is conscious, known and performed outwardly, but for what is lodged in the heart, repressed, unknown, and unexpressed. Judgments, once formed, must bring results. Bitter roots, not brought to the cross, must defile.

Bitter roots are perhaps the most powerful negative force in all our life, bringing destruction not only to us but to all our loved ones. As we unfold in this chapter the depth and power of bitter roots, let us be clear that we are not speaking merely of the power of psychological expectancy.

Psychology has caused us to ascribe too much to libidinal or subliminal forces with us, as though we had in our own persons the power to make things good or bad happen to us. Positive or negative thinking may indeed have some effect, but what we presently think or feel consciously and unconsciously is not the main determinative factor spoken of by St. Paul as a bitter root, springing up to cause trouble. Christians need to remove the blinkers of psychology and return to the Word of God. What is primarily causal in human life is not psychology but the law of God, "Be not deceived; God is not mocked: for whatsoever a man soweth, that shall he also reap" (Gal. 6:7).

Children, being small and loyal, not knowing yet the art of forgiveness, have little opportunity either to express angers, admit resents, or achieve forgiveness. Consequently, often repeated incidents form unconscious forgotten psychological patterns of expectancy; worse and far more causally, they set up judgments which act as seeds sown to be reaped in due time. The fact of conscious and hidden inner judgments is perhaps the most determinative factor in our lives apart from the mercy of the cross. In countless ways we form judgments and suffer accordingly. "Honor thy father and thy mother . . . that it may go well with thee" (Deut. 5:16) is consequently no nice "ought" or "should." It is not optional. It is an absolute description of reality. In whatever area or way we cannot honor our parents, it will not be well with us. "Till heaven and earth pass, one jot or one tittle shall in no wise pass from the law, *till all be fulfilled*" (Matt. 5:18). Jesus has fulfilled all the legal demands of the law upon the cross (Col. 2:14). Unfortunately, however, that fulfillment must be claimed by specific confession, else all is truly fulfilled by the law of sowing and reaping.

We cannot say why some things are surely and quickly accomplished at our first reception of Jesus as Lord and Savior, nor why other hidden sins of judgment must be revealed and confessed specifically, else we reap the full extent of the law. God does know.

A man whose father had been severely critical of him came for counsel. No task accomplished met an embrace or affirmation from his dad, but only attacks. This man could never hold a job. Bosses always reviled him and made life so miserable that no matter how hard he tried, in the end he would have to resign or be fired. Recently he had taken a new job and performed well. The boss thought, "Sam's been doing well. I'll go in and sit down and have a chat and compliment him." Within five minutes the boss found himself ripping Sam up one side and down the other. The boss left shaking his head, wondering what had happened. "I didn't want to do that at all; what made me do it?" Sam's attitude, his remarks, his expectancy to be criticized didn't help at all, of course, but these alone could not be enough to so divert and pull off-balance the other's mind and heart. Sam was continuing to reap the bitter judgments of his heart. Any boss is a father figure, and so steps into that sowing and reaping. By the law of increase we sow a spark, to reap a holocaust, or a wind to reap a whirlwind. Sam's boss stepped north into a hundred-and-fifty-mile-an-hour gale only to turn and run south before the storm. He could not keep from criticizing Sam.

At a mission in a church I (John) was impressed by the Holy Spirit that at a moment of prayer, the Lord was moving to heal someone's birth experience. I described under anointing, by the gift of knowledge, how someone was being held back by a doctor's hand while a twin was brought forth first, and how that person had always thereafter been beset with fear of death. A lady burst into tears. The Holy Spirit had described her birth exactly. Her twin brother had been brought forth first. Both from that experience (Ps. 58:3) and from constant sibling rivalries she had been held in the grip of bitter expectancy that she would always be held back; others would receive first, and what good things were coming to her would go to another. Life dutifully manifested her pattern of expectancy, even to her having to stay home while her husband went off long months to Alaska. His attentions were given to other women, and others received all manner of blessings in prayer groups while she suffered seeming neglect by God. Neither God nor her husband wanted it so. But life could go no other way so long as her unconfessed judgments set the channel for the flow of the river of return.

A beautiful woman came to us who had had three horrendous marriages. Each time she had dated a loving, gentle man, had been unable to become interested in him, and had ditched him to marry a drunken, violent bum. We could see that the present likelihood of marriage would turn out the same way. For a long time she came for counseling. We could find in her relation to the man she called her father nothing so vitiating as to create such a pattern. One day she came muttering again and again (while rocking back and forth), "I don't have a father. I don't have a father." Then she admitted what she had never been able to tell us before, that her "father" was in fact her stepfather, and that she had met her natural father only once, when she was eighteen. He had been a drunken, violent bum who had beaten on her mother again and again while her mother carried her. When she was six months old in the womb, her father climaxed his violences by pinning the mother's arms behind her while the mother screamed, "I hate you. I hate you. I'll kill you," whereupon the husband left and never returned. The baby came out of the womb with totally ambivalent feelings. First, there was a great need for her own father, for which reason any violent, drunken man could reach depths and stir responses no gentle man could. Second, virulent, hidden judgment ("men are like that") and bitter expectancy that the man of her life would be a drunken, violent bum ran rampant below the level of consciousness. No man who could upset that judgment could be allowed close enough to threaten that inner world; therefore, gentle men had to be ditched before they became close.

It was not this pattern alone which caused her husbands to become drunken or to beat on her. It was already their nature to be that way; that is what made them appealing to her. But what determined whether she would help such men change or drive them further into it was what was in her. Her bitter root defiled the many around her. The law of sowing and reaping thus had an easy field to bring forth its tares in abundance. For her husbands, marriage to her was like stepping into a cascade through a gorge; the law of sowing to the waters reaped a roaring river of destruction.

This example was not only vivid to us by its starkness but by its revelation of the hiddenness of sin, even while the woman was yet in her mother's womb (Isa. 48:8; Ps. 58:3). When we saw the depth of the pattern, we explained it to her and asked her to forgive her natural father. She would not believe that anything so stark had actually come upon her, especially that far back. She had no conscious awareness of hatred for her natural father, whose debilitated condition when she was eighteen had only evoked pity and shame. That day I (John) was ministering to her, and so I said, "Okay, let's just enter into prayer." After a while I said, "Now, will you say to the Lord, 'I forgive my natural father'?"

She began to tremble and shudder violently, and finally struggled to say, "I can't do it. I just can't say it."

"Now do you see, Betty, you really do judge and hate him?" She saw it. We prayed. And the Lord is healing her heart. She left the area, and to this day we do not know whether she has married again, but we have faith for her that the Lord who came to destroy the works of the devil (1 John 3:8) is setting her free to have an abundant life.

So long as judgments remain hidden in the heart, they swing like an ever-increasing cycle of a pendulum to greater and greater retribution. For this reason David prayed, "Who can understand his errors? cleanse thou me from secret faults. Keep back thy servant also from presumptuous sins; *let them not have dominion over me*: then shall I be upright, and I shall be innocent from the *great* transgression" (Ps. 19:12, 13). And Jesus promised, "Fear them not therefore: for there is nothing covered, that shall not be revealed; and hid, that shall not be known" (Matt. 10:26). Jesus spoke then of the false accusations of men, but the principle holds true that God in His mercy will reveal whatever troubles our own heart that we may be delivered from it (Ps. 51:10-12). That is how we are to obey the command: "See to it that no bitter root spring up." Not by repressing or struggling unaided against what we are, but by simple confession and forgiveness and the hauling down of inner strongholds (2 Cor. 10:4, 5).

Few have such dramatic roots as some we have chronicled

here. But all have countless little roots which trouble mightily. Paula and I, being normal, with good parents, had many (and still have some). Paula had healthily rambunctious brothers who continually did "dumb" things which added gray hairs like a snowstorm to her parents' heads. That angered her, and unbeknownst to her, built a bitter root judgment that men would always be doing "dumb-dumbs." Her favorite expression in place of a curse word still today is, "Oh, brother!" (Paula then and now loves her brothers, and remembers many hilariously happy times, and today admires her brothers, but the judgment had already been lodged in her heart.) When we first married, I discovered I had a propensity from the pulpit to say unnecessary, shocking "dumb-dumbs." Paula would say to me, "You aren't going to say something startling today, are you?" And then of course I "had" to, if only to declare an immature independence.

When I was invited to teach, away from home and away from Paula, I was surprised to discover wisdom flowing from me. I didn't have to say "dumb-dumbs." That puzzled both of us. At last the Lord revealed that Paula's bitter expectancy was corrupting me. When she repented of her judgments on her brothers, I was free, in her presence or out of it, to preach and teach in wisdom—and to make my own mistakes!

Having been told in a dream, before she knew she was pregnant with me, that she would have a son who would be the Lord's servant, my mother had time to think before I was born. She decided to say nothing to me before the Lord called me (which He did when I was seventeen), and to work me harder and to discipline me more severely. I had no awareness of her motives, only anger (now appreciation) for the work and discipline. We had cows, chickens, an orchard and large yard and garden, which became mine to take care of. Work never seemed to have an end. She used to promise me that if I would just do this one more thing, I could go play. Almost immediately play would be interrupted, and there would be mom with another, and yet another chore. My younger sister revolted and wouldn't do the work (it was too much for her, young as she was), and my mother made me do her work as well. It seemed that every time there was a promise and opportunity to play, there was another task! And again if only I would get this one more thing done, then I could go play.

You should see my brother and me play cards—fast! Play had to be gotten in quickly, or something would interrupt. I judged mom for all those "unfair" demands. My bitter root expectancy was that God and life would treat me like that. There would always be more work. I would never get to play and enjoy life. Life was and would be work, work, and more work.

What's more, when opportunity to play did come, I could never relax. On vacations Paula would be furious because no sooner had we set up camp than I would be finding some camper in trouble to counsel or help some way—all the while blaming God that He wouldn't let me rest! I couldn't let God bless me with a restful time, for that would blow all my inner mind's judgments. That bitter root defiled happy time after happy time for the family. Our children one day said to Paula, "Dad's definition of heaven is a line a mile long sitting outside his counseling office while he tries to save them one by one! And dad's definition of hell is a lovely, restful place with a deep armchair, a good book, nothing else to do and everybody waiting on him to do things for him."

Not until I quit blaming my mother, gave thanks for her sternness, and asked that the Lord haul that bitter root to the cross did things begin to change. We die slowly, so still today we get swamped with work, and I keep at it when God would have me rest. But at least He has taken the self-glory and self-pity out of it. I now know it's my sin, not God's requirement.

In the church I continually had to pick up strands others had left lying around. In ministerial alliances, other men would sometimes fail to carry the ball and I would take up the slack. Earlier, at work at Delta Airlines (Midway Airport, Chicago), as a foreman, I would drive myself far harder than any of the workmen, far more than what was necessary. This was not something to be proud of, but a defilement of others, as it prevented them from coming into the fulness of their own responsibility.

Our Protestant ethic exalts industriousness so that I could cloak my bitter roots behind "noble" motives. Unfortunately I am so far from being unique as to be representative of most men in our work-oriented culture. This very thing is one of the most destructive aspects of our Western heritage, seducing men into too many long hours away from their families. The point being that we fail to heal by hammering at men to set their priorities right and spend more time with their families. That may help, but unless the *heart* is turned to the children, the family is not restored. Each father needs to be helped to see what bitter roots defile his family life, so that the real judgments and bitternesses that find their expressions in too much work can be taken to the cross.

My father (Paula's) is a grand guy. He loves us, and when he was home, everything was fine. But he was a traveling salesman, gone two weeks at a time. The heart of a child is not as magnanimous as the mind. The mind says, "My daddy has to work; I'm proud of him; he works so hard for us." But the heart says, "I need him. Why can't he be here for me?" Unbeknownst to me I had formed a bitter judgment: "The man will not be there to defend me. I will have to defend myself, by myself." And, "My man will always be gone when I need him. Something else will take him away."

When we first married, John continually found himself making house calls much later each day than necessary, coming home late to supper night after night. I would reason and plead and scold and demand, and he would promise—and soon fall back into the same habit. We both thought it was something in John. Finally the Lord revealed my own bitter judgment, and I repented. Immediately John found himself easily coming home on time.

John never seemed to notice what the children were doing. His being absent-minded, a dreamer, and totally capable of tuning out all noises so as to be able to concentrate made it seem obvious that it was simply John; he didn't notice what he should, and left me to handle the children. I felt the over-burden of discipline, and soon fell to haranguing the children, taking out my anger on them.

It seemed totally unfair and misleading when John would respond to my accusations by saying, "But you are angry at your father." How could I be? He had been such a perfect father. I loved him and never knew a moment's anger at him. And besides, I could point out to John that at least when my father was home, *he would* discipline, *he would* notice, compliment, and defend me. At last I could dodge it no longer, and faced the fact that bad trees in our lives obviously had some roots in me as well as in John, and by faith asked the Lord to remove whatever bitter roots were lodged in me against my father. I never did feel any anger, repenting by faith only. John quickly took up his rightful headship. Not only was he determined to discipline; the Lord would break into his concentration in the study and he would come roaring out of the office to insist that the children obey me. Truly, my bitter root had coupled with John's (his father was also away from the home a good deal), to defile our family.

My parents (John's) received inheritances and Osage oil money so that for periods of my life we were quite well off. But they had a genius for losing money! In the day before theft insurance, they opened a jewelry store, and were robbed three times. They started a fine gift and furniture store in Joplin—just before Joplin went into a financial depression. And so it went, again and again. Little blame could justly be attached, but that didn't keep my sinful heart from doing it. My picture of life and God were formed unconsciously in bitterness. God would go bankrupt as far as I was concerned. I would not be consistently provided for. Some emergency would always bring likely prospects to defeat. I would never have enough, and would have to work extra hard all my life only to lose anyway.

Neither God nor life could go against the deep levels of my will. Life went that way. Always there was some emergency just when it looked like clear sailing. Three congregations dutifully starved us. My psychological projections streamed messages to trustees' boards, but though that helped to turn away salary increases, the reaping of judgments was what pushed them not to be as expansive as they would have been. Not until the Lord revealed the depth of my sin did things change. Whereas I had blamed congregations for being unloving and stingy, now I saw that I had defiled them. I had prevented them from receiving the blessing of giving to God's servant. My bitter root had cheated them more than me. I repented, and claimed God's faithfulness. Not only did God provide the gift of our wonderful home (*The Elijah Task*, pp. 55-57), He has caused people to shower gifts upon us consistently since that date. We have lived on nothing but faith for over five and a half years. We never charge for counseling nor ask for an honorarium for speaking. We give, and God causes men to give into our bosom (Luke 6:38). And God has provided at a rate three times above anything given us as pastor and wife in the church. Our children suffered unnecessary lacks, and worse, received a picture of the church and of God which failed to sanctify the true generosity and faithfulness of either. Again, my bitter root had defiled the many.

I (Paula) was the first child of five, and felt the responsibility to lead the family by performing well. Two normally rebellious brothers, full of pranks, followed. Jerry and Stan got into so many escapades that seemingly a great deal of parental attention went to them. Though they were brilliant, they seldom received better-than-average grades; life was too much fun, and mom and dad praised their C's and said little about my A's. Jerry now directs a nationwide computer service corporation, and Stan is news director of a TV station. But in that process of struggle with the boys, it was an unconscious (and sometimes conscious) bitterness to me that my straight-A cards and dependability seemed to be taken for granted. Small incidences in school added to my judgment that I would achieve but not be recognized. In the first grade I was placed in the second soprano section because I could harmonize; somehow I translated that to mean that I was considered second best. I sang my heart out and never got out of the second soprano section. In the second grade I proudly spelled my name in cursive writing on the blackboard only to be called "stupid" for not spelling it "Pauline" (that was never my name), and a bragger because we weren't supposed to be writing in cursive style yet. I hated that teacher! I was allowed to carry the Maypole for the May Day celebration—why didn't the teacher know how well I could have danced? One year I sang with a special girl scout caroling group. The next year I didn't make it; I didn't know that my voice had matured to the point that it would not blend with children's voices, and I felt rejected.

In high school it seemed I was usually on the effort end of projects rather than the glory end. Elected to student council office I rejoiced, and then felt fourth when a friend said, "Oh, I thought you should have won and you only got treasurer!" It was trained into me at home that it was a sin to cheat. But at graduation a large scholarship went to a classmate who openly bragged that she always hid the answers to test questions on a paper slipped into the top of her stocking. Actually I found out years later that my classmates thought of me as a "big wheel."

And I know my parents were inordinately proud of me. But my bitter roots were already grown by confusion, circumstance, and sinful reaction—all mine.

That bitter root set me to compete with John unconsciously, and expect he would get the credit for what we did. As late as last year, after many aspects of this root had been dealt their death blow, people were still saying to John what a wonderful talk he had given (that we had given together) while neglecting to say anything to me, and even consistently complimented him for remarks I had made. Introducers gave John's name and left me sitting beside him. People, conversing with both of us, would say to John, "That *Elijah Task* is a wonderful book you wrote, John." Having invited both of us to speak, pastors would lay hands on John and anoint him, neglecting me. John would prompt ". . . and Paula" and they wouldn't hear him, or act on it. I was truly the invisible woman. Were people really that deaf and blind? Not at all. The stream of retribution is that powerful. "With what judgment ye mete out, it shall be meted unto you again." My bitter root had jeopardized others, putting them in the position of failing common courtesy. Now that my repentance is more complete, that pattern has ended. I am honored in my own right, for my own life.

In the church I always had trouble procuring teachers and helpers for daily vacation Bible school, or whatever else I was in charge of. And people would let me down. The very spring the Lord began to reveal my bitter root, and I repented, I was asked to head the daily vacation Bible school again. Instead of the previous tedious phone-calling, we merely put a sheet of paper on a table in the narthex and announced that anyone who wanted to volunteer to teach or bring refreshments could sign up accordingly. That year for the first time in the church's history we had team teachers for every class and more people signed up for more refreshments than we could use. No one let us down or failed to show up, and we all had a glorious time! I wonder how often we pastors and wives have reaped our own sowing in the church, and then blamed the church for failing! Truly the judgment of God begins at home, in the heart.

I (John) seldom received affirmation or compliments. My mother, having grown up in Oklahoma ranch culture, would say, "Well now, you never worked like Uncle Leon. He would have been up by 3:30 and had a day's work done by breakfast. You slept in until 5:30!" There was almost never a thank you or an approval. Rather it was, "But why didn't you do this that way?" or "Okay, you did that, but I also told you to do this," or "Look at that (whatever) you missed. You have to learn to do things right, and do it right the first time." I was angry and bitter. Three congregations dutifully seldom complimented me, I thought, and criticized whatever I did. The truth was they were quite complimentary, but I had set my sails not to catch those winds and so didn't hear, or couldn't. It seemed that people were absurdly critical of the very things I had done well, and almost never mentioned an area in which I had in fact erred terribly. That fact completely bamboozled and upset me. I never seemed to be able to please (though, in fact, people were often pleased and said so). I seemed doomed to lose no matter how hard I tried.

Then the Lord revealed the truth of my bitter root, and I repented. Now, almost no one ever falsely criticizes me. If someone has a criticism, they say it appropriately, kindly, and directly to my face; it helps me and I appreciate it and love the people for it. My attitude had kept me from hearing the compliments that were there, and had spawned criticisms, but more than attitude, the law of retribution swung through people to me. I came to see, in the process of healing, that it was the very people who loved me who could be so influenced to criticize. I saw again that my bitter root had jeopardized God's people, for His discipline falls on those who dishonor His anointed. (Every pastor having been set aside and consecrated in the ceremony of ordination, is especially His anointed, though we ought also to understand that anyone whom God calls to a task is for that moment His anointed.) Merely confronting a servant of the Lord is not to be taken as dishonoring. The Lord's servants need honest people. "Iron sharpens iron, and one man sharpens another" (Prov. 27:17 RSV). The Lord looks on the heart. Finding pretexts to criticize, or excuses to attack, in order to avoid obedience to God's Word is to dishonor. Or simply to disrespect and scoff, or slander. My repentance that I had hurt God's people by causing them to revile me does not totally exonerate them nor excuse, nor prevent me from rejoicing when men begin to revile and persecute falsely (Matt. 5:11, 12), for the law of judgment (Matt. 7:1) is not the whole story. But my repentance can keep the law of bitter roots from defiling any more of God's people.

One question begs before we leave the subject. The law says, "With what measure ye mete, it shall be measured to you again," which seems to denote equal and exact return for judgments given. But we see in actual fact continual and grievous reaping far beyond what seems the measure sown. We don't understand fully, but we suggest these possibilities. One, perhaps the extent of our judging is far more vitiating than any of us suspect, so that God's justice is equal. Two, perhaps the law of increase is understood but not said explicitly, so that the Lord did not mean equal and exact retribution, but retribution measured as a harvest of grain is a multiplication of seed sown and nurtured. In such case, God is yet fair, for the law works equally to increase rewards for righteous deeds, and shall we say that it is fair to reap increase of blessing but not discipline?

Behind all this operation of inexorable law lies one blessed fact that so outshines all of history that everything else in all the universe pales beside it. God has fulfilled all that legal demand of law in His own Son's body on the tree. We have only to repent and claim that fact to be free and happy.

How good God is that He prompts us untiringly until we do

some good thing, and then rewards us an hundredfold as though that thing had been all our own idea. And the Father laments for us in the Spirit until we hear and repent so that He can pay the whole price of evil for us in the Son. Nothing is more sure than forgiveness. The Christian family need never fear exposure of evil and conviction, for that moment is the moment of release. Having received forgiveness, we may yet have to resist the old habit form in our nature, but once forgiveness is claimed, it is as though someone had been ringing the town bell for all to hear, and though it may continue to swing and ring awhile, no one is pulling on the rope any longer.

12

BALANCE THROUGH
THE FULCRUM OF CHRIST

Most of us can remember a time when as children we played on a teeter-totter. If we could find a playmate just our size it was fun with no hassle, and we enjoyed relaxed hours of going up and down in the sun. But it was another matter when we weighed sixty pounds and our friend weighed one hundred. Then our play necessitated all manner of shifting of weight forward and back until an easy balance could be achieved. Sometimes in our immature anxiety to satisfy our own desire for pleasure, we entered into wrangling for a position:

"Come on, you have to get closer to the middle."

"Well, that's no fun. You get all the good ride!"

"It'd be okay if you weren't so fat."

"I'd rather be fat than a runt like you!"

"If that's the way you feel, then I'll find someone else to play with."

And so our bigger friend hit the dirt as we jumped off. Once in a while an older brother would find us in our impasse, soothe our ridiculously ruffled feelings with affectionate chuckles, and assume a position at the center of the fulcrum, holding a balance for us with the magnificent power of his legs. So long as he remained in that position, we could relax and enjoy ourselves, neither shape nor weight nor position being important any longer.

As married couples we are as those two dissimilar children on opposite ends of the same teeter-totter. We will simply by token of those dissimilarities force the other to compensate for what we are or are not. In some areas of life one is heavy and the other light and in other areas and instances vice-versa. Jesus Christ is our elder brother. Only as He is the power at the center of our lives can we relate to one another without strain from the extremities of our differentnesses. Without Him we tend to accuse the other of being overbearing when indeed he is unconsciously compensating for our timidity. Or we are angry when the mate abdicates his responsibility, not recognizing a tendency in us to take over and crowd him out. In marriage we are called to be one with each other, and we need to become aware of the automatic, unconscious dynamic of balancing one another which occurs in the process of living together. We need to come to real repentance and forgiveness, else we will increase in our compulsion to accuse and the power to drive the other to become more of what we condemn.

We are called in a marriage relationship to complement one another, not to change one another, though change will naturally occur as a result of sharing strengths and weaknesses. God did not create us to be compatible; rather, we are opposite and conflicting. Some sameness of interests, goals, likes, and dislikes may help, but we will find that our natures are as opposed as plus and minus; most often we are sure we are the plus and our mate the minus. But we need that differentness. In the first place, life without it would be boring. Someone has said that if two people always agree, one is unnecessary! More to God's purposes, He uses that conflict to force us to see ourselves, face our sin, and die with Jesus on the cross to what we are, that His new oneness of flesh may be formed.

St. Paul wrote that through fear of death we are kept in lifelong bondage (Heb. 2:15 RSV). The death we fear most of all is not the physical, but fear to die to what we are. When we fear death and thus refuse to change, we fear the other's differentness that calls for it. Thus we encastle and defend our own ways to the exacerbation and death of our marriage. Truly he that would keep his life will lose it (Matt. 16:25).

The answer, however, is not for either to jump off the teeter board, either by copping out from oneself by becoming all that the other thinks he wants, or by divorce. It is only the Lord who can break down dividing walls of hostility and so make peace (Eph. 2:14). It is only as He gives sufficient grace (namely love) to cast out our fears (1 John 4:18) that we gain the freedom to laugh at what once threatened us, and enjoy the jagged edges of the other without need to polish or correct.

In what specific ways do we push one another to counterbalance what we are? John and I share from our own lives, inviting the reader to identify both with our sin and with the unmerited grace of the Lord which enabled freedom and transformation that we might strengthen one another.

John's nature was to be impulsive and adventuresome to the point of being courageously foolhardy. Every dare instantly became a challenge, every warning an invitation to overcome. My nature (Paula's) was to be more cautious, practically weighing and considering before choosing, and then carefully proceeding. The intensity of John's nature caused me to dig in my heels till the path of our lives could be traced by big black skid marks. At the same time, my caution caused him to press forward all the more. We lived that tension, each unwilling to let go for fear of ceasing to be our own person, risked in a position not of our choosing. When the Holy Spirit called my cautious stance "fear and untrust," and revealed that John's rushing forward came from overcompensation for the same root, and we individually repented, the Lord established for us a healthy, easy balance. I am now free to be spontaneous and to venture, whether it be in a car on a mountain road or in the freshness of some new spiritual revelation. And John can hear a word of caution without having to surge ahead to prove independence and capability. In the grace of Jesus Christ our differentness has become a mutual support as we offer what we are to one another through Him.

John's logicality naturally dictated to him that the only way to paint a wall was to begin at the upper left hand corner and proceed methodically left to right until the entire area was covered, finishing at the lower right. But I am an artist and to me that has always seemed a boring procedure. I prefer to paint here and there in what John calls interesting but impractical "swigglies"—and then fill the spaces in between. That difference, which symbolizes the variance in our approach to much of life, stood as a bone of contention between us for a long time. I judged him to be stodgy; he judged me to be disorganized, and we drove each other to the extreme—until we learned to accept one another in Jesus. Now He enables the two of us to contribute who and what we are, and He does the blending. John outlines the edges and the corners; I paint the middle, and the war is over. We share many activities—yard and garden work, redecorating, traveling, speaking, writing, whatever there is to do. Mutual judgment and criticism having been confessed to the Lord and forgiven, I can now accept with appreciation John's more structured way, and he is able to enjoy himself more in mine. More than that: we find emerging between us a new way which surpasses anything either of us previously defended as "the" way.

John was so absent-minded that as a child if he were sent

upstairs to get something, he would not only forget what he was to find, he would forget he had been sent! That quality combined later with an ability to concentrate deeply with impenetrable, imperturbable single-mindedness. This was developed as a necessary virtue during seminary days when most of his studying was done as he waited for cab fares in taxi stands all over Chicago, or tried to read in the midst of the noise of crowded apartment living. My training had always been to be aware of people around me, to be conscious of and responsive to their needs. As a child it had been too easy for me to become lost in a book or some self-interest, and I had accepted as a part of growing up a sense of responsibility not to indulge in that fault. When John and I began early to produce children, we found that these qualities, while virtues in appropriate situations, were often enemies of family peace and harmony. I was easily aware of what the children were doing, and because I had been the oldest of five, could discipline our children instantly. But I believed that John as head of our home should also discipline. I resented his not being alert to the activities and needs of our offspring, and his seeming to be content with letting me take charge. Unconsciously I began to overdiscipline to fill the vacuum. John retaliated consciously by criticizing the way I "drove" the children. Mercifully, the Lord broke through what would have been a vicious circle (and a whirlpool for the children) and enabled me to see that my judgment of John for not taking hold and my quickness to control were tremendous blocks to the Lord's calling him into account. I repented for my sin, John for his, and the Holy Spirit was quick to release him to grow into the freedom to discipline in strength and love without my prompting. Until then we had entrenched each other.

"Let not the sun go down upon your wrath" (Eph. 4:26b) was for many years my scriptural apology for pushing John to settle all arguments or misunderstandings yesterday if not before. I *had* to settle everything immediately. John's inclination was always to mull privately for a while and then discuss matters when he had worked them through on the inside. The more urgently I would insist that we get things out in the open, the more he would retreat. "John Sandford, come out and fight with me!" (Silence followed.) "You must like it there in that cave!" (an imaginary clanging of a very real, invisible steel door within him). And my indignant self-righteousness would stand outside the door of his, both of us wishing we could erase the whole episode and begin again. And then the Holy Spirit revealed himself in the person of Jesus Christ standing at the doors of our inner beings knocking politely, courteously entering, sensitively identifying with us where we are, patiently inviting us until we choose freely to trust and walk out of our self-centeredness with Him. And I knew that to be the only way to meet another person without violating him or insisting on my own way. I could reread the Scripture and know that it is my wrathful response which is called to instant account, not the settling of all things. I am rather called to support persons caught in unsettled affairs and people unwilling or unable at that moment to face or discuss a thing. My inclination to hurry to talk things through is still there, as is John's to withdraw. But as we have learned to trust the Lord to do the convicting, the calling to account, the establishing of meeting time and ground, and the interpreting between us, the urgency to attack, to defend and to retreat is gone. Our differentness has ceased to be our disunity. It has been transformed into that which protects the other. I now appreciate that John will not be stampeded into premature conclusions. He treasures that I will love him enough to venture into his hiding places to draw him out with patience. And it is a blessing to find less and less occasion for this new trust to be tested.

We were like many couples who measure well-being by the behavior responses of the mate. By doing that we subject ourselves to periods of unnecessary anxiety which can compound hurt to effect actual destruction of the love relationship. Only as we look to the Lord for primary security are we able to rest trusting while a mate exercises his yet immature or unhealed areas. We need to know that the Lord is in sturdy position on the teeter-totter, that he will preserve our life in balance as we grow together, and that the unresolved struggle of the moment need not threaten or consume us. The only real threat is in the perpetuation of that struggle by cherished resentment, angry accusation, vengeful tit for tat, or continual reinforcement of defensive walls to hide behind.

Perhaps one of the most frequent complaints we hear from wives is that their husbands are so completely occupied with work and sports and TV that they neglect their spiritual life. "How can I look to my husband as spiritual head of our household when I'm way ahead of him in spiritual matters?" Our answer to that is simply (1) There is no "ahead" or "behind" in the kingdom of God. God calls each person uniquely and individually to be where He wants Him to be. All measuring of ourselves over against our neighbor is fruitless. We play against our own individual par set by the Lord, not against each other. The only valid question is whether or not I am where God wants me to be at this moment. And only He knows the answer to that. We have no business measuring our mates by where we are; (2) If a wife is on a pedestal of thinking she knows more than her husband and living closer to God than he, she must abdicate that position if her husband is ever to come into his own full spirituality. Her super-spiritual stance will necessarily call for him to unconsciously or consciously counterbalance by being super-earthy or even worldly. A wife can never pray or drag her husband into vital relationship with the Lord. But she can win him without a word to that voluntary giving of himself by her "reverent and chaste behavior" (1 Pet. 3:1-5). Spelled out concretely, I believe that means letting him know by words and deeds that she loves him and honors him. It means a well-ordered home, a consistent and unqualified expression of affection and sympathy, especially when he doesn't deserve it. It calls for interest and participation in pursuits that bring relaxation and refreshment to him. It means forgiving and blessing, complimenting and rebuking in an attitude of respectful caring. It means activating him in his God-ordained position by relating to him in an attitude of celebrating his being already the spiritual head whether there is any evidence of his having any awareness of that fact or not. Many wives who have begun to ask their husbands the questions they used to ask their pastors have been astounded at the wisdom issuing suddenly from their spouses. And countless husbands have then scrambled to the Word and to mature counsel for wisdom to share.

If a wife makes a judgment upon her husband that he "just isn't the spiritual type at all," that is both untrue and tends to lock him into that stance. But if she believes the truth, that her husband was created with the breath of God in him, that he is already consecrated through her belief (1 Cor. 7:14), and that he may be better than she is, else God would have called him first (1 Cor. 1:26-31) (or the other way around), then her humility before God and her servant position to her family will free the hand of God to move upon her husband and children as He already desired. But she must wait patiently in faith, continuing to serve the family with love. And she must be earthy with them, lest that dynamic of counterbalancing force the husband to be too much earth to her spirit.

As we see diagramed on the next page, if a wife has the love of Jesus over her, and moves under her husband, that love has now come over him.

Marriage must be worked at. We train for years to play athletic games and study more years to become competent in a profession. But somehow we think that the most important factor in all our lives—our ability to live as families—will just

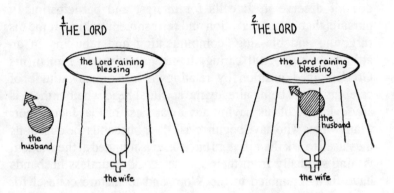

happen. It will not. Daily death of selfishness and resurrection into His gentle nature is a discipline which must be steadfastly endured or we shall reap hell rather than blessing. All too many families do not know there is a price to pay. On the teeter-totter of human life the cost is daily giving to the other's joy. Fifty-fifty is a balance for divorce. One hundred per cent given for the joy and well-being of the other is the only viable formula for the life of Jesus in our midst.

13

RESTORING THE BIBLICAL FUNCTIONS OF THE FAMILY

And I will make of thee a great nation, and I will bless thee,
and make thy name great; and thou shalt be a blessing:
And I will bless them that bless thee, and curse him that
curseth thee: and in thee shall all families of the earth be
blessed. (Gen. 12:2, 3)

When the materialistic mind-set convinced men that only the demonstrable is real, an erosion of biblical mentality resulted in the loss of many vital functions of the family. Biblical functions in a family depend upon awareness of the needs of spirit and soul. When these are no longer regarded as primal, all those practices in the family which were designed by God to nurture and shepherd the spirit and soul atrophy and die.

The family is not to build the soul; God does that. But He planned to build the soul through what happens in the family. Satan desires to destroy whatever would build the soul (John 10:10); therefore, he has set himself to destroy whatever God would establish for the soul's nurture and care (i.e. church, school, and home).

In previous chapters we have sought to restore proper understanding of what happens to personality and character in a Christian home, and to reveal what damages, and how the cross and resurrection heals. Now we would rediscover to parents what are those biblical functions specifically related to the nurture and care of children's spirits and souls.

Perhaps the most important gift a father has to bestow is his blessing. The blessing of a father directs the flow of God's munificence. God has so placed fathers that their prayers give Him access, or block His graces. The principles are simple. God has given us free will. He has given the care of our children into our hands. He will not interfere or invade; He is a gentleman. Therefore, the children's blessing waits upon our invitation. Without it, though God wants to help our children more than we do, He restrains His hand. Consequently a boy without his father's blessing wanders in a spiritually arid and fruitless land. A man more than twenty-one, born anew in Jesus, is not so vulnerable to his father, having come to his own relation with his Lord. Even so, though the negative effect of a father's curse can no longer so greatly prevent him, he cannot have the fulness which could be if his father's blessing rested upon him. A father's blessing opens the floodgates of heaven (Gen. 12:3). "That *in blessing* I will bless thee, and *in multiplying I will multiply* thy seed as the stars of heaven, and as the sand which is upon the sea shore; and thy seed shall possess the gate of his enemies; And *in* thy seed shall all the nations of the earth be blessed; because thou hast obeyed my voice" (Gen. 22:17, 18).

Jacob connived with his mother against Esau for their father's blessing and won.

> And he came near, and kissed him: and he smelled the smell of his raiment, and blessed him, and said, See, the smell of my son is as the smell of a field which the Lord hath blessed: Therefore God give thee of the dew of heaven, and the fatness of the earth, and plenty of corn and wine: Let people serve thee, and nations bow down to thee: be lord over thy brethren, and let thy mother's sons bow

down to thee: cursed be every one that curseth thee, and blessed be he that blesseth thee. (Gen. 27:27-29)

Observe that Isaac's blessing upon Jacob is not general banalities but cogent specifics. Jacob is to prosper as a farmer; people will serve him, including his brethren, and everyone he blesses will be blessed, and whom he curses will be cursed. Precisely those things are yet being fulfilled today. A father's pronouncement of blessing is God's spoken word through his son for that man's sons, and God's Word will not fail in the purpose whereunto it is sent. It will be accomplished (Isa. 55:11).

Jacob later cursed and blessed each of his twelve sons (Gen. 49). Each pronouncement was a judgment and a prophecy. Each was terribly specific and powerful unto destruction or discipline or mercy and blessing. And each has and will yet be fulfilled in every detail. God will not violate the free will of his sons, nor let His Word through them fall to the ground.

Esau, having failed to receive his blessing, cried out "with a great and exceeding bitter cry":

. . . Bless me, even me also, O my father. And he said, Thy brother came with subtilty and hath taken away thy blessing. And he said, Is not he rightly named Jacob? for he hath supplanted me these two times: he took away my birthright; and behold, now he hath taken away my blessing. And he said, Hast thou not reserved a blessing for me? And Isaac answered and said unto Esau, Behold, I have made him thy lord, and all his brethren have I given to him for servants; and with corn and wine have I sustained him: and what shall I do now unto thee, my son? And Esau said unto his father, Hast thou but one blessing, my father? bless me, even me also, O my father. And Esau lifted up his voice, and wept. And Isaac his father answered and said unto him, Behold, thy dwelling shall be the fatness of the earth, and of the dew of heaven from above; And by thy sword shalt thou live, and shalt serve thy brother; and it shall come to pass when thou shalt have the dominion, that thou shalt break his yoke from off thy neck. (Gen. 27:34b-40)

Again Isaac's blessing is both specific and prophetic. He prophesies that eventually Esau, later known as the father of the land of Edom, would be free of Israel's yoke, but as to the blessing erroneously given, what had been said, being God's word, could not be unsaid. What was done was done, and would happen as predicted by Isaac's blessing.

Those who are older can remember when none would think of marrying a girl without asking for her father's consent and blessing. More recently, some may remember *Fiddler on the Roof*, in which Tevye's three daughters came one by one for his permission and blessing. To the first he gave gladly both his permission and blessing. To the second he gave permission and added that they hadn't asked his blessing but he would give it anyway. The saddest scene in the movie occurred when Tevye could give neither his permission nor blessing. His youngest daughter, the apple of his eye, became then a no-daughter-at-all to him. How have we fallen so far from God's Word as to lose this greatest and most cogent of a father's tools?

I (John) was visiting in the home of a Christian psychiatrist when his daughters and son came at bedtime and knelt before him for his blessing. As he laid his hands on them and prayed, my spirit leapt for joy, and my eyes filled to overflowing. God was rediscovering to me the glory of His gift. Since then Paula or I pray blessings over our children before they leave for school. Our son Loren, having learned at home, laid his hands on his wife's abdomen each night to pray for their unborn child. Loren asked my blessing before marrying Beth. He often phoned long distance for prayers of blessing for the work in his church in Sacramento, and God prospered.

When we were writing the first chapters of this book, Paula and I felt as though in the writing itself we were slugging it out against the powers of darkness in intercession. The battle grew heavier and heavier. We kept asking God and receiving Nehemiah 4:10: ''. . . The strength of the bearers of burdens is decayed, and there is much rubbish; so that we are not able to build the wall.'' Then my father moved from Joplin, Missouri, to live with us, and in prayer with Rev. David Dengler and Professor Bill Johnson it was revealed that God had sent him to pray for us and for the writing. Immediately the anointing was full, the work was light, and we were refreshed. We were then writing the chapter, ''The Importance of a Father's Love''!

My father almost died several years ago and had an out-of-the body experience in which the Lord sent him back for three reasons, the second of which he then remembered was ''for the writing of books.'' He had thought he was to write. But it was because God wanted this book to be the result of a family, and knew we would need my father's blessing.

Parents should pray for guidance, and when sure of the leading of God, pronounce specific and prophetic blessing upon their children. There is no loss of power if parents want to consult with the children first, asking whether and what they want. Unity is the prerequisite of power (Ps. 133).

Throughout the Old Testament God speaks of the descent of trouble and sin from generation to generation (Exod. 20:5; 34:7; Lev. 26:39; Num. 14:18, 33; Deut. 5:9; Job 21:19; Isa. 14:21; Jer. 32:18; Lam. 5:7; and so on). But the Word also speaks of inheritance of blessing, both through Christ and through man. Of Christ: Rom. 8:17; Gal. 3:29; 4:7; Titus 3:7; Heb. 1:14; 6:17; etc. And through man: Gen. 12:1-3; 15:1-6; 17:1-8; 22:15-18; 26:24; 27:1-40; 49:1-28; Prov. 13:22; Ps. 103:17; Ezek. 37:25; etc. More is passed from generation to generation than we could ever fathom.

Blessing descends three ways by inheritance. First, through the genes we inherit both bodily health and propensities toward good character. Second, we receive a blessing by psychological emulation and formation. Third, by the law of sowing and reaping, for what a man sows that shall not only he reap, but his children's children will reap as well.

No one understands the mystery of the genes and the fulness of inheritance, despite our science. The Word is both specific and cryptic. "And *in* thee shall all families of the earth be blessed" (Gen. 12:3b). Note that little word, "in." More profoundly and mysteriously in Hebrews 7:9, "Levi also, who receiveth tithes, *payed tithes in Abraham.*" Abraham was the father of Isaac, who sired Jacob, who was the father of Levi. Yet St. Paul speaks of Abraham's actions as those of Levi and Levi's as those of Abraham! *In* Abraham? He speaks as though in some mysterious way Levi actually had something to do with or participated in his great grandfather Abraham's actions from within his loins! Can there be a mystery of integration and inheritance far beyond our mortal ken?

I speak of a mystery far beyond us all, but let me (John) suggest at least a line of thought by testimony. I was raised in Joplin, Missouri, and Kansas City, Kansas, in the midst of people of great racial prejudice and fear. It should have lodged in me. But from some mystery within me, I could not receive it. I take no credit for that. My heart is as perverse as anyone else's. It is simply unaccountable to me that black was always beautiful. And I could not explain to myself why I always felt, deep within, a strange and unaccountable gratitude for black people. It did not cover all that depth of feeling to know that my first words were said from behind the skirts of a black housekeeper whom they say I loved.

In seminary I drove a cab at night in Chicago. When I began, a great scare had just occurred, and all the white drivers were afraid in the black sections of town. By law they had to carry their passengers into these areas, so they rolled up their windows and locked their doors and shot through stop signs to get back to the white neighborhoods. The law of supply and demand meant that there was plentiful business in the black areas, so I drove there most of the time. I never refused a passenger. All around me my taxicab buddies were being held up. One was even left standing in nothing but his shorts way out "in the sticks" in sub-zero weather! Not only was I never held up, no one even gave me a rough time. Those black people were gracious and kind to me, and often visited and chatted. I enjoyed being with them. Sometimes in the midst of squalor they had an essence of dignity I could not fail to sense about them.

I puzzled often why I felt as I did and why I was treated so well. I seemed to have some sort of blessing or aura of protection about me. Then one day after my father came to live with us, he began to reminisce about his World War I experiences which he had never shared before. Upon arriving in France his company of marines was called out name by name and marched off to the front, all except dad. His name was not called. Somehow it had been omitted. There were no orders for him. The lieutenant responded, "Son, you'll just have to make out for yourself. Find somewhere to stay and someone to feed you and hang around till orders come," whereupon he marched off also and left him, an eighteen-year-old young man alone in a foreign country at war, with no money and no place to go. Two companies of stevedores were there to unload ships, one an Italian crew off the streets of New York, full of fights and knifings. And a black crew from the Southern farms. Dad went to the blacks, who took him in, treated him with great kindness, protected him, and fed him until much later his orders came. He used to sit and listen by the hour as they chanted in deep rhythmic voices as they swung crates and boxes from arm to arm.

As he spoke, I knew by the leaping of recognition in my spirit and the anointing of God, why I had had such love and gratitude for black people and one of the reasons why their singing always moved me so deeply. If Levi truly paid tithes in Abraham, is there a mystery of my father's experience being mine? Did I somehow know it in my spirit? Or is it merely some kind of "descendancy" of blessing by inheritance?

Then I began to recollect and my father added much I had not known before. It turns out that the Sandfords of my line were plantation owners in Kentucky; they owned slaves. They had been exceedingly kind to their slaves, and the slaves had loved them greatly. When one of my ancestors tried to set his slaves free and move to Missouri without them, they pleaded with him not to, and he relented and brought them somewhere north of Kansas City. Then he again tried to release his slaves to freedom.

On the other hand, it was a John A. Sandford of New York State, of our family, who owned and abused the Negro, Dred Scott, from which came the celebrated Dred Scott court case and Supreme Court decision—which greatly helped to precipitate the Civil War!

Can all this "descendancy" be mere coincidence? How much blessing and propensity do we inherit? I don't believe we need to know or understand the mystery of what actually descends in racial memories. But I believe God wants parents to become aware that what good they do and encounter descends as a specific gift and function of their parenthood to their children.

Again, I (John) was raised in a heavily Protestant, anti-Catholic atmosphere. Much prejudice, fear, accusation, and confusion was expressed all around me (not so much by our own family as by our friends and neighbors). Again, unaccountably it did not find a lodging place in my heart. I could take no credit; I tried to think as others did, but couldn't make it stick. I found myself drawn toward the Catholic church. In seminary I studied especially the Jesuits and St. Francis Xavier and found that such study touched unexplainably deep chords in my heart.

When the Holy Spirit came upon me, I soon found myself ministering much among Roman Catholics. Strangely, though I had never in my youth attended a Catholic Mass, I felt greatly at home in Catholic services. To my knowledge there were no Catholics in my family, yet I found myself being most happy and fulfilled in a Catholic charismatic Mass.

In 1968 my deacons' board decided I was becoming too tired, and they advised me to ask others to accompany me whenever I went somewhere to speak. (At that time Paula was busy being the mother of small children.) Camp Farthest Out invited me to speak in July at Tiffin, Ohio. I asked several friends in the Midwest. In the end, only Ami, our eldest daughter, and Barbara Shlemon (a Roman Catholic laywoman then of Chicago, later the author of *Healing Prayer*) could come with me. As we rode into town we sighted an interesting church. Being early, we decided to stop. As Ami, Barbara, and Hal Spence, son of the camp chairman, and I entered the church, the Holy Spirit fell on me with an anointing the like of which I never had experienced before. Ami looked at me and exclaimed, "Dad, what's happening to you?" The church was St. Mary's Roman Catholic Church, and the Holy Spirit began to make it known to us that He was calling us to intercede in repentance for the great historical division between Roman Catholics and Protestants!

During that week whenever we could grab a moment's time between speaking and counseling, we would pray for the healing of history, repenting for all the lynchings, burnings, recriminations, and battles throughout church history. One day we prayed for all those of either persuasion who married across the lines and then were excommunicated. That evening my mother reached me long distance—it was my birthday and she had hunted across the states to convey congratulations. I shared with her what had been happening. She said, "Oh, Jack, I never told you. You always knew my mother as a Methodist. But she grew up a very devout Catholic. All the Osage Indians of our family were strong Roman Catholics, converted by Jesuit missionaries. When your grandmother married your grandfather, they 'churched' her. In those days that meant they excommunicated her. That's why she became so ardent a Methodist."

Unbeknownst to me I had that day prayed for the healing of my own beloved grandmother! Was that only coincidence? What *do* we inherit? Could that have been why I felt at home in the Mass? Perhaps not? But it is certain to me that the blessing of love for the Roman Catholic church descended from my heritage.

All this testimony leads to one point. Many Christians have asked us, "What can we best do to help our grown children?" We say, "Purify your hearts. There is nothing that can happen to you that does not bless or afflict your children." Note that when Achan stole the devoted things, the Israelites stoned not only him but all his family and cattle and burned all he had (Josh. 7). Again and again the proscription is given in the Old Testament to destroy a man *and his sons* lest pollution descend in Israel (2 Sam. 12:14; 1 Kings 14:12). Today we have the cross to deal with that pollution. But until the sin in a family is brought to the cross, whatever happens to a parent either purifies or muddies the flow of God's waters to our children. It is as though we stand in a river, our children being downstream. Whatever cleanness is ours sweetens their waters. Somehow both before their birth and after, *"in"* us they are blessed. Would that every parent, whether or not he can understand all this, could grasp by faith that great blessings descend upon our children the closer we approach to God! "A good man leaveth an inheritance to his children's children" (Prov. 13:22a).

The biblical function we would restore by resurrecting our sense of inheritance is none other than holiness. Holiness is a thing in itself, "Having therefore these promises, dearly beloved, let us cleanse ourselves from all filthiness of the flesh and spirit, perfecting holiness in the fear of God" (2 Cor. 7:1). But notice that here it is connected with the two last verses of 2 Corinthians 6, that of becoming sons and daughters. And in Hebrews 12 in the context of God's chastening and of our seeing to it that no root of bitterness spring up and "thereby many be defiled" (v. 15a). Our personal holiness thereby becomes a function of our providing blessing to our children, most especially that we not defile the waters in which our children and children's children will swim to eternity. Thus our personal holiness is directly a function of our children's nurture and care.

There is no such thing as a private, individual, secret, or hidden sin. Nor any blessing or consecration which is ineffective or wasted. No good deed, however secretly done, is ever lost. Our children inherit by immutable law. We pray that mankind may recover this corporate sense of belonging in the family of mankind.

We have spoken already to restore discipline (chapter 5), and to restore authority (chapter 7). We only add that every parent needs to see that his discipline and authority are functions of nurture to the spirits and souls of his children. Such are not merely physical responsibilities. Nothing can happen through our body which is not an expression of our spirit. God's Word becomes flesh in a spanking, a command, a rebuke, a chastisement, a discussion, or even an argument. We cannot escape incarnation. We bring forth God to our children at all times. Therefore St. Paul commands, "Children, obey your parents *in the Lord*; for this is right. Honor thy father and mother; (which is the first commandment with a promise;) That it may be well with thee, and thou mayest live long on the earth.

231

And ye fathers, provoke not your children to wrath: but bring them up in the nurture and admonition *of the Lord*'' (Eph. 6:1-4). Mark those words, ''*in* the Lord'' and ''*of* the Lord.'' Obedience needs to be ''*in*'' the Lord. Authority, discipline, and nurture need to be ''*of*'' the Lord. Neither can happen by our Lord in us unless both children and parents are daily given to the discipline of living by His Spirit in the way He would act. Only so do we incarnate the life of Jesus in our midst. Giving vent to selfish screams and demands and self-righteous angers is not in or of the Lord and gives Him no glory. Parents must take the lead. Somehow we think to be careful to express courtesy to outsiders, but anyone in the family is often fair game for whatever undisciplined emotion arises. Courtesy must begin at home. We need to be more gentle and sensitive within the home than anywhere else, not the other way around. And we need to see that such gentleness in Christ is a specific function of Christian nurture of the souls and spirits in our care.

We have also written concerning sex (chapter 7). We add that husbands and wives need to see their sexual life as a function of the care of the souls and the spirits of each other and their children. We have discovered through counseling that most parents have almost no awareness of their relation to each other as a function of their care for their children's souls and spirits. By blessing of inheritance and by example our children's spirits learn to flow through and express to others, especially later to their own mates, by what we are and do. Can it be accident or something I could take credit for that I have never raised a hand against Paula, and only once in all our married life raised my voice to her? Can it be coincidence that I never utter a word in disrespect of Paula nor ever curse at her or call her names? Or she me? Could we take credit for that when both our fathers are gentle, kind men who carefully treated their wives with great respect? Their lives were nurture to our souls and spirits.

Both of us watched our parents express warmth and affection, banter and tease. Both of us watched as unintended slights did not call forth inflamed responses. Both of us continually watched good-bye and hello hugs and kisses. Neither of us as children ever saw an open, uncontrolled argument between our parents. Both of us saw love expressed as affection continually in the home in our parents' relation to one another.

Does the above make real what we say about personal holiness as a function of nurture to children? Holiness is not uptight rigidity according to law. Holiness is the life of love lived momentarily day in and day out in a family. Religiosity can never pass for holiness; that only is holy which is personal love, personally expressed in a home.

Sexual intercourse is of course something private, and should be kept so by the parents. Infant children ought not to be in the same room with parents in intercourse for the same reason as we have shown, that children's spirits are well aware before the mind is formed. Sex is holy and beautiful, but precisely because it is, and is distinctly a private wonder, just so children need not to be exposed to sights and sounds before the guardianship of understanding can handle it. Privateness, and a proper sense of modesty, are thus also functions of care and nurture of children's souls and spirits.

Noah's two sons, Shem and Japheth, carefully backed up and covered him when he was drunk and exposed, whereas Canaan was cursed because he disrespected his father's nakedness (Gen. 9:20-27). Parents need to be careful about nudity or overexposure around the house. Not that there are taboos and fears but that there is a holiness of person that needs to be respected.

Although sexual intercourse is private and hidden, inheritance of blessing applies as firmly to it as to all else. Parents need to know that their care, delicacy, respect, and cherishing of each other in sexual intercourse also provides a blessing of inheritance to their descendants. So many times we have discovered in counseling that daughters of frigid mothers tend also to be frigid, and that warmly free and sexually expressive mothers most often produce daughters like unto themselves, that we are tempted to proclaim it as a maxim. Fathers who are failures or successes as lovers almost always produce sons like themselves. Other factors may intervene, but if nothing does interfere, inheritance will run true. Prayer can improve things, but how much better if parents add to their own healthy desires the knowledge that the more improved their own sexual life, the more of blessing descends, and the less has to be overcome and replaced by Jesus.

Since all that we are descends to our children, every skill and talent is also a nurture of our children's souls and spirits—the way we love to work or malinger, our neighborliness or lack of it, our generosity or stinginess, our diligence with chores or sloppiness, our timeliness or tardiness, and so forth.

After we receive Jesus as Savior, it takes many years before His lordship transforms pattern after pattern in our life "line upon line, line upon line, here a little, and there a little" (Isa. 28:10b). Let us remember that wherever we yet fail to express His nature, His grace abounds. And realizing He gave us our children, knowing how messed up we are, let us plod on to know Him, and knowing Him, to love Him more fully, that His life in us may affect our children more fully. Our prayer life is our first and most powerful blessing which descends to our children!

14

SURVIVING PARENTS, DIVORCEES AND SINGLES

Learn to do well; seek judgment, relieve the oppressed, judge the fatherless, plead for the widow. (Isa. 1:17)

Pure religion and undefiled before God and the Father is this, To visit the fatherless and widows in their affliction, and to keep himself unspotted from the world. (James 1:27)

Today, when divorces are shattering more and more homes, the church needs more than at any other time to rediscover its ministry to singles, divorcees, and surviving parents. That ministry was always clearly spelled out in God's Word. Unfortunately today when the church needs it most, we have been tardy in reactivating what has been laid out for us to do.

Singles in biblical times lived with parents, or made their own way as the prodigal son did (Luke 15). Divorcees returned home to the care of their parents whenever possible. But care for widows and the fatherless was most explicitly developed within the Word.

First was the protection of God's law. "Ye shall not afflict any widow, or fatherless child" (Exod. 22:22). "Thou shalt not pervert the judgment of the stranger, nor of the fatherless; nor take a widow's raiment to pledge" (Deut. 24:17). "Remove not the old landmark; and enter not into the fields of the fatherless'' (Prov. 23:10). Prophets thundered when men forgot or failed to protect the widow and the fatherless (Isa. 1:17; Jer. 22:3; Isa. 58:6-10, etc.).

Secondly, the Lord made specific practical provisions. ''And the Levite (because he hath no part nor inheritance with thee,) and the stranger, and the fatherless, and the widow, which are within thy gates, shall come, and shall eat and be satisfied; that the Lord thy God may bless thee in all the work of thine hand which thou doest'' (Deut. 14:29). ''When thou hast made an end of tithing all the tithes of thine increase the third year, which is the year of tithing, and hast given it unto the Levite, the stranger, the fatherless, and the widow, that they may eat within thy gates, and be filled . . . according to all thy commandments which thou hast commanded me . . .'' (Deut. 26:12, 13). It was for this reason that the Lord demanded, ''Bring ye *all* the tithes into the storehouse, *that there may be meat in mine house* . . .'' (Mal. 3:10a). Provision for widows and the fatherless was not from the king's treasury but from the Lord's house! Today regrettably the state has had to fill the vacuum, and so we are overburdened with cumbersome and wasteful social machinery as the state tries to do the job of God's people. Perhaps we cannot answer for the general body politic, but every church should take care of its own. If God's people were obedient, serving God rather than mammon, by tithing as commanded, there would be abundance of meat in God's house for the care of widows and the fatherless!

Thirdly, the Lord provided for the guidance, care, and counsel of widows. When a husband died, the law stated that his brother or next of kin must marry his widow.

If brethren dwell together, and one of them die, and have no child, the wife of the dead shall not marry without unto a stranger: her husband's brother shall go in unto her, and take her to him to wife, and perform the duty of an husband's brother unto her. And it shall be, that the firstborn which she beareth shall succeed in the name of his brother which is dead, that his name be not put out of Israel. And if the man like not to take his brother's wife, then let his brother's wife go up to the gate unto the elders, and say, My husband's brother refuseth to raise up unto his brother a name in Israel, he will not perform the duty of my husband's brother. Then the elders of his city shall call him, and speak unto him: and if he stand to it, and say, I like not to take her; Then shall his brother's wife come unto him in the presence of the elders, and loose his shoe from off his foot, and spit in his face, and shall answer and say, So shall it be done unto that man that will not build up his brother's house. And his name shall be called in Israel, The house of him that hath his shoe loosed. (Deut. 25:5-10)

It was for this reason that Ruth came to the threshing floor *by night* and Boaz ordered that no one make it known (Ruth 3:14). They did nothing immoral. Ruth had chosen Boaz, and Boaz desired her for his wife, but Elimelech, as the next of kin, had the first right and duty of marriage. If Elimelech had known they desired each other, he could have extorted money from Boaz rather than taking off his sandal to indicate rejection (Ruth 4:8), therefore, the secrecy.

When polygamy was stopped, it yet remained the responsibility of the next of kin to counsel and watch over the widow and her children. When a man who had no brothers or other close surviving relations died, the elders of the city would call for men of the city to candidate for the position of counselor.*

Such men acted as stewards over the house, with authority to advise, even to buy and sell for the widow. Some unscrupulous men desired such positions, in order to plunder widows' houses.

* From notes taken while studying under Bishop K.C. Pillai of India.

For this reason Jesus said, "Which devour widows' houses, and for a shew make long prayers: the same shall receive greater damnation" (Luke 20:47). Such men, appearing before the elders and knowing they would watch for several days before making the appointment, made sure to dress carefully, attend the synagogue regularly, and make long prayers so as to seem to be pious and holy men.

Today we need not reinstate the specific practices of the past, but we need to obey the intent. Every church should have elders, or deacons, whatever such men might be called, who are designated and recognized as dependable, mature and honest men for the counsel and care of widows, divorcees, and single women in the congregation. Such men should be not only available but take initiative to offer help regularly, once or twice a month. Few divorcees would take first steps to ask for such aid. Such counselors should receive training to offer aid in several areas.

One, widows and divorcees usually need advice and protection concerning financial matters. Women alone should be advised never to sell property or buy or make major financial decisions without the counsel of wise and unselfish businessmen. Insurance and investments especially should be subject to counsel. "In the multitude of counselors there is safety" (Prov. 11:14). One of the most frequent and grievous things Paula and I hear across the country is that it is often "Christian" men who take advantage of widows and divorcees and plunder their houses! Again and again, wherever we speak of this across the country, numbers of women come forward to confirm, "Yes, that's what happened to me." We are mortified, ashamed, grieved, and furious! If we, who only have mere human hearts are so angered, how shall the heart of God the Father not be deeply, grievously offended? Truly His judgment will be thorough! The church must repent sorely, and quickly, and arise to its task.

To our further shame, it is often secular and unbelieving bankers who act in proper righteousness to protect women. And sometimes lawyers and family doctors whether Christian or not. When will the church hear the cry God commanded us to hear?

Second, such elders need to be there simply as listeners. Such women need men solely to talk to, even more than they need what is advised. To avoid confusions and temptations, such counselors should either work in teams or, at best, with their wives. These counselors need training in the rudiments of counseling at least. Pastors and elders especially need to comprehend the difference between grief and sorrow.

Grief is a specific and temporary wounding of the heart and mind and spirit due to loss and concern for the other. Grief is soon healed by faith. Sorrow is what rises from a more lasting wounding of the inner being due to loss. The recurrent emergence of sorrow is not a mark of lack of faith. It is rather a sign of healthy, normal attachment and emotions. Many immature counselors have insensitively berated women who continue to suffer occasional healthy sorrow, or failed to discern and be firm to stop inappropriate grief and pity parties. Recurrent sorrow arises from a very real ripping and tearing of the inner psyche. When a mate dies, it is as though half the being is suddenly torn away and the other half hangs out raw and touchy For months and even years thereafter there may be continual upbursts of hurt and tears, quite normally and healthily.

Counselors should explain to widows that they may suffer recurrent sorrow and perhaps even experience some deep depression for perhaps as long as two years. Unless the bereaved know this, and understand how sorrow arises from that very real ripping of the inner psyche, they struggle with fears concerning their faith. They feel that something must be the matter with them that they "don't seem to be able to get over it." They need to understand it is the little things which will catch at their hearts and reopen the well of tears—finding his old work shoes tucked under the stairs, bringing in the newspaper only to realize there is no longer anyone to give it to, or something that triggers into a fond memory like a favorite song. Christmas and other holiday times are the worst, for they are suddenly empty.

Such tears, if simply lived through, are a blessing. They say the heart is normal and healthy. Absence of tears, often ascribed to the effect of faith, may in fact be quite unhealthy, a suppression of real feeling. As persons in hospital beds need nurses who are attentive but detached, who do not moan or weep with them, so widows need those who can hear and understand but who do not encourage the widow to be weak. Normal sorrow can easily become something to "trade on" or turn into a pity stance. Simply being there, momentarily empathizing, and then turning the mind and heart into something alive and different to do is enough.

Divorce is a far greater wounding than death. Divorcees may have the same recurrent sorrows plus all the woundings of rejection. Divorcees often feel ugly and unwanted, undesirable, and they feel they are a burden to others. Particularly wounding both to widows and divorcees is to feel like a fifth wheel among erstwhile comfortable couples' groups. This is especially so when the woman senses that each wife now instantly has a protective air about her husband when she is present. This is more acute and aggravating to divorcees because women often feel that a widow, especially one who has had a good man, may not yet, because of love and sorrow, want to replace him, whereas they expect a divorcee to be a huntress for a good man to heal a bad experience.

Singles' groups in church may not be the best answer. Usually these devolve to a group of women who still lack male companionship. In such groups, women tend to entrench hurts rather than get over them. Rather, we believe that women who are alone for whatever reason should be brought into Christian

240

church support groups where there may be couples, other single people of both sexes, and a variety of interests and problems. Self-centeredness and lack of outreach into other lives are deadly traps for persons living alone. Singles' groups do not offer a necessary range of interests and activities, and tend to become marked as mate-hunting clubs—which creates a false atmosphere for relaxed getting to know one another before thinking in terms of finding a mate. At least, if a single person is in a singles' group, he should find a better range of interests and deeper security by belonging at the same time to a support group in a church.

Thirdly, counselors need to be available for women alone raising children. Trying to be both father and mother is terribly wearing. If an uncle or grandfather can step in to be a surrogate father, at least advising concerning discipline, well and good. Otherwise the church should provide a man and wife team, available on a regular basis, so that the single parent is kept from feeling like an unwelcome chore. She should know that that time belongs as a gift of God to her as her time with friends who are "closer than a brother," for her family problems to be aired. "Should I let Bobby go out for football? If I do, how about accident insurance?" "Last night Ben got into trouble with the law. How do I handle it?" "Mary wants to date this fellow; I just can't see her with him at all. What do I tell her?" "Should I let Margaret take piano lessons? I don't know if we can afford it."

Fourth, such counselors should have access to adequately supplied funds from church tithes, to assist in cases of hardship. We believe it is wrong to let our beleaguered families find their aid from the state's treasury when the Word of God is explicit that it is for this very reason that God has commanded His people to tithe. A committee or board can handle such a fund and mete out its resources according to their judgment. Last week, a young husband suddenly died of a cerebral hemorrhage. The church instantly informed his widow that they would see to it that she lacked for nothing. Probate time is a difficult time for widows.

Fifth, such elders should be given opportunity by the single parent to give words of warning or blessing concerning possible remarriage. A scoundrel recently played up to a wealthy widow we know. Her friends saw and tried to advise. I (John) came and saw, and perceiving she could not hear their advice, could only caution her to go slowly, give no money and wait for time to reveal the truth. Last week she called me to report that though he had said all the right Christian words of faith, he had managed to cause her to give him $11,000—whereupon he took off for parts unknown! Here the problem was not the lack of advisors. She wanted so much the touch of a man that she was unwilling to hear good counsel.

Counselors must avoid control and dominance. Widows and divorcees need to learn to stand on their own feet. Some would be all too willing to cop out from all responsibility by putting too much on the counselor's shoulders. Some won't lean enough. The task of counselors is to do themselves out of a job. Their aim should be to stand beside the lone woman avoiding doing so much that she fails to mature, while doing enough to protect and guide so she grows into unfamiliar areas safely and maturely. Among the many blessings God would bring out of the fires of suffering is maturity. Counselors must be careful not to comfort so much that growth is prevented.

No one who has not lost a mate can know the depth of loneliness of those who have. The never-married know an aloneness, but never having been married, they cannot know the poignant power of lonesomeness for the one who had been joined to another. Sometimes among older couples, for whom life has been full, the pain is lessened for the sense of nearness to eternity and reunion. Sometimes newlyweds have not had time to cement the bond. It is those from thirty to fifty, especially those who have children to raise alone, who need our most diligent care.

Finally, we have spoken mainly of women, but men are often as needy. Women need support, companionship, and practical guidance, whereas men can usually handle the practicalities; but in the heart, men are often far more devastated than women. Worse yet, normally, men have not been as able, because of their cultural training, to be in touch with their real feelings. Therefore, they handle the world of feelings far more inadequately than women. Men need support groups where both men and women can have the opportunity to make men see what they really feel.

Widowers and divorced men seem to be far more vulnerable to "sirens" than women are to gigolos. Such men need to commit themselves to being with a support group at least once a week; the women in the group can help him spot a vamp and warn him accordingly. Men need homes which are open to them for meals and quiet evenings of visiting. A man alone often gravitates to taverns for company, and finds there only those women who know a kind of life that is not what he and his children need.

We believe that counselors should avoid the temptation to become matchmakers. Having under counsel many lovely young women and strong young men, Paula and I have often been tempted to get some of them together. The few times we have succumbed when it seemed so obviously right, the results were disastrous! Now we see that counselors should help lonely people face the fact that what is in their hearts attracts trouble to them, and then let God bring His choice to them by His "coincidences." We have found that if the counselee lets God and His servants truly set the heart right, it is usually not long before He somehow brings the one who turns out to be just right for the counselee.

One word of comfort to the already divorced who fear remarriage because of the teaching on adultery. "Whosoever putteth away his wife, and marrieth another, committeth adultery: and whosoever marrieth her that is put away from her husband committeth adultery'' (Luke 16:18). We would not lessen any law of God; our Lord straightly warns against that (Matt. 5:19). We always work to save marriages. But let us not be caught in legalisms, which exalt the law above our Lord's mercy. Of course our Lord does not want us to divorce or be divorced. And of course our Lord is grieved by our rising divorce rates. But let us remember that when the legalistic Pharisees exalted the law of the Sabbath above His mercy, our Lord again and again healed on the Sabbath and told a man to rise and carry his pallet, knowing the Pharisees would accost Him for healing and the man for carrying his bed on the Sabbath day (John 5:1-16). By many such actions, Jesus was saying that God is eminently merciful and practical, and that it does not sanctify His loving nature before men when we insist on obedience to the letter rather than mercy and new life in Him. We have known some couples who have been so crucified by the legalistic within the body of Christ that it would *seem* more practical to murder a mate and be forgiven and then remarry, than to divorce, and not ever marry again or remarry and be condemned forever by immature Christians.

Paula and I cannot answer the dilemma of divorce. Would that it would never happen anywhere. But when men stumble and fall, can we not choose mercy rather than the letter? We plead with the church for a humble heart, that we not lay on the broken-hearted even heavier burdens, and that we at least examine each case for the fresh present will of our merciful and gentle Lord.

A word to families concerning unmarried older offspring who remain in or keep returning to the home. Most often it is not wise for their sake to allow that. Some young adults feel duty bound to ''take care of the folks.'' Whenever parents perceive that their very real needs have become excuses for their progeny to cop out from finding and living their own lives, they should make every effort in Christ to find some other way to be helped, and set their children free to go on to their own destiny.

Some young adults seem unable to get over homesickness, and keep returning, like a satellite that can't quite escape the gravity of home base. A simple truth to remember is that if as a child, one receives enough affection, affirmation, training, and discipline, he can leave home as an adult easily. If an adult child continues to return, saying, "I just love you folks so much, I can't bear to leave," the truth is the opposite. That child has not received enough (whether or not it was offered) and does not truly love or feel loved. Real love sets free. What passes for love—domineering concern, criticizing and controlling—clips a child's wings so he cannot fly as an adult. If a parent discovers his failure in this, he should pray that God would fill his son's or daughter's heart with love that will strengthen with might in the inner man. And then he should sit down and talk with that one candidly, kindly, lovingly, confessing these faults and asking forgiveness. He should then clearly express his unqualified and steadfast love for that grown child, and give assurance of his belief in the child's abilities to take hold of life and achieve as the Lord continues to nurture him and open doors of opportunity. That being done, he should insist that the child leave home and find his own way! That is the kindest thing a parent can do—it is not kind to allow a child to lock himself or herself away from life in the security of the home. I (John) can see in the eyes and facial expressions of young adults, when they begin to register that "kept" look. Seeing it in the eyes of a twenty-four-year-old man, I warned his parents and told them not to allow him to stay. They couldn't bring themselves to be that "cruel." Now, four years later, the more cruel fact is that they have a confirmed bachelor on their hands who most likely will never seek his own life and his own wife. The security of the home can become a psychological trap, subtly curbing healthy desire for independence and marriage until the urge dies altogether.

Home should always be there, a sense of security for adults so long as parents live. But wise parents will watch to see that that base never disrupts a marriage or prevents a fledgling from using his wings. Wise is the eagle mother who tears up her nest when the eaglet fails to fly.

15

A PLACE FOR FANTASY

Take heed that ye despise not one of these little ones; for I say unto you, That in heaven their angels do always behold the face of my Father which is in heaven. (Matt. 18:10)

Out of the mouth of babes and sucklings hast thou ordained strength because of thine enemies, that thou mightest still the enemy and the avenger. (Ps. 8:2)

Our birth is but a sleep and a forgetting: The Soul that rises
with us, our life's Star,
  Hath had elsewhere its setting,
    And cometh from afar:
Not in entire forgetfulness,
And not in utter nakedness,
But trailing clouds of glory do we come
  From God, who is our home:
Heaven lies about us in our infancy!
Shades of the prison-house begin to close
  Upon the growing boy,
But he beholds the light, and whence it flows,
  He sees it in his joy;
The youth, who daily farther from the east

Must travel, still is Nature's priest,
And by the vision splendid
Is on his way attended;
At length the man perceives it die away,
And fade into the light of common day. (William
Wordsworth, "Ode on Intimations of Immortality")

A child's spirit often soars free of "the prison house" and
uses his imagination to portray wonders far beyond our adult
minds.

Parents of a seven year old, driving in six lanes of freeway
traffic, suddenly had to swerve, causing the rear door to fly
open. Their child flipped out and rolled head over heels across
four onrushing lanes! Miraculously, every car stopped
instantly, and the child was unhurt even by the hard pavement.
When the parents managed to stop and rushed back, they found
the child exclaiming, "Daddy, mommy, did you see them? Did
you see them?"

"See what, honey?"

"Did you see the angels? Did you see them stop the cars and
catch me so I wouldn't be hurt?"

Was it "only" imagination? Or did the child, more free yet in
his spirit, in fact see the angels of God? "He shall give his
angels charge over thee, to keep thee in all thy ways. They shall
bear thee up in their hands, lest thou dash thy foot against a
stone" (Ps. 91:11, 12).

We maintain that it is from the active spirit of a child that his
imagination arises. He needs to find some way to express what
his spirit senses or knows. Consequently our counsel to
Christian parents is, "Do not suppress the imagination of your
child." So often we hear of parents who have called out, "Go
back to sleep. It's only your imagination," as though
imagination were something unreal, unimportant and childish.
Parents thereby teach their children not to trust their primal

apprehensions of life, to turn from and disrespect intuitive and imaginative faculties.

If a child cries out, "Mommy, there's a man in my room," mommy needs to listen. A father or mother can usually tell by a few minutes of quiet talking with a child whether the imagination has been kindled by TV, a book, stories between playmates, or whether in actual fact something is going on in the child's room. Samuel ran three times in the night to Eli before Eli knew something real was happening. Then Eli carefully and rationally instructed Samuel how to answer (1 Sam. 3:1-10). Eli neither scoffed nor spoke so crossly as to cause fear in Samuel to prevent the Lord's approach. Parents ought neither to give license to wild flights of imagination nor to call out roughly, "Go back to sleep, silly, it's only your imagination!" Our children's imaginations are a most precious commodity to shepherd, certainly not to be scoffed at. A child may sense or see something we adults are not aware of because we are too imprisoned in the flesh.

When our family moved to Wallace, Idaho, our children would not play in our upstairs back bedroom. They kept saying, "There's a man up there." Loren, sleeping there, would sometimes have nightmares and cry out in the night. I (John) would run up to pray for him and Loren would say that someone was choking him and he couldn't breathe. Finally, Paula and I decided there could be something beyond mere imagination at work. When we went into prayer, the Lord showed us a picture of a large, heavy-set man with a mustache and bald head whom we knew by the gift of the Spirit to be a cruel man who had used that bedroom. We prayed, "seeing" the angels of God carrying that man away. The next morning we asked some of our parishioners and discovered that the parsonage had in fact been occupied at one time by just such a cruel man who looked very much as we described him, and who had died in that room. Whether that man's ghost had been there, or a familiar spirit of him, we do not know. What is important is that our children's imaginations, informed by their more sensitive spirits, had been right all along. Loren never again had trouble sleeping there, and the children could play freely in that bedroom after that.

Perhaps it should be taught that Paula and I did not act immediately after our first suspicious experiences with the evil presence in the room. We did not want to teach the children to honor wild imaginings. Rather, we talked about their experience with them, and let them know that sometimes we sense something real, and sometimes things are only fantasy. We said, "Let's wait and see," and told them by our unhurried manner that even if something was there, it was not something to be greatly feared. Only after Loren was bothered a number of times in the night did we do an exorcism, and then we did the exorcism quietly, apart from the children. We reported to them that we had prayed about it, and that God had settled the matter so that they should have no further worry.

If a child calls out, "Daddy, there's a cat in my room," we should respect that child's perception. Maybe something *is* there, interpreted by the child's imagination as a cat. We do not have to know exactly what is there or not there, nor do we need to be afraid or convey fear to a child. We can simply talk matter of factly, honoring our child's imagination as real. "What's he doing, honey? Is it a good cat or a bad one? Does it make you afraid?"

"I don't want him here, daddy."

"Well then, we'll just tell him to go away. Now in the name of Jesus Christ you just go away and leave my Billy alone. He wants to sleep. Thank you, Jesus. You are here with your angels to watch over Billy."

Our manner in such instances should be calm (no matter who excited or fearful we ourselves may feel). Children need to see that we are not upset or intimidated by whatever may or may not be real in the unseen. Someday, by practice, they will learn to discern for themselves what is real and what is only fantasy. We need by our deportment to allow a child's imagination to live, without giving it either overdue license or abuse or scoffing.

Not everything a child imagines has objective reality to it. Children often project their inner problems into fantasy dramas. Lonely children sometimes "people" their world with imaginary play children, or creatures such as Winnie the Pooh. Sometimes these grow to have their own names and personalities and even seem to control their creators. We need not fear such imaginative activity, and above all should not accuse the children of lying. It is usually quite healthy and often acts out at the conscious level ideals and noble aspirations which by such early practice may later become cemented in what the child has indeed become. How many eventual ministers and lawyers have in childhood saved how many countless thousands of infant Guineveres or Maid Marians?

Sometimes children punish dollies or tear up comic book faces to express unacceptable repressed angers at parents or teachers. Some parents overscold for that, or worry too much about it. Continual such activity may signal real inner trauma. Praise God for readable signals and available counselors. But occasional fantasy anger is merely a blessed steam vent until the soul learns the release of prayer.

We do not have to know what is actually transpiring behind our children's fantasies. God did not call us to be psychoanalysts, but parents. We need only talk *with* our children, and whether we truly understand or not, they will read our heart's desire to love and appreciate. Our stance and tone will tell them whether we treasure their imaginations as valuable assets. That support alone will help them to sort out what is real from what is illusory. On the other hand, if we regard fantasies as immature, or somehow reprehensible, or if we are threatened by those moments when our child does confuse imagination with reality, that lack of trust and fear is what we convey no

251

matter what we say, because we cannot trust our child to wade through to maturity. Normally, children given loving support will naturally grow out of the world of unreality. Attacked children may entrench, hide that "other reality," and so retreat into an unassailable private world.

Christian parents often express concern about the Santa Claus and Easter Bunny myths. We advocate that if the parents are believing, teaching, and living the life of Jesus in the family, the children can enjoy some of the fun of the myths surrounding Easter and Christmas without losing sight of the historical facts which began the celebrations.

We never told our children that a rabbit could lay eggs. They knew quite early from their own observations that chickens are responsible for those, and that bunnies can only beget bunnies. But once we had taught our children the exciting truth of Christ's death and resurrection, and explained to them as clearly as possible the abundant life made available to them by those events, we saw no harm in celebrating with Easter eggs. Eggs are obvious symbols of new life. New life comes in as many colors and designs as there are people on this earth. As God's children we are part of the creation of that color and design and also of the discovery of bright new life which we need to search for and be alert to find. In our family we experienced no distraction from the reality or reverence of Easter in the egg coloring project which involved the whole family, or in the after church hunt to find those eggs. We were careful to focus our attention first on the reason for the celebration so that it never became a thing in itself.

Christmas in our home has always centered about the historical birth of the Son of God and the joy of the fact of His living in us. Our little ones grew up in the delight of being a part of a birthday party for Jesus, all gifts being given in His name. We knew and taught we could love and give only because He first loved us. Christmas morning in the Sandford household begins with a rush of excitement to appreciate for a moment the wonder of all the array of gifts under the tree, then settles quickly into a quiet sharing of prayers of thanksgiving and partaking of family communion. Then the packages are opened slowly, one at a time, each one appreciating, thanking, loving and sharing with every other member of the family. Sentence prayers are offered around the dinner table. This is the substance of the celebration, the Spirit of Christ born anew in our family in the midst of the giving and sharing. Family participation in the music and candlelight worship services at church bring into sharp focus the meaning and priorities of Christmas. And around the fringes dance the myths—Santa Claus and all his entourage introduced to our children not in the attitude of awesome wonder the gospel stories create, but with a twinkle in the eye that in itself invites delightful fantasies to play with and gracefully leave behind with the passing of other childish things. To our children we said, "Because of the birth of Jesus we have Christmas. Because God gave Him to us we give to each other in His honor. St. Nicholas was a Christian saint who gave himself to honor Jesus. The St. Nicholas, or Santa Claus, you hear about goes about giving in that same spirit, to bless little children."

Hearing of Santa in this fashion, our children did not feel at all betrayed to find that mom and dad were really Santa, and the jolly old elf representation was only a fiction. They took delight in discovering the truth of the game we had been sharing, and slipped easily one by one into the role of playing Santa for the younger children. One of the funniest and fondest memories we have is of our teen-age son Loren running around outside our home in the dark ringing sleigh bells and shouting "Ho Ho Ho!" for the sake of the little brothers and sisters whom he loved. Now they do the same for our grandchildren.

Maturity results from practice in handling imagination. All babies of all species in nature play, imagining battles to fight and tusseling and wrestling with one another. Parents who treat imagination as something to be scoffed at, something to be grown out of quickly, destroy creativity and spontaneity, inhibit intuitive and sensitive faculties, and disparage initiative and social graces.

Imagination is so far from being valueless or impotent; its misuse was the very reason God destroyed mankind. "And God saw that the wickedness of man was great in the earth, and that every imagination of the thoughts of his heart was only evil continually" (Gen. 6:5; 8:21). St. Paul listed as a most important task of Christians, that of "casting down imaginations" (2 Cor. 10:5a). On the other hand every good invention springs from the soil of creativity through imagination. Every creative idea finds its wings in imagination. Imagination is listed as one of the five "wits" deemed precious by the ancients, and from which we still use the idiom, "keeping his wits about him." Imagination being one of the most valuable gifts God has given to mankind, and the higher the gift the more mankind can pervert it; therefore, the importance that Christian parents learn to shepherd their children's imaginations more than any other faculty.

One Saturday morning while Andrea, then three, was still asleep, a man came whose wife had been receiving counseling from us. Filled with hate and anger, he sat on the end of the couch and villified us for two hours. We had been trying to turn his wife's heart to accept him again, and he was so confused that he was threatening to sue us for alienation of her affections! He left before Andrea awakened. As I (John) carried her downstairs when she awoke, she pointed at the couch where he had been sitting, eyes widening with fright, and cried out, "That bad! That bad!" And she clung to my neck like someone drowning. That night something jumped on her in her sleep just as Loren came home. He heard, woke us up, and together we cast it off of Andrea and exorcised the house. What did her spirit sense and her imagination portray? What attacked her in the night? We have no idea whether a demon remained when the man left, or his own presence, or what. Whatever it was, Andrea could see it and we couldn't. Had we scoffed or scolded, Andrea's trust in her own perceptions could have been greatly wounded. We handled it matter of factly, even in casting whatever it was away from her, so as not to convey to her that unseen, harmful things are any more out of the ordinary or any less acceptable as reality than unseen love or hope. More than that, she knew by the experience that her parents would defend her and not put her down by ridicule.

One day a lady came to my office (John's) claiming she was inhabited by a demon. I didn't believe she actually was, but because she believed it, I said the words of exorcism. Had I really believed her, I would have prayed to cleanse my office afterwards. That night Ron, our son-in-law, and Jason, our grandson, were playing in the living room. Jason, then two, made a game of trotting down the hall toward my office and running back to jump on his daddy. Passing the office he suddenly stopped in fright, and came streaking back crying and screaming, "That bad! That bad!" Ron looked up, and by the gift of the Spirit, saw something standing in the door of my office. He exorcised the office, prayed for cleansing, and comforted Jason. How did Jason's imagination portray that demonic thing to him? Or did he in fact, without imagination, see what was there? Whichever, he could "see" naturally what the Holy Spirit had to open Ron's eyes to see. Had Ron ridiculed him, Jason would have been thrown into confusion between his own honest perceptions and what the adult world would have said was real. Again, Ron simply handled it as a fact of life to be dealt with, which also said by inference to Jason that his reactions were normal and acceptable. Moreover, this said to Jason that such things are not fearful to the adult world, or something adults are upset about, and that his father could be trusted with Jason's emotions.

Countless parents could tell many stories of children's awarenesses. Our materialistic culture has taught mankind generally not to value what cannot be verified in a test tube or fit within the nice, neat boxes of what we have learned to accept as reality. What a shame and loss that is. When Jesus said, "Suffer little children, and forbid them not, to come unto me: for of such is the kingdom of heaven" (Matt. 19:14), to what did "of such" refer? We take it to mean "of the natures of children" which possess blessed trust of parents and vivid imaginations. When He said, "Verily I say unto you, Except ye be converted, and become as little children, ye shall not enter into the kingdom of heaven" (Matt. 18:3), to what childlike qualities was He referring? Like unto a child's trust, love, imagination, simple, unadulterated belief in God? Whatever, parents need to treasure all such in their children.

Encouraging parents to treasure their children's imaginations does not mean they should give their child's imaginations *carte blanche*. Shepherding means to help them put on a bit and bridle, lest they run amok, while not undervaluing nor disparaging their imaginations.

Unfortunately, the church has been tardy in growing into a mature understanding of demons and other mystical realities. Therefore, many parents have far too little understanding concerning the stories we have shared here. We are writing both to novices in the faith and to the experienced. We do not feel we should fail to share for fear the immature might be frightened about these things. However, we cannot teach here fully concerning demons and exorcism. Suffice it to say that no Christian need fear the demonic world. Jesus Christ has once for all defeated and stripped the powers of darkness (Col. 2:15). He who is in us is greater than he who is in the world (1 John 4:4). The least Christian can defeat any demonic power simply by the word of faith—as we have sung so often in Martin Luther's mighty hymn, "A Mighty Fortress Is Our God": "And though this world, with devils filled, Should threaten to undo us, We will not fear, for God hath willed His truth to triumph through us. The prince of darkness grim, We tremble not for him; His rage we can endure, For lo, his doom is sure: One little word shall fell him."

Since the field is so little understood, and such things as newspaper stories of foolish attempts at exorcism, and the movie *The Exorcist,* have burlesqued exorcism into something weird and frightening, many not only have no knowledge, they want *not* to know! Since children are being more and more exposed every day to occult movies and TV series, as well as occult games at parties, parents can no longer claim to be responsible as parents if they remain ignorant of demons and how to protect their children.

Exorcism is done by simple faith and the word of command in Jesus' name. The demons all know that Jesus is Lord (Acts 19:15; Phil. 2:10). An exorcism does not have to be dramatic and emotional. It can be done in an atmosphere of dignity and reverence, quietly and rationally. If a parent feels ill-equipped and ill at ease, there are enough in the body of Christ who have the faith and knowledge required. In our case, being known as counselors, we are quite often called upon to exorcise. Consequently, we have had to learn how to protect our children and our home. That is our subject here, not how to exorcise, but how to shepherd our children's imaginations.

In the instances we have shared, in which something had to be cast away from Loren and Andrea, and a demon cast from my office in Jason's presence, the primary teaching of the children came through our own quiet, matter-of-fact faith.

Children's spirits, more than ours, already sense the reality of evil around them. How we handle that reality becomes the model for their lives. In each case of exorcism, Paula and I and Ron have remained calm, detached, and objective. There is never an aura of fear about us. The children see that a Christian handles such things as easily as a man swats a fly, because he battles an already defeated enemy.

We minister to the children's hurts and fears equally as calmly and easily. We hold them and love them and quietly tell them that, yes, there are bad old spirits that do want to hurt us but they can't do it becaus Jesus is our King and He protects us so that we don't ever need to be afraid. Since we rest in the perfect love of Jesus which casts out fear (1 John 4:18), they learn to take occasional scrapes with the demonic about as matter of factly as a bruised shin or a bumped toe in the dark. Today, Loren has grown up and is a minister who does exorcisms whenever the occasion arises. Ami is our receptionist for Elijah House, unafraid to greet wild-eyed people calmly and easily when they come for counsel. Mark is filled with the Spirit, and unafraid of the demonic. The younger children laugh and joke about some of the battles they have seen and heard.

Children who have learned to use their imaginations vividly, and from practice to distinguish what is good or bad, real and unreal, will have the stuff in them to become great prayer warriors for the Lord. It has been our experience that adults who say they never see visions in prayer have most often been raised by parents who prided themselves in being "down to earth," "realistic," "pragmatic," or "factual." There is nothing wrong with any or all of these if such parents also let spontaneity, imagination, and intuition live. But these parents thought it was their duty to scold their children if they fantasized about an imaginary partner or cried out in the night. They crippled their children's prayer life. But how wonderful that the Holy Spirit restores to His own the creative power of the imagination.

An engineer who has had many years' experience in many offices shared with us that he had observed that in every office there are two kinds of engineers, what he terms "the drones" versus "the live ones." Drones, he explained, never have a creative idea of their own. They copy and expand what others dream. He observed that the creative ones are usually the prayerful Christians who have kept a childlike quality of openness and imagination about them. What kind of parents could one suppose each had?

Paula and I both devoured children's books. My parents provided wondrous sets of graded reading materials—*Journeys Through Bookland, The New Wonder World, My Book House*, and all the children's classics—*Black Beauty, Little Men, Little Women, Moby Dick, King Arthur, Robin Hood, Tom Sawyer, Huckleberry Finn*, and so on. Created to be a prophet, inquisitively imaginative, intuitive and full of fantasy and day dreams, I consumed all such books like a "bookaholic" on a binge. From there I proceeded even in childhood to search out the *Odyssey* and *Iliad*, Greek and other ancient mythologies, and Indian and other folklore and legends, and loved every minute of it. I read *Robin Hood* thirty-one times and *King Arthur* thirteen. All such was good preparation to be a servant of the Lord.

Many zealous Christian parents tend to overcensor their children's reading. Let us see if we can establish two principles: First, the Scripture says, ". . . It is not the spiritual which is first but the physical, and then the spiritual" (1 Cor. 15:46 RSV). We take that not only to mean first life on earth and then heaven, but a principle that in God's order He would have us become first soundly earthy and physical, then spiritual. Therefore, we did not confine our children's reading materials to "spiritual" writings. Our advice to all parents is to let children enjoy the full range of good wholesome earth. Earthiness is not coterminous with worldliness. Jesus enjoyed the good earth. Earthiness is good. In J.R.R. Tolkien's trilogy, *The Lord of the Rings*, the Hobbits, a folk smaller than dwarfs, turn out to be more resilient, and tougher in moral fiber than heroic men, and more able to rejoice in trial than all others. Tolkien describes them as affectionate, lovers of good living, eating and partying and sharing gifts and stories at the slightest excuse. He makes it plain that their strength of heart came from their good life in the earth. We see that truth again and again in counseling. We would write it as a maxim: Only the fully, warmly human and earthy can be safely spiritual!

Being overly involved with spiritual life, Paula and I carefully avoided enlisting our children in too many spiritual things too soon. We gave them normal exposure to church and Bible and prayer, and then saw to it that they were free to experience the full range of life's good human experiences—sports, picnics, camping, play, work, swimming, movies, TV, etc. Though we avoided rank sex in movies, we purposefully took them to see some violence so that while they were in the home we could talk together about all of life so that they would not be oversheltered and, therefore, overcome when they left the nest. Imagination runs amok when the mind is prevented from knowing what is. We wanted our children to see life in all its richness—appropriate to their age levels.

The principle is that since children need to be freely, solidly earthy when growing up, squelching life by too much censoring shuts down the vitally important intuitive and imaginative faculties. Then imagination, prevented from portraying life as it is, not having sufficient matter to work with, concocts what is only illusion and false fantasizing. Imagination needs rich human matter to work with.

In incarnating His own Son, God did not find a grown man and invest him with Jesus' spirit. That is adoptionist heresy. He sent Jesus through a womb and childhood. We see the wisdom of God in Jesus' training in the warm earthy smells, sights, sounds, ideas, and touches of a carpenter shop. That was ideal grounding in solid human earthiness for the most spiritual of all men on earth. It can be historically documented that most of the great leaders and inventors of America have come from the farm and small towns in which rich experience fueled the imagination and built moral character.

The second principle was stated by Jesus in relation to the ritual washing of food, but it can be applied to all of life. "Not that which goeth into the mouth defileth a man; but that which cometh out of the mouth, this defileth a man" (Matt. 15:11). Christian parents have been incensed by much of what has been made available to our children on TV, and fearful lest the children become what they see. Statistical studies reveal clearly a close connection between violence seen and violence done. But many parents have overreacted in fear and rigid censorship which begs a counterbalancing word: Children who have been raised in an aura of affection and laughter, acceptance and freedom to enjoy the good earth, naturally throw off whatever evil is seen in drama. If the love of God has been expressed consistently as nurture to growing children, and the Word of God has been planted in their minds and hearts, they will have that discernment from within to recognize evil and the strength to choose to reject it.

Children who are raised in uptight, fearful, nonaffectionate homes have repressed angers and resentments. For them violent drama may trigger animosities and fuel the imagination to act out evil. But every Christian parent should hear—drama does not put evil in; it only gives opportunity for what is there to find recourse to action. *We* put evil in our children's hearts when we fail to express love, and when we behave in selfish, hurtful ways.

If a child is full of deep inner woundings and resentments, that storehouse of violence will be activated inevitably by exposure to the drama of life as evil exists in the adult world he grows into. For such a child, censoring of his reading and TV viewing will only postpone the explosion. The one cure is in the healing that will come by bringing him into relationship with Jesus and into the freeing experience of repentance and forgiveness in the family.

Pornography stirs more than imagination. It quickens sexual appetite in an inappropriate and unholy setting, hooks into unregenerate flesh, stirs passion for passion's sake, and sickens the spirit. Parents should not expose children to that at all. But where Christian nurture has been given, exposure to drama, occasionally even of violence, informs and thus prepares us to handle life by seeing it. "For wisdom is a defense, and money is a defense: but the excellency of knowledge is, that wisdom giveth life to them that hath it" (Eccles. 7:12). Evil portrayed can have a cathartic effect, so that drama, employing imagination, works like a steam valve to objectify and release the hidden tensions of anger and resentment we all have. In such cases drama (which in the Western Christian world was reborn in the late Gothic and Renaissance periods within the church as a teaching and cathartic instrument) acts as a therapeutic agent—indeed as an answer to prayer in many cases. Much healing happens through even poor or bad drama. For this reason drama is used in psychotherapy, and in many Christian camp experiences such as summer church camps and Camps Farthest Out.

Children, being loyal, normally repress any anger they feel toward us. Such evil needs to be seen and handled. That's why children laugh so uproariously at shows like the Keystone Cops. They feel a need to see authority humbled. In laughter they release tensions that could otherwise fuel resentments that could lead to excesses of rebellion. Christians need never fear that normal or even violent drama will hurt or greatly influence their children if not taken in large doses. Rather than copping out to blame movies and TV for influencing our children to violence, we should resolve to put the sort of consistent nurturing care and teaching into our children to develop in them a deep rooting in the love of God, a solid grounding in the laws of God, and a sharp discernment of mind and heart to make wise choices. Too often we have seen apparent model children leave a sheltered nest to crash on the rocks they didn't know were there. The strict discipline and protection of parents had been a structure and conscience imposed upon them. Because it did not provide exposure to all of life and build in the child by open discussion his own base of judgment, life on the outside became curiously attractive in its newness and strangeness. Vulnerability invited disaster.

We are not advocating the resigning of campaigns to clean the polluted stream of TV programing. We are heartily in favor of doing away with the garbage. John founded Citizens for Decent Literature in Streator, Illinois. But in that experience we discovered that such programs only scratch the surface. What we are proposing is that parents first of all face problems at the root level.

We surrounded our children with love and affection, prayer and laughter, while allowing them to watch *some* of most anything on TV. Now Tim will say to me if I sit down to watch something violent, "Aw dad, what do you want to watch that thing for?" How can children develop their own judgment unless it's through practice? Had we insisted the children not watch, like the Catholic church did some years ago, we could have created best sellers by banning them.

Fear is the enemy of life. Fear is a false damper upon healthy imaginations. Christian parents need to read to their children Hansel-and-Gretel-type stories (that have mean witches), *Uncle Tom's Cabin* (with villains galore), and *Huckleberry Finn* (with the wicked Indian in the cave). C.S. Lewis's Narnia series is a tremendous classic for children—full of witches and goblins and all manner of evils. Most especially children need the Old Testament with all its violence and heroes and villains. Children's spirits know there is evil in the world. Such stories portray, through the imagination, realities children know are there, and give them practice dealing with all of life's wild emotions within the safe environment of the home.

How many of us can remember, before TV, how vividly our imaginations portrayed "Gangbusters," "I Love a Mystery," "Inner Sanctum" ("The shadow knows . . ."), and so on—including Fibber McGee's closet? We suggest therefore that children be encouraged to read, lest TV rob them of their own richness of imaginative portrayal. Paula and I used to lie on the floor with Loren and Ami and make up stories to go with symphonies on the stereo. It was great fun, and it quickened our imaginations. For beginners, it is easy to do this with Ferde Grofé's "Grand Canyon Suite."

When children come home from school, thrusting some barely decipherable splash of colors at us, saying, "That's you, mommy," or "Look at daddy's funny tummy," we need at least not to belittle their work. Children often unconsciously draw what their real feelings are. Frowns, smiles, hair styles, posture, thick and thin figures can tell us a lot. Many mental institutions, especially for the young, are now hiring artists and teaching counselors to read what the drawings of inmates reveal. We should never criticize a drawing, or coloring, or finger painting. Artistic ability is not what is important. What it expresses is. Appreciate. Ask questions. Imagination is the window of the soul. Through it we can come to more understanding of our children than most any other way.

It should remembered that this book is addressed to the restoring of *Christian* familes. Families outside of God's church often tragically have given their children neither love nor training in the Word, so that their children's exposure to TV and movies is to them all too often a portrayal of what life *should* be! Drama has become for them a primary formation of their picture of life. TV and movies are for such often horrible teaching instruments, needing to be cleansed. But for Christian families—we are overcomers, not conditioned by what comes into the home, but using it to mature our children. We are *in* the world, but not *of* it, and we do not need to be afraid of it.

Let's take another look at our children, parents. Their spirits are more alive than ours.

PART III

16

DEATH UNDER THE LAW, BUT LIFE IN THE SPIRIT

Woe to you, scribes and Pharisees, pretenders—hypocrites! for you clean the outside of the cup and of the platter, but within they are full of extortion—prey, spoil, plunder—and grasping self-indulgence. (Matt. 23:25)

Every day our hearts are wrenched because Christians have not understood God's continuing work of grace daily to sanctify the heart. It troubles us to see countless families falter where a proper understanding of sanctification, or simply of themselves, could have saved them. We see men and women driven blindly by hidden sins of rebellion, hate and fear that long ago ought to have been brought to death on the cross. Therefore we insist that to cleanse the inside of the cup is to save the marriage. The church must cease to flee from comprehending the depths of grace *in the heart*, or today's pressures will succeed in destroying family life.

What then shall we say? That the law is sin? By no means! Yet, if it had not been for the law, I should not have known sin. I should not have known what it is to covet if the law had not said, "You shall not covet." But sin, finding opportunity in the commandment, wrought in me all kinds of covetousness. Apart from the law sin lies dead. I was once alive apart from the law, but when the commandment came, sin revived and I died; the very commandment which promised life proved to be death to me. For sin, finding opportunity in the commandment, deceived me and by it killed me. So the law is holy, and the commandment is holy and just and good. Did that which is good, then, bring death to me? By no means! It was sin, working death in me through what is good, in order that sin might be shown to be sin, and through the commandment might become sinful beyond measure. We know that the law is spiritual; but I am carnal, sold under sin. I do not understand my own actions. For I do not do what I want, but I do the very thing I hate. Now if I do what I do not want, I agree that the law is good. So then it is no longer I that do it, but sin which dwells within me. For I know that nothing good dwells within me, that is, in my flesh. I can will what is right, but I cannot do it. For I do not do the good I want, but the evil I do not want is what I do. Now if I do what I do not want, it is no longer I that do it, but sin which dwells within me. (Rom. 7:7-20 RSV)

This passage has mystified Christians for more than 1900 years. How could trying to live by God's good laws bring death? How could it "deceive me and by it kill me?"

Diagram one on the next page pictures what we call "a gate of ascent to action." When an impulse arises from within—a thought, idea, emotion, or whatever—we have a moment to decide whether or not to act. If we decide to act, we open the gate and let the conscious mind decide how and where. If we determine not to, we sit on that plug and push that impulse down.

DIAGRAM 1

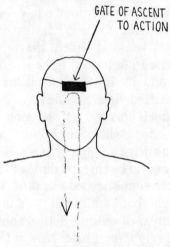

GATE OF ASCENT
TO ACTION

In diagram two we have added the crown of Christian character we are all trying to wear as new Christians.

DIAGRAM 2

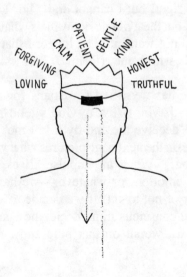

It would seem good to try to be all those things which the Ten Commandments, the Sermon on the Mount, and the fruits of the Spirit (Gal. 5:22, 23) lay out for us to be. In fact, God commands it. But let us see what happens when we try:

Papa discovers that the children have strewn his Sunday morning paper all over the house—again! What rises inside him? Anger and resentment. But he has determined to be loving and kind and calm. Therefore he pushes angry feelings down. Besides, it's Sunday. Mama calls everyone to breakfast, and no one comes—again! The colder the eggs, the hotter the mama; but she has purposed to be loving and forgiving, calm, and kind. So she stuffs the anger back down. Papa goes to wash his hands and finds mama's lingerie soaking in the sink again, after he asked her not to. What rises? Resentment which triggers into many other stored-up little vexations. But he has set himself to be loving and forgiving, gentle, and kind. So he represses those angry impulses. He will not let himself act on them. The children leave muddy handprints on the towels, again! But mama has agreed to be loving and forgiving and calm.

The price of control is fearsome. The unconscious mind never forgets anything. Normal families multiply irritations little and large by the hundreds in a week, by thousands in a month. Healthy, normal members of families become steam boilers ready to explode! We will explain later about the efficacy of prayer; for now we speak of those who intend to live as Christians but do not know the power of prayer. Whatever is not settled in us rolls around inside us gathering momentum. So without constant repair to the cross, we become explosions looking for somewhere to happen! (See diagram 3 below.) Therefore the law of sin runs rampant in Christian families.

Finally we no longer can hold ourselves in check. Someone does some silly little thing which normally we could throw off easily, and we explode. We "flip our lid," "blow our cork," "get it off our chest." We "let it all hang out." Now we are

DIAGRAM 3

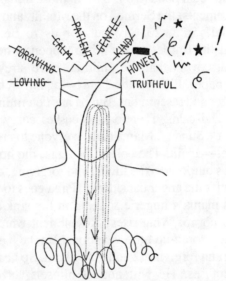

mortified. We have failed to be what we set out to be and most likely have disgraced our Lord. Forgiveness, kindness, gentleness, and all those good things have flown out the window. So we set ourselves even more determinedly! That probably will only mean that we may be able to store up more violence before we explode again. And so it goes. Apart from the cross, this dynamic is inescapable.

Whoever understands this dynamic of suppression and expression may comprehend the startling truth that the most dangerous thing Christians have ever done is to teach the church and the general public the *laws* of the Bible without imparting how to live *in HIM*. Whoever, apart from the cross, tries to live the Ten Commandments, let alone the much tougher Sermon on the Mount, is doomed to failure in ratio to his determination to try. Whoever says, as we have all heard so often, "Well, I figure if I just keep the Ten Commandments . . ." has never really tried, or he would have discovered that he can't. The hurrier we go the behinder we get! Violence stores up in us in direct proportion to the vigor of our effort to be good. This is one major reason why so many suddenly pick up shotguns and blast the family and themselves!

As counselors, again and again Paula and I see Christian families striving with all their strength to express the fruits of the Holy Spirit, only to become more upset, angry, and violent than families which do not appear to try at all. What has happened is that each day, as they set themselves to be kind and loving for Jesus, many irritations have caused resentments to begin to rise. Each instance required inner decision, either to act out the resentment or do something with it. Not knowing how to relinquish momentarily to the cross in prayer, they had no recourse but to suppress that emotion. The more such repressions piled on top of one another, the more difficult it became to maintain control, until finally some insignificant remark tapped a gusher and violence erupted.

All along there have been little healings, touches of love, instances of prayer, worship services, and acts of forgiveness. But they weren't enough to quell the rising storm. Unfortunately, many Christian families, ignorant of this dynamic of suppression and explosion, unaware of what is storing up inside themselves, and too negligent in devotional prayer, have thereby been less able to act like Jesus than some families outside the faith. The simple difference is the matter of *striving* to live the law. How helpful and relaxing it has been to Paula and me to learn that it was never our responsibility to accomplish the law. Once we accepted Jesus as Lord and Savior, we became His responsibility. It is the work of the Holy Spirit to express Jesus' life in ours. It is our work to cooperate in positive response to the Holy Spirit.

We have also counseled countless families who make no claim to be Christian at all, in whom the same dynamic of striving, suppression, and explosion was just as vitiating. To live by law is such a universal thing in the human heart that every group has its laws, whether such are spelled out or not.

Call girls used to ride in my cab in Chicago, complaining bitterly to me about the girls who did not live up to the code of ethics they thought call girls ought to have. Workmen on the job have their codes of conduct. The Mafia has inviolable laws. Every social club develops its own traditions and holds its members to them. We cannot escape from law by turning from the Lord. Law is everywhere around us. Whenever we strive to live up to the law, no matter what the context, choice requires suppression of emotions and desires. And suppression demands expression.

The remarkable difference is that where the strength of the Lord enters us by association with Him, we have more power to try harder, and thus if we do not have commensurate devotion and forgiveness, we march to explosion faster than non-Christians.

God has designed the Law precisely to show us our inability to keep it. He knew in commanding that none could live it. His plan was that whoever would try should discover his need for the Savior. "For no human being will be justified in his sight by works of the law, since through the law comes knowledge of sin" (Rom. 3:20 RSV). It is as though Adam and Eve had said, "We will not let you raise us. We will raise ourselves."

And God has said, "Okay, try it. Here are some rules to live by." God knew that the sooner and the harder we try, the quicker and more painfully we will discover we can't accomplish what we know we should. St. Paul, therefore, wrote that through the law sin deceives us and by it kills us (Rom. 7:11).

By logic alone, on the face of it, to live the law of God is impossible! As we see in diagram four, following, if we suppress anger and give a loving and forgiving answer, we have failed to be honest and truthful. But if we act out what we truly feel, we surely will fail to be kind, loving, and forgiving! By purity of logic alone, disregarding human frailty, the contradiction is inescapable. No one can be both loving and kind and honest, nor truthful and yet be gentle and forgiving.

DIAGRAM 4

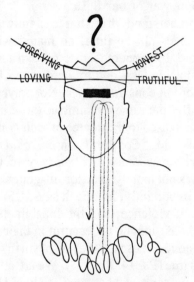

That simple equation demands another quotient, else it is unsolvable. That quotient is of course the cross. The essence of Adam and Eve's sin, and therefore ours, was to try to be gods, without the help of God's Holy Spirit. The essence therefore of the plan of God for our salvation is to write on our hearts again and again our desperate need both of the Savior and of His Spirit. The law is given to bring us again and again to that point. The contradiction between kindness and truthfulness, and our consequent bellyful of hurt, is why St. Paul writes in Romans 7 (RSV), "I do not understand my own actions. For I do not do what I want, but I do the very thing I hate" (v. 15). "I can will what is right, but I cannot do it" (v. 18b). "It is no longer I that do it, *but sin which dwells within me*" (v. 20b). "But I see in my members *another law* at war with the law of my mind and making me *captive to the law of sin* which dwells in my members" (v. 23). Put in psychological terms, that law of sin can be called the law of repression and expression operating in and through the power of our flesh.

We should understand that that dynamic of repression operates in all of us all the time, no matter what our stance relative to the Lord. In or out of Christ, that dynamic of repression will operate—until, unless, and to the degree of our ability to release to the Lord in constant prayer. Nonprayerful Christians will not only suffer the same dynamic as those in the world; in them it will be increased to the degree of their consecration. For this reason Amos said, "For they *know not to do right*, saith the Lord, who *store up violence and robbery* in their palaces" (Amos 3:10). It is not merely exterior, ill-gotten wealth that we store up. More importantly, as Micah says, "For the rich men thereof are *full* of violence, and the inhabitants thereof have spoken lies, and their tongue is deceitful in their mouth" (Mic. 6:12). Because none can escape the law of sin in our flesh, there is no one who is true (Ps. 14; Rom. 3). We are all liars, because we are not what we say and what we try to live. Underneath our face is stored a thousand and one remembrances of anger. This is why a gentle man, under the influence of alcohol, becomes a bear. No one can love purely. No one can be truly kind and gentle. Whoever acts it out lives a lie above a volcano. No wonder Jesus said, "Without me ye can do *nothing*" (John 15:5b).

This dynamic is one of the major reasons for the paradox that in the very time of the latter rain, when God is pouring out His Holy Spirit upon all flesh (Joel 2:28, 29), family tensions and divorces are drastically increasing, even among Christians. So long as we do not admit too much of the power of love in the Holy Spirit into us, we are not much impelled to try to live Jesus' way. But as St. Paul said, "Apart from the law sin lies dead. I was once alive apart from the law, but when the commandment came, sin revived and I died" (Rom. 7:8, 9 RSV). As the Holy Spirit increases hunger in us to live for Jesus, the moment we try harder, that moment sin revives in us by the dynamic of repression and we enter into death.

The answer is not to quit trying, nor as some psychologists would have us do, to lessen the law or do away with it. The answer is Jesus. As we see by diagram 5 below, we need such a constant walk of prayer that the moment of stimulation is the instant of silent prayer. Each stimulation to hurt and anger should find instant repair to the cross. "Jesus, I'm hurt. I'm angry. I'd like to belt him one. Please accomplish forgiveness through me." That way we have been emotionally honest. Hurt is not repressed. The heart is immediately refreshed. And we are then enabled either to rebuke kindly (Luke 17:3; Gal. 6:1) or to say nothing (Rom. 12:17, 18; 1 Pet. 3:9). It is then solely Christ's love for the other which prompts. It is then the Lord's life which pours through us, not our own.

DIAGRAM 5

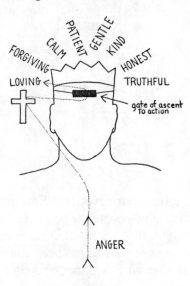

Our families are being torn apart in ratio to their distance from our Lord in prayer. When will we learn that the command to "pray constantly" (1 Thess. 5:17 RSV) is *necessary* to life, not a nice option?

Prayer, however, is not the full answer to the dilemma of Romans 7. The cross is, and our full self-death there. When we begin to try to live God's way, at first our desire may be for His glory, but what happens is that that attempt to be Christ-like becomes a thing in itself. As portrayed below in diagram six, our attempt itself becomes an idol, the thing we actually live for rather than God.

DIAGRAM 6

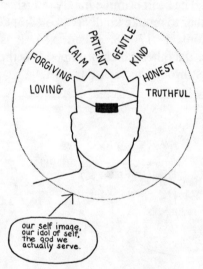

Fear of failure fuels our devotional fires at the altar of self. We want to make some people see and congratulate us that we *are* doing "it" right. If someone rebukes, criticizes or gossips, we can't take it because our god has been attacked. "How dare they—?" "And after all I've done for them—" "No one has tried harder than—'' ''How could he ever think such a thing of me?'' ''That just isn't my nature; I don't act like that.'' Whatever, it *is* our nature. We are trying to live something we aren't. So we become as the Pharisee who exclaims that he fasts and pays his tithes, not like the publican (Luke 18:12), and we do not go *home* justified.

Because the problem of evil in us is far deeper than our surface behavior, the answer of grace is far more profound than simple prayer. The entire attempt to live Christ's way is what we must surrender daily to death when we accept Jesus as Lord and Savior. It is no longer solely our task to make us express or become loving and kind and gentle. That is the job we gave to the Holy Spirit. We are His burden, His project.

The way up is the way down. The sooner we see that we have no righteousness at all (Ps. 14; Rom. 3; 1 Cor. 1:26-31) and lay the whole idol of self on the altar, the sooner our fleshly striving can die. Then indeed ''the law of the Spirit of life in Christ Jesus hath made me free from the law of sin and death'' (Rom. 8:2). The delusion we bought is that with God's help we could do it. We never could. When the process of Romans 7 is complete, we know that ''in me (that is, in my flesh,) dwelleth no good thing'' (Rom. 7:18). Then and only then do we begin to be free to let the Holy Spirit, rather than our striving, express Christ's nature in us. And what a blessed rest and freedom that is!

The deadliest thing extant in the church is the religious spirit. It was religious leaders who crucified Jesus. Today in the church and in our families it is usually those who are striving the hardest in their flesh to be what Jesus wants who are driving the church and their families to distraction and rebellion. But, ''There remaineth therefore a rest to the people of God. For he that is entered into his rest, he also hath *ceased from his own works*, as God did from his'' (Heb. 4:9, 10). We cease from our own works when we see how we have striven to be gods, however good we thought our motives, and claim momentarily

279

Jesus' death as our own. At St. Paul said, "I die daily" (1 Cor. 15:31), so must we. For the flesh resurrects easily, and soon plunges us into striving again, and the dynamic of repression and expression and explosion is on again.

Jesus is ours, and His life, when we believe *in the heart* that He has us; and call each practice of the old nature to death on the cross as and when we see it.

Fulness of love and life is ours when we believe *in the heart* that Jesus does truly inhabit us through His Spirit, and we set out to give each hurt to Him in prayer, and let His life cause us to express His forgiveness and love.

To die to self is not easy, for the flesh dies slowly. But it *can* happen, once we see that our problem is never that other fellow out there, but truly the log in our own eye (Matt. 7:4, 5). Life in the Spirit *is easy*. For that is the hallmark of the kingdom—no sweat (Ezek. 44:18). If we have to *try* to be loving, that is evidence that we are serving not God but the idol of our flesh. If kindness, love, and forgiveness flow from us easily and naturally, all credit goes swiftly and easily to the Lord, for His life is in us. So the presence of striving is always our first clue to the dynamic of Romans 7 resurrecting itself.

Because Christian families have not understood this dynamic of the law nor how the Holy Spirit would be the life of Christ in us, Christian families have often been more beleaguered and upset than families in the world. Men have asked us, "How come some non-Christian families seem to be happier and more relaxed than we are?" And Paula and I think ruefully, "Just wait till they start trying to do better." The answer is not to give up, but to surrender all our striving to death on Jesus' cross, that His life may truly be ours—and to be filled with His Holy Spirit.

Come unto me, all ye that labour and are heavy laden, and I will give you rest. Take my yoke upon you, and learn of me; for I am meek and lowly in heart: and ye shall find rest unto your souls. For my yoke is easy, and my burden is light. (Matt. 11:28-30) 280

17

NEBUCHADNEZZAR'S IMAGE

Thou shalt have none other gods before me. Thou shalt not make thee any graven image, or any likeness of any thing that is in heaven above, or that is in the earth beneath, or that is in the waters beneath the earth: Thou shalt not bow down thyself unto them, nor serve them: for I the Lord thy God am a jealous God, visiting the iniquity of the fathers upon the children unto the third and fourth generation of them that hate me. And showing mercy unto thousands of them that love me and keep my commandments. (Deut. 5:7-10)

There is no sin which does not involve idolatry. If we steal, we have valued whatever we took more than God. If we commit adultery, we have elevated that woman or that man as more important to us than God. If we choose not to be in church on Sunday, we have made an idol of whatever we wanted more than obedience—pleasure, business, repairing the house, laziness, etc. If we do not tithe, mammon is our god, no matter what we say. We may protest with our lips that we love God, that we are born anew, that we have all manner of wondrous experiences with God, but if we have not put our money where our mouth is, all our belief and experiences testify only to God's grace, not our faith. Apart from works, faith lies dead (James 2:17). Proof is written unequivocally in the history of our giving. "No man can serve two masters: for either he will hate the one, and love the other; or else he will hold to the one, and despise the other. Ye cannot serve God and mammon" (Matt. 6:24).

We all are inveterate idol-makers. We do it by nature. For example, all we need is an anointed worship service, and the next time we get together we will try to copy what we did last time. We are no longer seeking the Lord himself. We want that experience of power, and the goose bumps. These things have for the moment become our god, the idol we worship.

We often idolize pastors and other spiritual leaders. That is why we hate them so when they fall. They shattered our god.

If we check the many hundreds of little unconscious, unnoticed ways we break God's laws, we will see that even if we have tried, attended church and prayer meetings, and paid our tithes, we are still habitual idol-makers. How about when the wife is angry, so we don't tell her the whole truth, "just to keep the peace." Peace is now the idol we have served which justified lying. God said through St. Paul, "Do not provoke your children to anger" (Eph. 6:4 RSV). When we keep pushing the children away because they interrupt the ball game on TV, we have worshiped TV more than God. When the boss not only fails to compliment, but criticizes, and we blow up, it's a sure tip-off that we serve the idol of self. And so it goes, through every aspect of life. Idolatry is the first and greatest sin, behind all we do.

Idol-making is directly related to the family, for the command not to bow down to idols nor serve them (Deut. 5:9) is the only command of the Ten Commandments which includes a specific warning for families. Only two of the ten include remarks directly concerning the family. To honor the parents brings the blessing of long life and provides "that it may go well with thee'' (Deut. 5:16). But to worship idols visits the iniquity of the fathers from generation to generation (v. 9). It is not that God wants to hurt anyone. He always wants to bless. But His laws are inexorable; we *must* reap what we sow. Unfortunately the reaping comes also in our children's lives, as we have shown in chapter thirteen.

The longer we walk with Jesus by the Holy Spirit, the more our thousand and one idols will be revealed and, hopefully, left behind. But there is an idol-making that is central to all our living, which besets us every day, and destroys the family more than any other. That is none other Nebuchadnezzar's image.

> Then an herald cried aloud, To you it is commanded, O people, nations, and languages, That at what time ye hear the sound of the cornet, flute, harp, sackbut, psaltery, dulcimer, and all kinds of music, ye fall down and worship the golden image that Nebuchadnezzar the king hath set up: And whoso falleth not down and worshippeth shall the same hour be cast into the midst of a burning fiery furnace. (Dan. 3:4-6)

This passage never informs us, further than details of height and breadth, whose likeness the image of gold represented. Most likely because whether of Bel, Marduk, beast or man, it actually glorified Nebuchadnezzar. It is his image, his power, his glory, his idol of self. We are not different than he. His idol is our idol made visible. In the previous chapter, we began to reveal the idol of self we serve.

The significant dimension added here is fury. How shall we know when unconscious idols have ensnared us? By our furies. Whatever we defend with rancor is an idol. Whenever our furnace becomes heated up ''seven times more than it was wont to be heated'' (Dan. 3:19), we can be sure beyond a shadow of a doubt that it is not God nor anything noble we defend but our own idolized honor! What we get mad at tells us where our hidden idols are.

Nowhere is this more true than in the close confines of the family. In public we may be able to mask our idolatries. But at home sooner or later we are known for what we are, and when our beloved enemies refuse to bow down to our god (our idea, our view of the way things should go, our opinion of ourself, whatever), we sound our warnings—bagpipe, trigorn and lyre (v. 15 RSV)—and blow up!

When an idol is not behind what we stand for, we don't *have* to defend it. Suppose it is to accomplish something in the church, such as to win the church members to our idea of the way the youth program should be run. We want more leeway for the teen-agers to have fun, like dances, swim parties, and fun and games along with worship and Bible study. Some older, more fundamental folks can't see how those things should be allowed at all in a church program, much less in God's house. Right there, in such disagreements, is where the absence or presence of unconscious idols makes all the difference. If we are dead to self and alive to God in faith, we know that the Lord will work out in His own way what is good. And though we may have some anger and impatience, it does not overcome us. We can handle it easily, even without much prayer, and find ways to involve our opponents with us in the youth program, or talk with them until some peaceable way has been tried to the fullest. But if behind our service in the youth program lurks an unconscious picture of ourselves as the big cheese for God, our anger and impatience overpower us. We strut and huff and puff, insensitive to others in meetings, until everyone's back is up against us. We have blown our bagpipes, trigorns, and lyres and they ought to have been intimidated!—"Don't they know this is God's work!"; "Look how our youth attendance has increased; what would they do without me?"; "How can those old fogies be so blind!" Our fury is a sure sign of our idols. "Wherefore, my beloved brethren, let every man be swift to hear, slow to speak, slow to wrath: For the wrath of man worketh not the righteousness of God'' (James 1:19, 20). ''He that soweth iniquity [idol-making in this case] shall reap vanity: and the rod of his anger shall fail'' (Prov. 22:8).

On the other side of it, most likely the ''old fogies'' have some pretty stern idols too. Their image of church decorum is only an extension of their icon of their life with God, confused with God so that that young upstart's program threatens the way ''things (namely God, us, what's the difference?) have always been done around here!'' When no idol is present, we can die to self, share our wisdom, and be gracious if not heard (which is quite likely). But the presence of the idol calls forth our fury to defend.

The same dynamic happens in the family, only with more tenacity. Johnny's disobedience may threaten father's image of himself as a good father. Dad's idols may be hidden beneath noble aspirations to be the best father he can be for the Lord. Without idols, a father can be understanding and gracious, bending with the changing winds of teen-age lives according to God's wisdom in love. His discipline may be kind and appropriate. But unconscious idols of fatherhood generate the fury of the flesh, and Johnny is sacrificed on the altar of that god. ''NO SON OF MINE IS GOING TO ACT LIKE THAT!'' Notice, not ''That kind of behavior will be harmful for you,'' but, ''No son of mine. . . .''

Until husbands and wives become aware of their idols, much of their life together is a teeter-totter of dominance-submission, tit for tat, taking turns at giving in and getting mad. Self-righteous anger is a dead giveaway to the presence of an idol. For instance, if the husband continually comes in from the garden with mud on his feet, a wife dead to self can easily forgive, and her scolding, having no rancor behind it, is a blessing to her husband. But if an idol of perfect housekeeping is being continually tarnished, or an idol of self arises that says, "I ought not to be treated like this!", anger rather than grace takes hold. Then, however she may attempt to control her vocal tones, her husband will read the anger of her spirit and react accordingly. We cast our own into the midst of the fiery furnace whether or not we know we are doing it. Sometimes we may be totally unaware of our anger, but it is there nonetheless.

Our children's performances at school elicit responses from us. To the extent that our children have become extensions of our idols of success, we cannot abide less than the highest marks. Again, anger tells the difference, for where no idol is, compassion will rule our concern for the child, and what we do, however stumblingly, can be received as love. But idols of parenthood, or the idol of necessity to succeed vicariously through our children's talents, will often turn our admonishments to bitter demands and insults.

How do we handle Sammy's fears? With tenderness and firmness or with yells because our image of courage is dimmed? How about Debbie's ungainly walk and sloppy ways (especially in the dumpy time of early adolescence)? Do we feel fear watching her because our image of ourselves as parents of a graceful queen is being shot down? Or do we feel quiet understanding and appreciation of the "ugly duckling" before the graceful swan appears? Absence of threat usually indicates absence of an idol.

It is selfishness which is at the core in all disruptions in all families. But selfishness always has at its core idols of self which demand adoration. Pride is nothing else than the first offspring of idol worship. And fear is its first stepchild. We defend what we are proud of for fear it will either not be acknowledged, or be destroyed. Part of our fear arises from the guilt of innerly knowing that somehow we are wrong somewhere. But since the best defense is often the best offense, we heat up the furnace and attack!

The entire purpose of this short chapter is to give to every husband and wife, father and mother, one simple key—the blessings of our angers. Angers which rise so that we can recognize them, whether or not we successfully control them, reveal to us what idols need to be smashed on the cross.

Anger which rises as love in the Lord for the other always comes in the husks of compassion. Physically, we feel such anger as a burden in the chest and a flame of anointing love about the head. Anger which arises from the flesh in defense of an idol physically pulses in the temples, sweats in the palms, knots the stomach, shortens the breath, and we may feel hot all over.

Eyes informed by God's loving anger hold deep pools of His suffering in the other for us. Eyes of fleshly anger look flat and hard behind the surface—and there's a hundred-mile-an-hour freight train steaming down the track at us!

If Christians could learn to recognize their idols by their angers, much suffering and division could be prevented by grace. God wants to help, but He has to be invited in.

Shadrach, Meshach, and Abednego trusted God. They did not respond to anger with anger. They simply prayed prayers of blessing. (See the Prayer of Azariah, or the Prayer of the Three Young Men, in the Apocrypha.) Right then and there is when and where Jesus appears with us in the midst of the fiery furnace in our daily life in the family.

If Paula has not heeded my bagpipes, trigorn and lyre, and has failed to fall down and worship at my demand, and I have thrown her into my furnace heated seven times more than it was wont to be, but Paula simply silently prays, His grace comes into that fiery furnace—and I guarantee you I become a very startled Nebuchadnezzar! I expect her to crank up her own fiery furnace. If she does, I am off the hook. I can even justify my selfish angers. But if she lets her idols of self die (The idol is, "I don't have to stand for this kind of treatment!"), and humbly trusts in God and lets my fire flow all over her, His appearance with her there in my flames rebukes me thoroughly, and like Nebuchadnezzar I have to acknowledge that this God is truly God, not my image (my selfish desire). So I die, and am born anew in another needful area. On the other hand it may need to be mentioned that sometimes love requires that a mate rebuke sharply and expose the other's idol to him. But a husband or wife can only rebuke in effective grace if his or her own idol of self is dead. Let each begin with his own idols, not the other's (Matt. 7:3-5).

Our counsel is therefore twofold. Let us be quick to discover and repent of our own idols. Two, let us not be terrified of others' angers at us, but trusting in God, let Him cool those fiery furnaces by His appearance. He is faithful. He will always be there. Just so, we can turn all our spears into pruning hooks (Isa. 2:4)—for pruning hooks cut away living and dead limbs that prevent our bearing fruit.

18

RENUNCIATION, OR CUTTING FREE

If any man come to me, and hate not his father, and mother, and wife, and children, and brethren, and sisters, yea, and his own life also, he cannot be my disciple. (Luke 14:26)

Yesterday's good is tomorrow's evil. We mature and change and yesterday's harness won't fit tomorrow's task. Our relationships in the family change because we change. When we change, and relationships don't, there is hell to pay.

When we received Jesus Christ as Lord and Savior, that was a major change, which demanded an equally radical change in our family relationships. Jesus was speaking of that when He said, "If any man come to me, and hate not . . . ."

Hate, like love, is a word that has many moods. We say of an ice cream soda or a good book, "I just love it," and everyone knows that doesn't mean the same as a boy saying "I love you" to his father and mother; it certainly means something else than those identical words between lovers. Just so, hate means many things. Jesus uses the word here to mean renouncing or cutting free.

In the biblical setting, whenever a person entered into a new walk, it was understood that he must clearly leave the old, and sometimes must burn bridges behind him. Genesis 2:24 says, "Therefore shall a man *leave* his father and his mother, and shall cleave unto his wife: and they shall be one flesh." If a man does not leave his father and mother, psychologically and emotionally, indeed in every way, he cannot be joined to his wife, and the two cannot move on into the process of becoming one. Much tragedy results because one or the other partner still thinks primary loyalty belongs to mother and father. Truly yesterday's good becomes tomorrow's evil in countless marriages.

When Elijah called Elisha, he found him plowing with his team of oxen (1 Kings 19:19). Elijah threw his mantle over him, and Elisha said, "Let me, I pray thee, kiss my father and my mother, and then I will follow thee" (v. 20). Elisha meant that he be allowed to serve his parents until they died. "To kiss my father and mother" was an idiom which referred to a burial custom, as when Joseph "fell upon his father's face, and wept upon him, and kissed him" (Gen. 50:1). Elisha had for the moment forgotten, or disobeyed the rule that the call to the Lord's service supercedes all family duties. What Jesus said in Luke 14:26, "He cannot be my disciple," is exactly what Elijah then said to Elisha, "Go back again" (v. 20b). Elijah was saying, in our vernacular, "Forget it, you aren't willing to pay the price." But Elijah remembered that God had told him to call Elisha, so he gave him another chance by reminding him, "for what have I done to thee?" (v. 20c). At last Elisha comprehended, and did what he should have done in the first place. He "took a yoke of oxen, and slew them, and boiled their flesh with the instruments of the oxen, and gave unto the people, and they did eat. Then he arose, and went after Elijah, and ministered unto him" (v. 21). Elisha knew he must leave his father and mother, and because he had demurred at the first, now he must show his good faith; therefore it was not enough merely to leave home and farm, he slew the oxen, broke up his

Renunciation or Cutting Free

instruments, and invited all the family and friends to a feast. Now he could not retreat to the farm. Moreover, anyone who understands the cattle business would know that the beef of work oxen would be stringy and tough. It was not for the goodness of the meat that Elisha and the family participated in a feast. They were all joining in an agreement, sealing it with a covenant of salt with Elisha, that this was the way he was to go. His bridges were now totally burned; he could not return.

When Jesus called Peter and Andrew, "They straightway left their nets, and followed him" (Matt. 4:20). They knew the custom; the old must be left for the new. The call was to be "fishers of men" (Matt. 4:19). James and John were in a ship mending their nets with their father when Jesus called them (Matt. 4:21), "And they immediately left the ship and their father, and followed him" (v. 22).

But when Jesus had already arisen, and that fact was known to all the disciples, Peter said, "I go a fishing," and "They say unto him, We also go with thee" (John 21:3). No wonder they toiled all night and caught nothing. They weren't supposed to be there. Commercial fishing was what they had left behind, and they knew it. That was why Jesus said to Peter three times, "Lovest thou me more than these?" Jesus had called him to be a fisher of men and they had turned back to the old occupation.

When Jesus was in Capernaum, "his mother and his brethren stood without" (Matt. 12:46). "Then one said unto him, Behold thy mother and thy brethren stand without, desiring to speak with thee" (v. 47). We are not informed whether or not the man who said that intended to test and trap Jesus, but it *is* sure that the Pharisees and scribes were watching carefully. Had Jesus turned from God's ministry to see first to the comfort of His mother and brothers, they would rightly have cried, "See, he's no prophet at all. He turns back from following God to take care of His family, which He ought to have left." Jesus, fully aware both of them and of the laws, avoided the trap by saying,

291

"Who is my mother? and who are my brethren?" (v. 48); "And he stretched forth his hand toward his disciples, and said, Behold my mother and my brethren! For whosoever shall do the will of my Father which is in heaven, the same is my brother, and sister, and mother" (vv. 49, 50). Jesus also had truly left home for the new call of God and would not return; and in the process He outlined for us all what is our new calling—to be a family in Christ which supersedes the old natural allegiances.

It is not that having received the Lord Jesus Christ, we become callous or uncaring or have no feelings or duty toward our families. Rather that the old man has died, and therefore so have all the old ways of relating. Now, all the family and friends will have to be related to in new ways, and relegated to new priorities.

When we are born into this earth, our father, mother, brothers and sisters, relatives and friends, race, nationality and culture have become as a womb in which our character and personality were formed. All were shot through with sin. None of those who formed us, however good, is perfect. Like the nursery story of the crooked little old man who lived in a crooked little old house, we are all formed crookedly by a crooked people "in the midst of a crooked and perverse generation" (Deut. 32:5; Phil. 2:15)—until the Lord comes along and makes the crooked straight (Luke 3:5). "Behold, I was shapen in iniquity" (Ps. 51:5a) refers to this same fact of our formation.

When we are born anew, that means being born out of and detached from that womb of the past, to become "the escaped of Israel" (Isa. 4:2). If we do not cut the umbilical cord, the old blood of the old life will contaminate the new. Changing the metaphor, if having become new wineskins, we do not throw off the old, the old will cramp and sully the new. It sometimes seems to us that it ought to be automatic, that having died, all things would become new to us, for that we truly are new creatures in Christ (2 Cor. 5:17). Nothing could be truer in the life of our spirit, but all of our heart and mind must learn to claim that death and new life we already have in our spirit. Therefore the death of old ways is not automatic. Our salvation has to be worked out or made manifest in heart and mind as well (Phil. 2:12). We must claim that death and newness in every relationship in all our life. That is what Jesus means in Luke 14:26. If we don't cut free, and claim the new, we cannot go on to be His disciples.

As we have said before, all of human love is filled with use, manipulation, exploitation, and demand. However much we may exalt mother love, it is still imperfect, and finds its stopping place at the cross. When my (John's) mother used to come to visit, I underwent subtle changes. Mothers habitually do those things that put sons under control. Sons have learned to play whatever games keep the peace—or disrupt it in rebellion. So I would gravitate away from Paula and the children, ceasing to be husband and father to become son to my mother—and Paula would be furious! It was not a matter of jealousy over attention. It was that I was drawn into a role-playing which caused me to abdicate for a time my primary position and appropriate relationships. Then we learned this lesson of Luke 14:26, to renounce all old relationships as new creatures in Christ. That did not mean to hate my mother in any fleshly, wrong way. It did not mean to dislike her or disapprove of her. It did not mean to revile her. It meant by faith to cut free, to say in prayer, "I renounce and cut free from my mother."

What I was actually doing was to say to all the old practiced ways of the flesh by which we used to relate, "I now deny you." I was rejecting the habits, instincts, loyalties, belongings, and ways of loving which had belonged to the boy, and to the unregenerate nature, which were now invading and preventing my new freedom of life in Christ. I was rejecting what still broadcast from my mother's flesh (though she was and is a Christian), and what was still trying to act in my flesh. I was reckoning all that way of life as dead.

Jesus still calls us to love our mothers. I not only had not ceased to love her, I now could love her without trying to change her and without having to play the old games. Immediately, the next time mom came to visit, she still acted in all the old ways, but I was not bound to respond in the old patterns. I didn't have to try to remember not to react; what she said and did fell off my back like water off a duck. I truly *was* changed. The old ways which had manipulated my behavior found no lodging place at all. And Paula rejoiced that she still had her husband.

My mother didn't understand at all! She was sure, since I didn't play the old games any more, that I didn't love her. She went home in a huff. We must be willing to run that risk for Christ. Two years later Tommy Tyson and I spoke together at a C.F.O. in Kansas, while my mother was there, and she heard. "I have planted, Apollos [Tommy in this case] watered; but God gave the increase" (1 Cor. 3:6). Part of cutting free is to let go all those ways of acting and reacting by which we think to ensure our control of life so that people will keep on loving us. We must be willing to let go, trusting God, and "let the chips fall where they may."

Paula and I have now had more than twenty-eight years of an exceptionally good marriage. The candle of love has never gone out. We have labored together in the ministry over twenty-nine years. But we were not free. Our love carried huge waves of demand. I would come home thinking, "I'm going to give Paula and the kids a hug," and the moment I stepped in the door I would feel a wave of demand for affection coming through the air. Now I couldn't do it. My freedom to choose had been preempted. Paula wanted to have a nice meal and a refreshing quiet time ready for me, but my demand waves preceded me, upsetting the whole household. We must be free from each other in order to choose each other.

God himself refuses to demand from us, and pays the price every moment of every day for us to be free to stumble around so that all our choosing to love Him arises out of free hearts freely choosing to love. He cuts us free from Him, else He could have no real companionship.

Husbands and wives most often are bound up as we were in basically idolatrous relationships, demanding consciously and/or unconsciously that the other fulfill for us what only God can do. We want that comfort and strength which only the unseen God can give, and wrongly identify its source in what the seen mate is. The more vast the unregenerate love, the more immense the demand levels. No wonder the more the pressures of life increase, the more impossible our marriage relationships have become.

Paula and I learned from Brother Winston Nunes to renounce each other. Again, that meant only to cut free from the demands of the flesh in ourselves and in each other, to hate continuing carnal influence whoever and wherever it came from. We said in effect, I cut free from all your flesh and my own. I reckon as dead all that old way of relating. I reject all the old idols of our love relationship and set you free to be you.

The result was immediate and refreshing. For the first time we were free to fail each other. Neither of us any longer *had* to fill that mold of the ideal mate in the other's mind. Nor did we *have* to live up to our own. We were free to love, freely choosing each other in the sunshine of a new day.

Such a prayer to be cut free may need to be said afresh every once in a while. Some aspects of relationships may not die that easily. There may have to be some struggle to free ourselves of already broken chains. Seeing the traps, and discussing them, may have to be a regular diet for evening hours for quite a while. But the end result is worth it, for freedom to choose each other results.

Perhaps mainly from fear, we have all built false guarantees about us. We somehow think (or maybe grab without thinking) that demands will insure the love we count on so desperately. We put each other under guilt, to make the other move for us, just as mama did. And then we wonder why the other wants to be free of us when we "did everything, just everything for him." Our love was a prison, a bundle of chains by which we unconsciously sought to control the other so he would be everything we thought we wanted him to be. Only those willing to lose their lives will find them (Matt. 10:39; Luke 17:33).

This same dynamic works equally as powerfully within one individual alone as between two or many. We try to control and make demands upon our inner self even more fiercely sometimes than upon others. Until finally our inner "junior" revolts and goes on a sit-down strike in depression or rebels in some outwardly embarrassing revolution, like telling someone off or getting drunk or both. Therefore Jesus included, "Yea, and his own life also" (Luke 14:26).

One difference pertains. Until we receive Jesus, we have no life to lay down. We were dead in sin (Eph. 2:5). All our strivings and successes were but mere stirrings of dead leaves. But when Jesus enters our hearts, and we are born anew, then we do have a life to lay down. That life has become our Isaac. And God calls us to lay that Isaac on the altar.

Until we do, whatever that life is—our talents, our gifts in the Spirit, our office, our ability to love or to be a reconciler—whatever we have been given, becomes our idol (as we have shown in previous chapters). We demand that our ministry be recognized—after all, it's God's anointed work! Unconsciously we insist that others give devotion and homage to our talent. The surest tip-off to our idolatry (other than anger) is jealousy. The moment we sense lack of rejoicing, petulance or jealousy when the other brandishes some new toy in the Lord, that moment we may be sure our own gift has become our idol.

God would not have anyone be needed. None of us are needed. He is able to raise from the stones at our feet children to cry "Hosanna" to Him (Luke 19:40). We want a handle on God. How could God fulfill His Word to raise up countless millions from Isaac's seed if Abraham had sacrificed him? Abraham could have thought he had God in a bind. But God will have none of that. Therefore He put Abraham through the breaking of asking for sacrifice until Abraham knew in his heart that it is God alone who rules.

I renounced all the ministry of praying for the healing of the inner man, and not understanding, came home to announce that I would not receive any more people for counsel and healing. God only sent all the more. He didn't want the ministry stopped. He wanted *me* stopped. Until then the ministry had me. I *had* to minister. That single aspect of healing had invaded all my thinking. It had become all I could see of the life in Christ. Now the idol was dead and the Lord had the ministry rather than me. And I could be His disciple again, not merely the disciple of healing.

Whatever our life is, until we renounce it, it grows and has a life of its own, until it has us. Then the family suffers, for we are given to an "it" rather than to the Lord who would hold us in moderation and give us to our family. We cannot be His disciples until, like St. Paul, we have learned the lesson of Philippians 3, to "count all things but loss" (v. 8a). Indeed, he says to count all gain as "dung" (v. 8b). Until we do, we will not be free to seek after Him, to know Him and only Him. Until we learn this lesson, our children become our trap, and so Jesus includes in Luke 14:26 that we are to "hate" even our own children. Once we release them to the Lord, He returns them to us, for now we will no longer grasp them to us and so snuff out their own life. We will rejoice in that life He brings forth in them.

19

FORGIVENESS

For if ye forgive men their trespasses, your heavenly Father will also forgive you: But if ye forgive not men their trespasses, neither will your Father forgive your trespasses. (Matt. 6:14, 15)

Forgiving is not a nice option. The command carries a stern warning. If we do not forgive, we will not be forgiven. Countless times we have seen Christians enmeshed again in the same old carnalities because they refused to forgive others; all that had been forgiven and washed away came back upon them. When Jesus told the story of the man forgiven ten thousand talents who refused to forgive one who owed him "an hundred pence," He added, "And his lord was wroth, and delivered him to the tormentors, till he should pay all that was due unto him" (Matt. 18:21-35). We see that principle in action in families every day in counseling. Whoever has not forgiven father or mother, brother or sister is handed over to torment. Whatever we judge in another we are doomed to become or to reap in our own lives (Rom. 2:1; Matt. 7:1, 2). And whatever we do not forgive returns us to the mess we just came out of.

Given the countless continual irritations of daily family living, and the law of increase in sowing and reaping (see

298

Chapters 8 and 9 *The Elijah Task*), one can see that if the cross, through the act of forgiving, is not central to family living, every family will self-destruct. The capacity to forgive is an absolute *sine qua non,* the "without which nothing" for family living. Every resentment acted on or nurtured quietly in the heart is a sin which engenders an equal or greater response, which creates further reaction, and more and more. Only on the cross is there a stopping place, where for all things "It is finished."

Christian families (or any family) cannot afford the luxury of even one grudge. Whatever is not forgiven will work like a cancer to eat out the vitality of all the family life. Whatever is not forgiven will color like a drop of dye all other seemingly unrelated areas. A simple resentment for failing to come home on time for supper will affect the ability to express affection, the freedom of sharing in conversation, physical health, sexual responses, and so on. A grudge held is like sand thrown into well-oiled machines.

But the trouble about forgiveness is that we think we have when we haven't. We may say the words, but who can make his heart follow? Who can know whether it really has? The fact of hidden and forgotten resentment is by itself reason enough for the existence of counselors. For the first and major work of every counselor is to discover where grudges are lodged in the human heart—grudges which destroy present happiness. Truly the Grinch who steals our Christmas is none other than unforgiveness.

We fool ourselves and have no awareness of that fact. We say, "No matter," or "That's okay," and it definitely is not okay. St. Paul wrote ". . . without the shedding of blood there is no forgiveness of sins" (Heb. 9:22b RSV). Whatever hurts us registers in the heart and demands a response. The mind and lips may be convinced and say, "It's okay," but the heart knows differently. We cannot get at our heart to make it change. This fact alone guarantees our need of the Savior. Only He can change the heart, and this He does only by fulfilling the legal demands of the law in His body on the cross.

We may say, "It's okay" or even the good words "I forgive you," only to discover ourselves yelling, "And you did that same thing last week!" Or closed doors in the heart manifest in icy behavior while our mind is still convinced forgiveness has been accomplished. Taut lines in the face and hard eyes tell others the truth. Forgiveness is no easy matter. We cannot read our own hearts to know whether it has really happened or not.

Here then are some simple guidelines. One, if you have not made the hurt a matter of specific confession of resentment and hate in prayer, it is not done no matter what you think you feel. Only Jesus can sprinkle the heart with blood (Heb. 10:22). Only on the cross is anything ever finished. If it has not been relinquished in prayer, it is lodged in the never-forget-anything banks of our computer, waiting to be recalled to action somewhere sometime. Two, by their fruits ye shall know them, so watch for the tells. "Dis-ease" in relationships that formerly were more open and warm. Dreams of violence or of hurt to the other, even dreams where you are the hero saving the one who hurt you, are signals of a "dis-eased" heart. Three, impairments to health. Not every physical disease crops from seeds of hate, but physical discomforts along with other signs are a pretty good barometer of inner storms.

Not all things lodge in the heart. Sometimes hurts are caught in the moment and taken easily to the cross. Sometimes, unaccountably, large things which should hurt us just don't register, whereas some unintended slight tips the scales and scores deeply in our heart. Sometimes we don't even know we are being hurt till suddenly the heart won't respond to the other as it used to, or we surprise ourselves by making some cutting remark. We may have rationalized and excused the other, or made loyalty cover his faults until the heart is loaded unbeknownst to us.

When we discover that a seed of resentment is sending taproots into our heart, then we must enter into a discipline of forgiveness. Here we have found the greatest, most damaging ignorance. Too many Christians have not yet known how to let the Lord cleanse the heart in the art of forgiveness—or even that there is a desperate need and a work of cleansing required.

First, we need to identify the resentment. We need to face facts squarely. No euphemizing, explaining away, excusing, or painting with whitewash. If something was done which *should* have hurt us, we must not listen to our noble feelings when they send up no-hurt signals. It is far wiser to assume that hurt is there. If we have figured out logically why the other did what he did, and excused him, that is fine; it is a good exercise, but it is only mental, and most often our heart is not there at all. Again, it is wiser to assume that the heart does not agree with such surface magnanimity. If we assume wrongly, and the heart has not retained anger, exercise of prayer to cleanse the heart cannot harm. But to assume the heart has no angers and fail to pray, can only be a lazy gamble that can bear no fruit other than the surprises of dismay later.

Therefore, identifying angers does not mean being certain they are there, or not there, but being certain of what events could have produced resentment. It means to face history squarely, believing the worst of the heart. Looking at events, remembering in detail what happened, is not the same as recovering the feelings of the moment. If we happen also to discover what we actually felt, that is helpful, but neither most important nor necessary. What is important is fact. Given the facts, we can say to Jesus, "I don't know what I actually felt, Lord, but you do. Take every anger out of me to the cross. Don't let me hold any resentments, whether I am aware of them or not."

Today a prime example came into our office, a man who had

301

very good, responsible, hard-working farm parents of German lineage. He loved them and had worked alongside them all of his life. He could remember nothing at all for which to be angry at them. But he could never express love to his wife or children. His recent adultery had confused him about his feelings for his wife. His sister spoke of him as cold and unfeeling. And his eyes were filled with suppressed anger from his childhood. Questioning revealed that his parents had never expressed affection. The home was not filled with the warmth of laughter. The mind of the growing boy had only admiration and respect for his parents. But the spirit and heart were starving for love. He was innerly angry, and had no way of knowing it. But his life was now manifesting it. Piaget's moral law says that if a man commits adultery, he is angry at his mother. And his children were asking their mother, "Why can't daddy show us love?" His angers had never become conscious, and by that very fact were more vitiating to his inner being. Since his feelings had actually been hurt deeply and were too painful for him to admit to consciously, he had worked as a boy to turn off all his feeling centers so as to get through life performing by duty, not having to feel. He could no longer relate heart to heart with anyone. He had become the tin man coming to the Wizard of Oz to get a heart. That starvation left him vulnerable to the adulterous woman, who knew how to touch the heart beneath the barriers.

That example of hidden anger is so classic it is tragic. There are at least three levels to us—mind, unconscious mind (or heart), and spirit. Sometimes unbeknownst to us, while our outer being rejoices at the gift our brother or sister has just received, the inner heart is convulsing in jealousy or anger at the parents or God. Or we may be unaware that the reason the mind forgot to bring a present is that we didn't want to. And so it goes. The difficulty about forgiveness is that we seldom know what and when and whom to forgive. Therefore we must learn to use present problems like the outcroppings of silver veins to trace the mother lode in the heart. Present problems are almost always symptoms rather than causes. And we must track to facts, because the world of actual feelings will almost always surprise us and reveal that what we thought we felt was either only partial or false altogether.

When something has rooted itself in the heart, no easy, flippant "Oh, I forgive you" will suffice, nor will a moment's prayer dislodge it. We will not get out of that prison until we have paid the uttermost farthing (Matt. 5:21-26). There is a process of forgiveness which allows no shortcuts. Jesus, Lord of the heart, will not allow us access to freedom short of fulness of healing, even as He would not let the lady who touched the hem of His garment slip away until in front of the whole community she confessed and was received by all (Luke 8:43-48).

First, once we have discovered the facts—who, when and where—He calls us into Gethsemane. Gethsemane is that place of prayer where Jesus laid aside His righteousness and became all that we are. We are called to lay aside all our righteousness—until it is no longer important whether we or the other guy is right or wrong. As He became our sin, so we need to say, "Lord, make me to know my sin, and so identify me with the sin of all mankind that I may know my oneness with my brother at the foot of the cross." Peculiarly, people have often cried out to us, "Well, I could forgive him if he just deserved it, but do you know what that skunk did? . . ." as though to be forgiven required that you didn't need it!

What happens in anger is that we pull back from our brother, and differentiate, saying, "Well, I'm not like him, at least I don't go around. . . ." In so doing we elevate ourselves and become the Pharisee who says he pays his tithes and is not like the publican (Luke 18:9-14). We no longer want to be counted one with that brother. We are different. But we are not. The first task of prayer is to enter Gethsemane in order to rediscover our

303

oneness with the sin of all mankind.

If we go deep enough we may see that our bitter root has drawn our brother to hurt us, or some seed of sin sown by us has jeopardized our brother by causing him to be the one through whom we are reaping even less of evil than we deserve.

A Christian man picked up a hitchhiker. After a while the rider stuck a gun in his ribs and commanded him to pull over; he would rob him of all his money. As he stopped, the Holy Spirit convicted the Christian's heart and he began to weep.

The hitchhiker said, "Whasamatter fella, you yellow?"

"No, son, I weep in shame that you have ridden so long with me and still think you have to use a gun to get whatever help you need from me." The Holy Spirit caused the robber to see the reality of the Christian's repentance—and he received Jesus and went away with a gift of money as well! That Christian lived close to Gethsemane. The Lord could quickly show him his and mankind's sin and unite his heart with the brother who hurt him. Our visit to Gethsemane is not complete so long as we are still innerly marshaling our defenses of our rightness and cataloging the other's sins.

We would often rush directly to the cross with our hurts, but the wisdom of Jesus says, "No, my brother, you must come the way I did, through Gethsemane." If you do not come through the loss of our own self-righteousness and identification with ours and mankind's sin, we will never be free, for we will always feel noble and self-martyring that we forgave that fellow. And then each time we have to repeat forgiving, we will grow that much more self-martyring and noble and of course better than that fellow who keeps sinning against us. Our patience wears thinner and thinner until we cry out, "I can't do it any more. I don't care if it is seventy times seven, I can't, I'm done, and I won't." Forgiveness had never been complete, because we had never gotten off our pedestal. We were handing down mercy to someone less than we. Perhaps even God had to become one with our sin before forgiveness could be complete—else why not just forgive from heaven without having to come to earth! We need to begin our prayers to forgive by saying, "God, take me to Gethsemane with you until all those noble lines of who is right and who is wrong are lost in our sense of common shame at the foot of the cross." You see, behind all our hurt is the sneaky thought, "Noble me didn't deserve that kind of treatment; it isn't fair." That false nobleness and separation from our brother must be defeated at the outset.

Then we need to claim Jesus' act of forgiveness. Hopefully, every man will be so wounded some time that he will come upon the happy discovery that no man can forgive anybody anything at any time! We actually think we are pretty good fellows, and sometimes say, "Forgiving was always easy for me. I never could hold a grudge." There goes a self-deluded man. Forgiveness is never easy for any man. And no man can ever forgive another. Forgiveness is an impossibility for human flesh. The mind can fool itself, and outwardly gracious people can think they really are that way, but "the heart is deceitful above all things, and desperately wicked" (Jer. 17:9), and no man is capable of forgiveness.

We cannot get at our heart to change it. "Can the Ethiopian change his skin, or the leopard his spots? then may ye also do good, that are accustomed to do evil" (Jer. 13:23). Only Jesus, as God in flesh, can enter the human heart, and change it. For this reason "No man cometh unto the Father but by me" (John 14:6). And no man comes to any other but by Him for the same reason. Sin and resentment separate. But the blood of Jesus cleanses us of all unrighteousness (1 John 1:9).

Once we are in a position to receive the gift, forgiveness is abundantly simple. We simply receive by faith that Jesus has accomplished it for us. Again, if we still think forgiveness is something we do, we are neither in position to receive the gift nor have we died to our noble, forgiving self. People who

305

forgive cannot escape the pride of it. But those who come through Gethsemane know that neither the one who hurt them nor they themselves deserve it, cannot accomplish it, and receive afresh every time as an undeserved mercy of the Lord.

We claim by faith then that forgiveness is accomplished, and again do not go by feelings. If we still want to grind our teeth at the other fellow or find ourselves not liking him or any such thing, it is not that forgiveness has not happened. It is that we were robbed of it because we never got through Gethsemane to the foot of the cross with our brother. But we may not feel great love or release either. No matter. It is done, and we need to believe that fact.

Forgiveness, however, is not yet complete. More is required of us. In 1 Peter 3:9 we are told, "Not rendering evil for evil, or railing for railing: but contrariwise blessing; knowing that ye are thereunto called, that ye should inherit a blessing." We are called, that is, commanded, to bless those who despitefully use us. That means to pray all manner of good things for the one who hurt us. To invest ourselves in love for his benefit. Romans 12:14-21 says it even more cogently:

Bless them which persecute you: bless, and curse not. Rejoice with them that do rejoice, and weep with them that weep. Be of the same mind one toward another. Mind not high things, but condescend to men of low estate. Be not wise in your own conceits. Recompense to no man evil for evil. Provide things honest in the sight of all men. If it be possible, as much as lieth in you, live peaceably with all men. Dearly beloved, avenge not yourselves, but rather give place unto wrath: for it is written, Vengeance is mine: I will repay, saith the Lord. Therefore if thine enemy hunger, feed him; if he thirst, give him drink: for in so doing thou shalt heap coals of fire on his head. Be not overcome of evil, but overcome evil with good.

We are to overcome evil with good. When evangelists preached to some natives that they were to heap coals of fire on their adversaries' heads, they gleefully dumped hot coals on them while they slept! They understood that verse as little as most Christians do.

In biblical times, there were no gas or electric ranges, or matches. Fire was a precious commodity, scarce because fuel was scarce. Therefore one man in a village was appointed to keep a fire going all night. In the wee hours he built it up and let it burn down to hot coals. These he scooped into a metal brazier which he set on a wood block on his head. Then he went with tongs from kitchen to kitchen so every housewife could have hot coals for her day's cooking. It became an idiom that "to heap coals of fire on his head" meant to turn a man into a spreader of warmth in the community.

When God desires to reach a man who will not listen, one route to his heart is to allow him to hurt a Christian. That will plunge the Christian through Gethsemane to the cross for himself and the one who hurt him, and cause the Christian to pray for that sinner. Now a bridge is open, for the sinner's heart is engaged with the Christian's, and the Lord has an avenue to walk into the sinner's life.

What did Stephen cry out as they stoned him? "Lord, lay not this sin to their charge" (Acts 7:60). At whose feet were the clothes of the stoners laid? Saul's (Acts 7:58). The blood of the martyrs has always been seed of the church. Sergei Kourdakov in our day testified that the Lord struck his heart when an old lady prayed for him as he was about to bludgeon her with a club.

Until we complete the process of forgiveness by blessing the other, we have not overcome, and we have not followed through to resurrection life. Life issues forth in love. Until we cost ourself for the other, we have not stepped into the river of love and found life. Blessing the one who hurt us is thus not a nice option for those nuts who can do it, it is another absolute necessity if we would be whole—indeed if we would continue our walk with Jesus and the family.

Whoever would bless the one who hurts him must learn the same lesson—the flesh cannot do it. If we don't want to, if it does not flow as naturally and easily as a spring of water from a mountainside, then we have an unmistakable sign that the first steps of repentance in Gethsemane and restful receiving at the foot of the cross have not been accomplished in our hearts.

If we say, "Well, I've forgiven him, but I don't have to like him," we are only fooling ourselves. We do not have to like him in the sense of approving of his nature or what he does, but we do need to come to that point at which our heart hurts and yearns for him, and our spirit likes him. If we find ourselves not wanting to be with that person, we may not have accomplished forgiveness. There is no "may" about it if that person is a family member. With family, we must not allow ourselves to stop until the other is as precious to us as the dearest life we know. If we are wary of the other, and are reticent about being vulnerable again, we must overcome the reticence among family, while letting the wariness become a caution of wisdom in love, by which we do not tempt our brother at the point of his known weakness.

Sometimes much of the travail of prayer needs to be accomplished quite apart from our brother. But often the Lord will require that we talk. Herein more Christians have failed the fulness of forgiveness more than any other point outside of Gethsemane. Perhaps we are timid, or afraid, or unsure. So long as these are greater than the promptings of love, we have not prayed and acted it through to completion. Our brother needs to hear our forgiveness, our love, and our blessing.

Wisdom and restraint ought to prevent insensitive boldness in sharing, but fear or unworthy motives must not be allowed to inhibit altogether. We fool ourselves so easily. It may be easy to bless a brother in the privacy of the home. We may even feel grandly Christian. It is humbling to go and speak words of forgiveness and blessing, and more humiliating to ask the one who hurt you for forgiveness for your part in causing it to happen.

Again, there is no nice option. Failure to complete the process leaves unfinished business which either engenders further hurts, or concludes in isolation. And then the whole debt and prison is back on us.

But what a joyous grace He has given us. Paula and I have counseled non-Christians and people of other religions, and mark in them above all other faculties, the absence of the grace of Jesus to restore what is amiss. What five minutes of prayer restores to better-than-what-was-originally, takes years apart from Jesus only to begin to get back to less-than-what-was. Hurts remain irreparable outside of Jesus. How revealing of the wonderful love of Jesus for us that He continues to pay the price daily that we might be restored in joy to each other. St. Paul wrote that we should be subject to one another out of reverence for Christ (Eph. 5:21). Here is the final key for forgiveness, for what will propel us to continue through the entire process to fulness of forgiveness? Not the flesh. Not human love alone. Not will power. But the desire of our hearts to bless Jesus with His happiness, and not to grieve His loving heart any more than we have to.

Whoever loves Jesus cannot abide a grudge in his heart, for he knows it wounds His heart, and grieves His Spirit.

20

EAGLE CHRISTIANS

But they that wait upon the Lord shall renew their strength;
they shall mount up with wings as eagles; they shall run,
and not be weary; and they shall walk, and not faint. (Isa.
40:31)

What is the end product of Christian family living? We have
spoken of death; now let us speak of rebirth. God wants to raise
up from the ashes of our families His own eagle Christians.
Families are launching pads for eagle Christians.

Eagle Christians are a distinct breed. They are swift (2 Sam.
1:23; Jer. 4:13); they comprehend quickly and fly to do His
bidding. They see from afar (Job. 39:29). Gifts of counsel,
insight, and vision are theirs (Isa. 11:2, 3). When others see
only problems and rivet their eyes to circumstances, they see
beyond to the joy set before them, and despising the shame,
endure whatever cross must be borne (Heb. 12:2). They see by
the Spirit into the very depths of God (1 Cor. 2:10), seeing in
His nature the answer to all things (Rom. 8:28).

They "mount up with wings as eagles" (Isa. 40:31b). When
storms approach, with wind and thunder and lightning, lesser
fowl head for cover, but the mighty eagle spreads his wings, and
with a great cry mounts upon the very winds which drove the

lesser to cover. Storms are a joy to him, for on their mighty updrafts he soars to heights of glory. And he does it effortlessly, letting the wind carry him where lesser birds must beat with frantic wings to stay aloft. Just so, the eagle Christian sees behind the storm the surging, moving power of the Holy Spirit of God, and rises on wings of faith to rest in God's carrying power far above harm and destruction. He does not have to pump up his faith and talk himself into ephemeral moods of fleeting courage. He abides, restfully trusting the current of God's love, moving not by striving but by the soaring currents of God. The Lord himself bears him up. Others seeing, try to huff and puff to his heights, and cannot understand his restful, easy soaring, ascribing it to the eagle rather than the winds of God's love. But the eagle knows the currents and turns here and there to catch the rising flow of life.

"They shall renew their strength" (Isa. 40:31a). Every so often, some say every seven years or so, an eagle must renew itself. Its mighty wing feathers become laden with oil and dirt, cracked and worn with use. Beak and talons become calcified and brittle. Then it is that the eagle retires to a cave or hiding place high beyond the reach of predators. There he begins an arduous process of renewal. With his great beak he pulls the mighty wing feathers one by one. And then each talon, claw by claw. Until at last, having neither talons nor feathers, he is defenseless except for his great beak, which he then begins to bash against the rocks, until it too is broken off, piece by piece. There he trusts and waits until beak, talons, and feathers have regrown.

Above all, eagle Christians have learned flexibility of mind and heart. They have teachable spirits. As St. Paul said in Philippians 3, they count all things as refuse, pulling off old feathers and claws and breaking their beaks. Old feathers are old understandings and insights by which we have soared into experiences. Old talons are the old ways in which we rose to do battle. For example, we used to be sure to put on the armor (Eph. 6:11) and plead the blood before exorcisms, but when we learned the better way of the shield of faith, that He is our shield and buckler (Ps. 91:4), like St. Paul we "put away childish things" (1 Cor. 13:11b). We tore off those old talons; a new and better way to fight had come. Eagle Christians are flexible. They do not hang onto the old. Like the chambered nautilus of Oliver Wendell Holmes, they are always ready to "build thee more stately mansions, oh my soul." Old beaks are accustomed ways of perceiving and feeding on the Word. Eagle Christians seek fresh bread from the oven of God's love, knowing that yesterday's manna is filled with worms. They break off the old ways of perceiving what God has said, ready to see something new in the familiar passages of the Word. Eagle Christians keep the solid stable bones of doctrine and Word and pluck off whatever will not keep them soaring on the fresh winds of God's storms. They renew their strength.

Note, eagles are not like sheep which must be sheared of the old. They take the initiative. They renew themselves. How often God must wear us out with warnings and the ministrations of brothers before we take heed and let Him take away the old way! But eagle Christians know by the Spirit within when it is time, and move by Him to destroy their old way and regrow the new. It is not that they will not let others help, but they take the initiative to enlist that aid. They do not have to be badgered by others to get at it. They are already alert to see what needs to die, and willing to be at it quickly while the Lord is near (Isa. 55:6).

The Lord wants families which promote rather than frustrate the formation of eagles. Overprotective families produce chickens. Critical, hypertensive families create vultures. Maudlin, soft and sentimental families produce pigeons that strut and coo and overcomfort, who run for shelter in the storms. Ambitious, worldly families bring forth peacocks full of pride and flashy dress. Flippant families to whom life is a succession of parties spawn sparrows who flit here and there chattering meaninglessly. Over-busy, work-oriented families send out woodpeckers to bang away noisily at life, red-headed with embarrassment when there is no new crusade to peck away at in self-importance.

But an eagle family is something different. Its eyrie is set high upon the rocks of faith or in the topmost branches of the tree of faith. It is exposed to wind and weather and sun. To change the metaphor, God is not raising hot-house tomatoes, cultured and overprotected, but exposed. The Christian family is perched on the solidarity of God's Word, standing against the winds of current fashions and ways. If it is called to stand by a new black child, and take the abuse of "nigger-haters," it stands. If it befriends a Jew, it takes the winds of hate and is strengthened by the standing. When the children complain of discipline and parents come to haul a teacher before the board, Christian parents back the teacher and say, "If you get a spanking at school, you get one at home." When a child in an eagle home falls and skins his knees, his parents brush him off, love him up, doctor the wound, and say, "Back at it, kid, life's like that." No mollycoddling is allowed. Eagle parents demand work, and balance it with play.

An eagle mother trains her children to fly by an awesome process (Deut. 32:11). A mother eagle flutters over her nest, demonstrating by sight how to fly. Then comes a day when she gathers an eaglet onto her back and spreading her wings flies high—and suddenly swoops out from under! Down and down he plummets and perhaps begins to discover what his wings are for, until the mother swoops under him and catches him again on her back. Many times the process is repeated. If the eaglet is slow to learn or cowardly, she returns him to the nest, and tries again a few days later, and then perhaps again. But if he will not learn, she begins to tear her nest apart, until there is nothing left for the eaglet to cling to.

Eagle Christians

As Paula was growing up, her father told her again and again, "Whatever you set your heart to do, you can do." When I (John) was a boy, my mother said, concerning chores and work, "Watch what others do. Whatever you see someone else do, you can do." I was expected to learn, and learn quickly. As a Christian adult I took team members with me on missions where they were to counsel and pray with people, and lead prayer groups. I purposely never gave them advance warning. If someone came needing prayer, I would say, "Here, go with Ken. He will pray for you." Or I would suddenly ask someone to give a testimony or say a prayer, or read the Scripture, teach, do an exorcism, whatever. I figured if they had seen it done at home, and been taught, they could do it. The team members often teased and joked about being exposed and unprepared. But they liked it and grew rapidly. The Lord wanted eagles who would find their own wings in the rough winds of trial and error.

There was no overprotectiveness in my (John's) home. We were expected to fight our own battles, do our own chores, and stand to our own faults and chastisements. The same in Paula's. Falls and tumbles were to be endured and learned from. John's mother's counsel on the ranch in Oklahoma was, "If you fall off the horse, get right back up on him and ride, no matter how much it hurts or how much you are afraid," and, "You've got to show the horse who's boss!" None of that meant we never felt fear. Sometimes we were scared spitless. It was clear instruction what to do *about* fear—you let it call forth energies, and charge! Any courageous soldier knows that the difference between the cowards and the medal winners is not the absence of fear, but how each responds to it. Cowards plummet helplessly to death. Eagle Christians put out their wings and fly. Christian families build that kind of eagle nature by example.

Today as never before the world needs eagle Christians. In a recent movie, Lee Marvin played the part of the "king of the hobos" in depression days. An upstart came to challenge his

314

leadership, but proved to be cowardly and selfish. At the last, the upstart was caught by the cruel "bull of the trains" (Ernest Borgnine), who was beating him with a chain. The "king" jumped in, defeated the "bull," and threw him from the train. Then as the train pulled across a bridge over a river, the king turned suddenly and threw the young man over and down into the river. The movie ended as the king shouted back, "Give it up, kid. You'll never make it. You gotta have *heart!*–You gotta have *heart!*—You gotta have *heart!*" Eagle Christians have to have heart. We have found that those families that give love and laughter but do not overprotect create heart. Men and women with natural heart can stand the breaking and the crushing which produces saints. Those from other kinds of families, if they get there at all, do so over a much longer and harder route. God wants eyries for eagles.

21

THE FAMILY OF GOD

And He gave some as apostles, and some as prophets, and some as evangelists, and some as pastors and teachers, for the equipping of the saints for the work of service, to the building up of the body of Christ; until we all attain to the unity of the faith, and the knowledge of the Son of God, to a mature man, to the measure of the stature which belongs to the fulness of Christ. As a result, we are no longer to be children tossed here and there by waves, and carried about by every wind of doctrine, by the trickery of men, by craftiness in deceitful scheming; but speaking the truth in love, we are to grow up in all aspects into Him, who is the head, even Christ, from whom the whole body, being fitted and held together by that which every joint supplies, according to the proper working of each individual part, causes the growth of the body for the building up of itself in love. (Eph. 4:11-16 NAS)

The production of eagle Christians is not the end but the beginning. For God gives them as gifts to the church. They are pivotal to His plan, for through them God designs to edify the church, until *all* come to the unity of the faith and to such maturity that, no longer tossed to and fro, we all stand as that perfected Zion which upbuilds itself in love and becomes God's demonstration to all the principalities and powers (Eph. 3:10—"This is how I created life to be!")

The Holy Spirit has now poured forth His latter rain upon the earth (Joel 2:28, 29). God is moving to restore the unity of His church (Dan. 12:7), ending the scattering of our power. At present we have the unity of the Spirit (Eph. 4:3). But God intends to move us into unity of the faith—something far greater (Eph. 4:13)! And the key to that is eagle Christians—the fivefold ministry of apostles, prophets, evangelists, teachers, and pastors. Eagles are known for their ability to soar alone to the heights. But they do it to see far for food for the young. Christian eagles exist for the family of God, to establish the corporate life of the body of Christ. When St. Paul prayed for individual Christians to have power to comprehend with all the saints the height and length and depth and breadth of the love of God that they might come into all His fulness, he set that prayer into the context of "whom every *family* in heaven and on earth is named" (Eph. 3:14-19 RSV).

God is working out a mystery of individuation and union in corporate life. He is leading on to the marriage feast of the bride and the Lamb. Lone individuals who can never become one with the family will find neither place nor joy there. On the other hand, those who would cop-out from their own life to become and do whatever sells them to the company will find fear and trepidation there. Paradoxically only those who know how to soar high on their own wings will be able to fly in tandem with others. And only those who have ridden on the back of mother church will have learned to soar lone and free to the heights. God wants whole people who because they can stand alone can submit also to others, and because they can submit to others can fly alone.

It is in the natural family that God builds that capacity to enter the larger human family. If the family is a bow, what is the mark? Corporate life in the kingdom of God, the brotherhood of mankind, and the fellowship of His creatures is the mark. Sin is to miss that mark.

From the womb a child learns first dependency and at birth begins his pilgrimage to independence. That pattern is repeated over and over as pupil depends and graduates and teaches, woos and weds, lives on and serves and forms his own, gives birth and instructs only to release again. In and out, the dance of life commands that each partner learn to insist and resist, lead and follow, learn and teach, give and take, receive and give out. All the movements of life demand inner cores of tough, resilient bone and outer flexes of feathers and tendons.

God can build corporate life only where strength has produced meekness, and men are as unwilling to override another as to be overridden. The family of God comes into unity where none dominate and none would allow a Hitler anyway.

That flex of give and take which upbuilds can only happen in love. That love of God among men can only happen where the river of God's love has firm banks of character in men in which to flow. Firm character is built only in families founded upon the rock of God's Word.

Love and forgiveness are the power and guarantee of strength and flexibility without which men cannot join hand-to-hand to build. God restores the family of mankind in order to restore earth to liberty from its bondage to decay and to the fulness of the sons of God (Rom. 8:21).

The cross is therefore central to all God's planning. For without the continuance of death of sinful ways, the new cannot be resurrected. Rigidity must set in to thwart the new where prayer does not haul the old to the body of the Son on the tree.

The Holy Spirit would sing a mighty chorus of praise not only through all the redeemed family of man but through every bird and beast. "And I heard *every* creature in heaven and on earth and under the earth and in the sea, and all therein, saying, 'To him who sits upon the throne and to the Lamb be blessing and honor and glory and might for ever and ever!' " (Rev. 5:13 RSV). There is a family of more than men to whom the love of God would marry us.

The end product therefore is the whole family of all creation, reunited and singing glory to God the Father and the Son—but it starts with Jesus in the local human family, setting free each individual to become.

CASSETTE TEACHING TAPES
by John and Paula Sandford

UNDERSTANDING THE CHRISTIAN FAMILY SERIES
1. The Demon that Rises With Us
2. A Heart of Flesh for a Heart of Stone
3. Man and Woman Becoming One Flesh
4. Animus and Anima
5. Fathers, Sons and Daughters
6. Mothers, Sons and Daughters

RESTORING THE CHRISTIAN FAMILY SERIES
1. Importance of a Father's Love
2. Getting at Roots of Bitterness
3. Balance through Jesus Christ
4. Biblical Function of a Family and A Christian View of Sex

LORDSHIP OF JESUS CHRIST SERIES
1. The Lordship of Jesus Christ
2. Why We Can't Stay with Jesus
3. Living in the Perfect Will of God
4. A Covenant People
5. Giftings, Blessings, Cursings
6. The Blessedness of Brokenness

THE FATHER'S LOVE SERIES
1. Importance of a Father's Love
2. The Gift of a Father's Love
3. Functions of a Father's Love
4. Authority of a Father's Love
5. Defend the Fatherless
6. At Home with the Father

CHRISTIAN DISCIPLESHIP IN FREEDOM SERIES
1. Who Disciples Whom?
2. Prerequisites for Discipleship
3. Sanctification

4. Coming to Life in Discipleship
5. Questions and Answers
6. Kinds of Ministries

REFRESHMENT OF FORGIVENESS SERIES
1. Forgiving and Overcoming—
   Coming into Jesus' Presence
2. Getting at Roots of Bitterness
3. Balance through the Fulcrum of Forgiveness
4. How Forgiveness Issues in Unity and Coming into
   Fulness of the Father

THE POWER TO COPE SERIES
1. Power through Blessing and Praise
2. Power of Forgiveness
3. Power in Granting Forgiveness
4. Power of Intercession

THE PROPHETS SERIES
1. Standing on the Word
2. Prophets—Then and Now
3. Prophets—God's Gift to Man
4. Prophets—Seeking Judgment
5. Prophets—Inner Healing
6. In Jesus' Name (by Loren Sandford)

THE PEACE AND REST SERIES
Part I by the Sandfords
1. The Giver of Rest
2. When We Lose our Rest
3. Coming into Mental Rest
4. Coming into Heartfelt Rest
5. Coming into Spiritual Rest
6. Into Rest in God's Family
7. Into Rest in the Good Earth
Part II by "Rev. Ev" Carter Spencer
1. Cause Me to Come
2. Renewed Mind

3. No Ground
4. Don't Bind God
5. Going Back "Home"

COMING ALIVE IN CHRIST (Four tape series)
1. How God Sets Us Free
2. Freedom from the Pit
3. Freedom from Hidden Roots
4. Freedom from Snares and Traps

SINGLE TAPES
1. Cutting Free
2. Performance Orientation
3. Sex in the Marriage Relationship
4. Widows and Orphans
5. Restoring Basic Trust
6. What is Submission?
7. How We See God
8. John 14
9. *Dying* to Performance Orientation

Music by Loren and Beth Sandford
LP Stereo Album—"There's a Sweet Spirit"

Available from: Elijah House, Inc.
P.O. Box 14758
Opportunity, Washington 99214

Prices: Each single tape: $4
—Tape series are packaged in plastic book-type bindings at no additional cost. Postage and handling included in price quoted.

Stereo album: $6.95
The Elijah Task $4.00

Also by the Sandfords: *The Elijah Task*

For free information on how to receive
the international magazine

LOGOS JOURNAL

also Book Catalog

Write: Information - LOGOS JOURNAL CATALOG
Box 191
Plainfield, NJ 07061